THE BOXING COMPANION

AN ILLUSTRATED GUIDE TO THE SWEET SCIENCE

THE BOXING COMPANION

AN ILLUSTRATED GUIDE TO THE SWEET SCIENCE

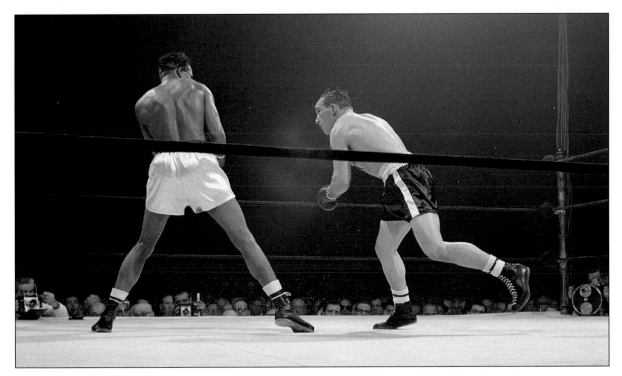

RICHARD O'BRIEN

MALLARD
PRESS

MALLARD PRESS

An imprint of BDD Promotional Book Company, Inc.
666 Fifth Avenue
New York, New York 10103

Dedication

To my grandfather, Frank O'Brien, the St. Louis featherweight

A FRIEDMAN GROUP BOOK
Published by MALLARD PRESS
An imprint of BDD Promotional Book Company, Inc.
666 Fifth Avenue
New York, New York 10103

Mallard Press and its accompanying design and logo are trademarks of
BDD Promotional Book Company, Inc.

ISBN 0-7924-5297-6

THE BOXING COMPANION
was prepared and produced by
Michael Friedman Publishing Group, Inc.
15 West 26th Street
New York, New York 10010

Editor: Sharon Kalman
Art Director: Jeff Batzli
Designer: Kingsley Parker
Photo Researcher: Daniella Jo Nilva

Additional photo credits: p. 2, © Cheryl Dunn; p. 3, © Hy Peskin/FPG
International

Typeset by Classic Type, Inc.
Color separation by United South Sea Graphic Arts Co.
Printed and bound in Hong Kong by Leefung-Asco Printers Ltd.

Acknowledgments

I would like to express my thanks to all those who helped, directly or indirectly, with this book: First, to Pat Putnam, for making it possible in the first place and for all the encouragement along the way; to Ed Schuyler and Earl Gustkey; to Emanuel Steward, Lou Duva, and Angelo Dundee; to Irving Rudd; to Leslie King of the USAABF; to Ed Brophy of the International Boxing Hall of Fame and Museum in Canastota, N.Y.; to my editor, Sharon Kalman, for her help, advice, support, and patience; and finally, to my wife, Lolly, and to our daughters, Daisy and Valentina, thanks for putting up with the whole thing.

Scores of books and magazines were consulted along the way, all of them helpful. I would like to cite the following as being of particular value:

The Ring Magazine; Boxing Illustrated; The Ring Record Book; A Pictorial History of Boxing, by Sam Andre and Nat Fleischer; *Boxiana,* by Pierce Egan; *Fifty Years at Ringside,* by Nat Fleischer; *The Sweet Science,* by A. J. Liebling; *The Encyclopedia of World Boxing Champions,* by John McCallum; *Boxing: The Records,* by Ian Morrison; *Shadow Box,* by George Plimpton; *The 100 Greatest Boxers of All Time* and *100 Years of Boxing,* both by Bert Randolph Sugar.

Table of Contents

ROUND | ONE
A Long and Glorious History — page 8

ROUND | TWO
Between the Ropes: What Goes on in the Ring — page 16

ROUND | THREE
Training — page 28

ROUND | FOUR
The Ten Greatest Fighters of All Time — page 36

ROUND | FIVE
The Ten Greatest Fights of All Time — page 62

ROUND | SIX
Ring of Dreams: Five Great Fantasy Fights — page 84

ROUND | SEVEN
The Undercard — page 96

ROUND | EIGHT
The Business of Boxing — page 106

ROUND | NINE
Ringside — page 114

Appendix — page 121
Index

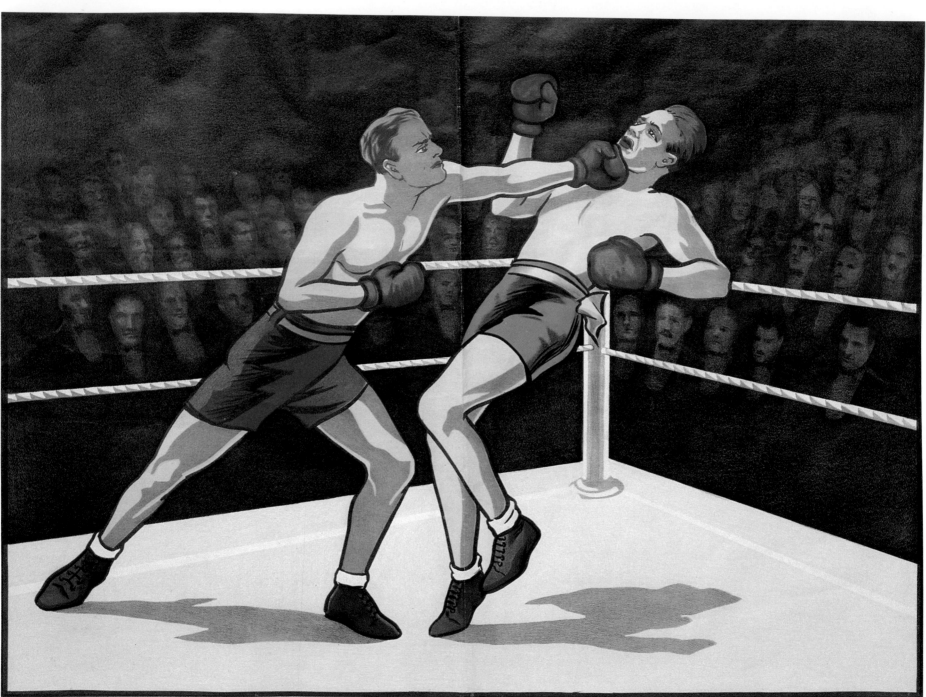

ROUND

A Long and Glorious History

*I*n the vast central room of the National Museum in Rome there is a bronze sculpture of a man seated on a rock, his arms resting across his knees. The dark naked figure, heavily muscled, is clearly fatigued. His head is turned up, revealing a weary, battered face—a flat nose and heavy brows. His hands, clasped in front of him, are wrapped with thick straps across the knuckles. The statue, which dates from the first century B.C., was uncovered in Rome in 1884. It is known as the *Seated Boxer.*

Boxing, in its rawest form, probably dates back to the day two men first figured out how to make a fist at the same time. And indeed, pugilistic activity of a sort can be traced as far back as the ancient Sumerians, who were throwing punches at each other some five thousand years ago. However, as with so many of civilization's finer elements, boxing truly came into its own with the Greeks. A fresco found on the isle of Santorin, dating to 1500 B.C., shows two athletes in combat wearing a form of boxing gloves (along with, strangely enough, light-blue hats). The gloves, like those worn by the *Seated Boxer* of a much later period, evidently were made up of a soft leather pad across the knuckles with thongings of ox-hide wrapped around the wrist and forearm. Hands were protected and so, to some extent, were faces—although a study of the *Seated Boxer*'s profile suggests that blows still left their mark.

In 688 B.C. boxing was incorporated into the Olympic Games, becoming, according to contemporary accounts, a great favorite of the people. The boxing on display at Olympus was not all that different from what we see these days in Atlantic City and Las Vegas. The Greeks, however, never bothered with weight classes, and there were no rounds as such. Contestants fought until one gave up, raising a hand in defeat. One intriguing feature of Greek boxing matches was the refereeing. Vase paintings of the period show a third man in the ring controlling the action with a forked stick, which he used to poke or slap offending boxers.

Greek boxers also trained much like their modern-day counterparts. Antyllus, a writer who lived in the second century A.D., described a sort of heavy bag or "punch-ball," filled with flour or—"for stronger men"—with sand. In practice bouts combatants wore padded earguards and heavy gloves. In real competition, of course, there was no such protection, and through the years the sport grew increasingly brutal.

The Greeks were also quite fond of wrestling, and eventually devised a third combat sport, a vicious hybrid called *pankration,* which was introduced into the Games in 648 B.C. Imagine *Wrestlemania* with real blood. In the *pankration* a contestant set out to inflict as much damage as possible on his opponent, even killing

him if he could. The event became enormously popular.

The Romans, with their thirst for spectacle and zest for combat, readily embraced both wrestling and boxing. They developed the Greco-Roman style of wrestling, a stylized, less brutal form of the sport still seen in the Olympic Games today. Roman boxing was another sport entirely. And one that, thankfully, has not

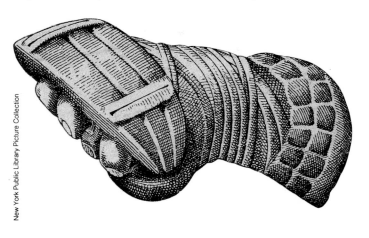

New York Public Library Picture Collection

Bound to hurt: Under the Romans, boxing rapidly evolved into a brutal, killing spectacle, exemplified by the notorious *caestus (above).* This primitive boxing glove featured leather strappings and bands of iron across the knuckles, bringing new meaning to the term "everlast."

▼ight of the century—the sixth century B.C., that is. As this painting from an ancient Greek vase shows *(above)*, boxing was a highly structured exercise, complete with leather handwraps and stick–toting referees. Note the "peek–a–boo" defense of the boxer on the right.

▼he "Seated Boxer," a first-century B.C. bronze sculpture discovered in Rome in 1884 *(opposite page)*, captures in timeless fashion the pain and fatigue of a career in the ring. Note the heavy, studded handwraps and the boxer's battered face.

survived. In Roman rings, the soft leather thongs worn by the Greeks were replaced first by a hard leather strap across the face of the knuckles and then by the infamous *caestus*—a leather strap weighted with lead. Later versions of the *caestus* were studded with iron spikes. Any semblance of skill or science disappeared, and the first solid blow was almost always the winner—and often the killer.

As bloody as this sounds, it was merely a warm-up. Gladitorial combat appeared in 264 B.C. and quickly became the favorite Roman entertainment. True pugilism was to disappear for several centuries before it would flourish again in a marginally less brutal setting.

© Bridgeman/Art Resource

British Boxing

Modern boxing was born in the British Isles— fittingly enough a former Roman colony.

Take a look at another work of art: An early eighteenth-century painting by William Hogarth of a man named James Figg. Here is Figg, in his heavy coat and ruffled sleeves, fists in front of him, a determined expression on his broad face. He is the model of the sturdy English sportsman, ready to take on all comers. It was with just that spirit of national pride that the sport of fisticuffs flourished in Britain in the eighteenth and nineteenth centuries. England, expanding its empire and feeling its strength, was eager to celebrate the tough, even violent, image of the fighting man, a bulldog with bare fists. Figg, a master fencer and an expert with the quarterstaff, opened a school of self defense in London's Oxford Street and began to teach sparring. He was acknowledged as the first English champion in 1719. Though there is no evidence that Figg himself ever engaged in a true boxing match, he has retained the title of Father of English Boxing.

Figg resigned his championship title in 1734. It was in that year, coincidentally, that a future champion by the name of Jack Broughton introduced a set of rules for the increasingly popular sport. Broughton's rules called for rounds to end whenever one man went down. Contestants then had thirty seconds to return to the mark "or be deemed a beaten Man." Hitting below the waist or when down was reckoned a foul, as was seizing one's opponent "by the ham." Of course, there was still plenty of room for mayhem. Under Broughton's rules a fighter's seconds could drag their man to scratch virtually unconscious and hurl him in against the opponent in a desperate attempt to protect their bets before the referee declared their fighter beaten.

Broughton also reinvented the boxing glove, introducing a pillowlike hand covering that came to be called a muffler. Mufflers of course were used only in practice, to preserve the faces of the gentry now gravitating to the ring.

If Figg was the Father of Boxing, Broughton, six feet (183 cm) tall and weighing 190 pounds (86 kg), may legitimately be called the Father of *Scientific* Boxing. He shunned the accepted pattern of toe-to-toe battering in favor of feints, blocks, and when the occasion demanded, retreat. He also introduced the classic English style of the left lead followed by the right hand. Fighting under the sponsorship of the Duke of Cumberland, Broughton won the title in 1740 from George Taylor, a former pupil of Figg's who had succeeded to the championship upon the master's retirement. Broughton held the title for ten years. His rules continued to govern the sport in Britain until 1838 and the advent of the more humane London Prize Ring rules.

> *"Boxers when striking an opponent grunt as they deliver the blow, not because they are in pain or their courage is failing, but because making the noise concentrates all their powers and the blow lands with greater force."*
>
> Cicero

Following the departure of Broughton, the sport fell on hard times. Broughton's conqueror, Jack Slack, also known as the Norfolk Butcher, was notorious for his backhand punch (called the "chopper") and for his alleged crookedness. The Fancy, as boxing spectators were known, lost faith in the game. In the words of Pierce Egan, the great chronicler of the sport, "The championship was in a very unsettled state, and knocked about quickly from one nob to another."

When Men Were Men and Nicknames Really Said Something

Benjamin Brain—Big Ben
Peter Crawley—Young Rump Steak
John Jackson—The Napoleon
　　　　of the Ring
Jem Mace—The Swaffham Gypsy
Daniel Mendoza—The Light of Israel
Stephen Oliver—Death
Hen Pearce—The Game Chicken
Jack Slack—The Norfolk Butcher
Bill Stevens—The Nailer
George Stevenson—The Coachman

The series of nobs included a parade of colorful, if not overly impressive, champions: There was Bill Stevens, called the Nailer; George Meggs, who bought the title from Stevens; Baker Milsom; Tom Juchan; Bill Darts; Waterman Lyons, who retired two weeks after winning the championship to return to his job ferrying people across the Thames; Peter Corcoran, the first Irish champion, who in 1771 knocked out Darts in less than a minute; and Harry Sellers, who supposedly paid Corcoran to lie down. Things finally began looking up in 1783, when a "remarkably round-made" Yorkshireman by the name of Tom Johnson won the championship. Johnson, in the words of Egan, brought dignity and courage back to the ring and restored the public's interest.

Johnson's reign, however, was but a prelude to that of boxing's first superstar. Daniel Mendoza, five feet, seven inches (170 cm) and 160 pounds (73 kg), "a keen-featured, long-haired beauty" of Spanish-English descent, was boxing's first Jewish champion. Mendoza, a master boxer who was known as the Light of Israel, actually held the title for only a year. He is best known for his three battles with Richard Humphries, the "Gentleman Boxer."

The first fight between Mendoza and Humphries was in Odiham, Hamsphire, and today remains one of the most famous fights in history. "No sporting kid that could muster the blunt was absent," wrote the ubiquitous Egan. "HUMPHRIES and MENDOZA were to fight, and that was the only consideration." The match ended after twenty-eight minutes and fifty-four seconds of fighting when Mendoza, struck in the neck, went down hard on the turf and sprained his ankle.

It was after this victory that Humphries dispatched his famously laconic note to his patron, a Mr. Bradyl:

"Sir: I have done the Jew, and am in good health.—Richard Humphries".

Mendoza, Humphries, and boxing were all the rage in England. The Prince of Wales and the Duke of York turned up at ringside, and boxing schools opened throughout the country. Mendoza went on to defeat Humphries twice before losing the title to Gentleman John Jackson. Jackson, five feet, eleven inches (180 cm) and 195 pounds (88 kg), was a fine all-around athlete. It is said he could write his name with an eighty-four-pound (38-kg) weight suspended from his little finger. More important, perhaps, he was an extremely stylish boxer. Jackson was followed by Jem Belcher, the grandson of the blackguard Jack Slack. Blinded in one eye during a friendly game of racquets, Belcher lost the championship on December 6, 1805 to Hen Pearce, "scientifically denominated the Game Chicken." The Chicken, termed by Egan, "the very acme of perfection in a pugilist," retired undefeated.

The years that followed marked the heyday of the English Ring, even as fighters from other countries began to find their way between the British ropes. Two black Americans, Bill Richmond and Tom Molineaux, became favorites of the Fancy, though neither won the championship. Richmond was knocked out by English titleholder Tom Cribb in 1805, while Molineaux lost twice to the durable Cribb, the second time before a crowd of twenty-five thousand.

Female Pugilism

The fighting spirit during those heady early days of the English ring was not confined to the English man, it seems. Pierce Egan, writing in 1812, made note of this advertisement, which had appeared in "a diurnal print" in June of 1722 (during the reign of James Figg):

CHALLENGE

I, ELIZABETH WILKINSON, of Clerkenwell, having had some words with HANNAH HYFIELD, and requiring satisfaction, do invite her to meet me on the stage, and box me for three guineas...

ANSWER

I, HANNAH HYFIELD, of Newgate Market, hearing of the resoluteness of ELIZABETH WILKINSON, will not fail, God willing, to give her more blows than words...she may expect a good thumping!

There is no record of the outcome of the proposed match.

Following Cribb came a series of less prominent champions, until 1833 when James (Deaf) Burke claimed the crown. Burke, known as the "Deaf 'un," became the first English champion to campaign abroad, fighting in New York and New Orleans. Burke's most famous bout was his 1833 match with Simon Byrne. The longest fight on record, the bout went ninety-nine rounds and lasted three hours and sixteen minutes. Byrne died three days afterward.

The English Fighting Spirit

April 10, 1750, Jack Broughton vs. Jack Slack.

The great Broughton, both eyes swollen shut by a lucky punch, gropes helplessly about the ring in a vain search for Slack. Broughton's patron, the Duke of Cumberland, shouts, "What are you about, Broughton? You can't fight! You're beat!"

Replies Broughton, "I am blind, not beat! Only let me be placed before my antagonist and he shall not gain the day yet!"

Courtesy Boxing Illustrated

The end of the bare–knuckle era. John L. Sullivan and Jake Kilrain squared off in Richburg, Mississippi, on July 8, 1889—the last heavyweight championship fight held under the London Prize Ring rules. This rare photograph captures the action in the seventh round. The Boston Strong Boy *(right)* won on a knockout sixty-seven rounds later.

© Joseph Martin/Scala/Art Resource

The Sweet Science in full bloom. This Currier & Ives print, "The Great Fight for the Championship," shows the John C. Heenan–Tom Sayers fight of 1860 at Farnborough, England. The bout was in the forty-second round when the crowd rushed into the ring and ended it.

By 1850, the English Prize Ring was in its decline, the battles grew more and more brutal, and the public more and more outraged and distanced. Yet two English heroes remained.

The first was Tom Sayers, a bricklayer from Brighton. At five feet, eight inches (173 cm) and 155 pounds (70 kg), Sayers was a middleweight by today's measure. He was one of the greatest British champions, winning the title in 1858 with a twenty-one-round knockout of the much larger Tom Paddock. With Sayers, boxing became a truly international sport, when, on April 17, 1860, he met the American champion, John C. Heenan in the most famous prizefight of the nineteenth century—and the first true world-championship match.

Heenan, six feet, two inches (188 cm) and 195 pounds (88 kg), had inherited the relatively young American championship the year before when Irish-born John Morrissey retired. The match, for a prize of one thousand dollars, was to be fought to the finish. It seized the public's imagination as none before it had. The fighters preparations received extensive coverage by both the British and American press. Under threat of police intervention, both fighters trained in secret. On the great day, two special trains were chartered to bring the spectators (each bearing a two-pound ticket printed, "To Nowhere") to the secret site of Farnborough, outside London.

With William Thackeray and Charles Dickens at ringside, Sayers and Heenan fought thirty-seven bloody rounds before the ropes were cut by the crowd and a riot ensued. The referee fled, but the principals continued for five more rounds before the fight was called a draw. The decision was argued for weeks in the press.

Heenan became the acknowledged champion of the world when Sayers retired, and, though Heenan soon lost his title, it was clear that boxing glory had crossed the Atlantic.

Only the great Jem Mace, the Swaffham Gypsy, a cabinetmaker from Norfolk who held the title three times, remained to buoy English spirits. And finally even Mace left the increasingly restrictive British Isles for America, boxing's New World.

The Marquess of Queensberry

John Sholto Douglas was born into a noble sporting family in Dumfriesshire, in the Scottish Lowlands in 1844. At the age of fourteen he became the eighth Marquess of Queensberry. Though his name was to be forever linked with the prize ring—and though he himself was an amateur lightweight champion as a youth—Douglas' first and greatest passion was not boxing, but horses. He loved to ride to the hounds and was quite successful as a gentleman jockey and owner of horses.

Still, Douglas was never far from the ring. As a young man he went to London, where he spent much of his time in the public houses and clubs where the Fancy met, drank, sang, and watched the rough and tumble bouts of the time. As a sportsman used to the more genteel ways of the horse set, Douglas was distressed at the corruption and terrible conditions of the prize ring. He became convinced that if the Noble Art were to survive, it needed the sort of regulation and leadership that horseracing had in the national Jockey Club. It was an ambitious goal, but Douglas was a young man of vision.

Shortly after the end of the Civil War, Douglas traveled to America—on a sort of fistic fact-finding trip. He and his companion, Arthur Chambers (once the lightweight champion of England), spent several months studying conditions in the American prize ring. When they returned to England, the two friends drew up a list of a dozen rules which were passed in 1866 by a committee of the Pugilists' Benevolent Association. Within a generation, they would be, with slight revision, in universal use wherever boxing matches were held.

Douglas died in 1900, most of his family's 30,000-acre estate broken up and given away, yet his name lives on, honored with every opening bell.

The Original Marquess of Queensberry Rules

Rule 1. To be a fair stand-up boxing match in a twenty-four foot (7.3 m) ring or as near that size as practicable.

Rule 2. No wrestling or hugging allowed.

Rule 3. The rounds to be of three minutes duration and one minute time between rounds.

Rule 4. If either man fall through weakness or otherwise, he must get up unassisted, ten seconds to be allowed him to do so, the other man meanwhile to return to his corner, and when the fallen man is on his legs the round to be resumed and continued till the three minutes have expired. If one man fails to come to the scratch in the ten seconds allowed, it shall be in the power of the referee to give his award in favour of the other man.

Rule 5. A man hanging on the ropes in a helpless state, with his toes off the ground, shall be considered down.

Rule 6. No seconds or any other person to be allowed in the ring during the rounds.

Rule 7. Should the contest be stopped by any unavoidable interference, the referee to name the time and place as soon as possible for finishing the contest, so that the match must be won and lost, unless the backers of the men agree to draw the stakes.

Rule 8. The gloves to be fair-sized boxing gloves of the best quality and new.

Rule 9. Should a glove burst, or come off, it must be replaced to the referee's satisfaction.

Rule 10. A man on one knee is considered down, and if struck is entitled to the stakes.

Rule 11. No shoes or boots with springs allowed.

Rule 12. The contest in all other respects to be governed by the revised rules of the London Prize Ring.

Between the Ropes: What Goes on in the Ring

"Sweet Science of Bruising!" Pierce Egan, Boxiana, *1824*

Not always so sweet, and at its best more art than science, boxing remains the most demanding of sports. Once in the ring, the boxer is alone. He has no teammates, no ball, bat, or racquet to hide behind. He can't stop the clock by stepping out of bounds or by calling time. His success or failure—and in the ring, failure can mean not only a loss, but humiliation and serious injury—depends solely on what he does with his own fists and feet.

Blow by Blow

All boxers, even the most gifted—the improvisational artists like Sugar Ray Robinson, Willie Pep, and Muhammad Ali—work with the same basic tools. The great ones, of course, do more with those tools. But, whether he is a world champion or a club fighter, the boxer must learn a specific set of skills, a kind of language of the ring; the language of attack and defense. The boxer's tools—the punches, the slips, the footwork—have all evolved over the past two centuries from the natural movements of hand-to-hand combat, although now they are stylized and specially suited to a conflict within a roped, twenty-foot (6-m) square. When a young boy walks into a basement gym in any city and says he wants to box, he is shown the same stance, the same punches, and the same moves that the sport's greatest champions have been using for millennia. With time he begins to make them his own, and then, perhaps, there is a new champion.

What follows is a look at some of the basic punches and movements in the ring.

The Jab

The jab is the basic building block of the ring. A quick, straight punch, snapped out from the shoulder, the jab creates openings, starts combinations, and often establishes a boxer's rhythm and pace. The jab can be a defensive weapon as well, keeping an opponent off balance. When James J. Corbett challenged the great John L. Sullivan for the heavyweight championship in 1892 he was an underdog by odds of 5 to 1. No one gave the smaller, lighter-hitting Corbett any chance against the hulking Sullivan. But Corbett never allowed the champion to set himself, jabbing his left into Sullivan's face round after round until Sullivan, weary and frustrated, began to crumble.

A superior jab can win a fight. Just ask anyone who ever saw lightweight champion Benny Leonard in action. Or take a look at some films of Muhammed Ali in his prime. Ali, with a slight flick or twist of the wrist at the end of the punch, turned his jab into a deadly slicing weapon. An Ali jab could bring on the end of a fight as suddenly as any knockout punch.

A handful of heavyweight champions have possessed jabs as powerful as most other fighters' Sunday punches. Joe Louis, Sonny Liston, and George Foreman frequently rocked their opponents with heavy, thudding jabs. Two years before he upset Mike Tyson for the heavyweight title, Buster Douglas knocked Mike Williams down twice with the left jab.

A fighter with a good left jab is a fighter with confidence. Just ask Philadelphia Jack O'Brien, the great light heavyweight champion of the early 1900s—who had one of the best. Writing of his attitude approaching a match with Stanley Ketchel, O'Brien put it very simply: "I had heard that Ketchel's dynamic onslaught was such it could not readily be withstood, but I figured I could jab his puss off."

The Manly Art of Mayhem, c. 1926 *(opposite page).* Harry Greb and Tiger Flowers in one of their less elegant moments.

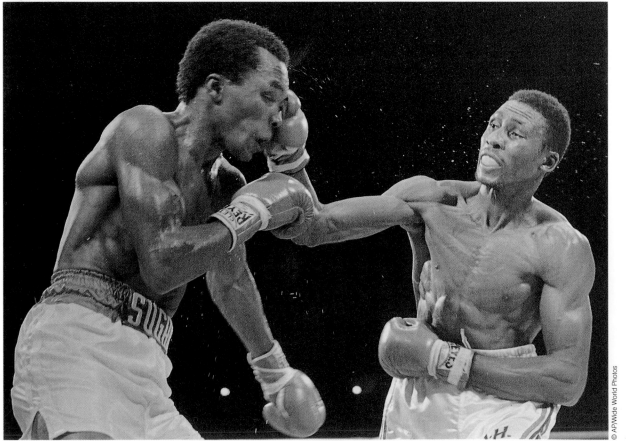

The Right Cross

This is the fighter's bread-and-butter punch. From either side the principle remains the same: A long, straight punch thrown over the straight lead leg, power coming through the entire length of the body. For most fighters, this will be their hardest punch, the one they must land to score a knockout.

Joe Louis, who had a pretty fair right himself, was undefeated until, in 1936, he ran into the right hand of Max Schmeling. Schmeling, by then an ex-heavyweight champ, had studied films of the young Louis's earlier fights and come away saying that he "saw something." What he saw was Louis's low left hand, an invitation to a right cross. Schmeling knocked Louis silly with the punch all night, finally stopping him in the twelfth round. A good right can be a tremendous equalizer.

Many fighters, in fact, have proved successful —at least for a while—with little or nothing more than a good right hand. Heavyweight champion Max Baer, though big and strong and a popular performer, had little in his arsenal besides a stunning right cross. Another heavyweight champion, Ingemar Johansson, was nearly useless in the ring until he could maneuver himself into position to land his vaunted right hand, nicknamed "Toonder and Lightning." It was with that punch that Johansson knocked Floyd Patterson down seven times and won the title.

It would be hard to imagine a more perfect example of the classic straight right hand than

■In a champ's eye. Muhammad Ali *(above, on the left)* used his superb jab to frustrate Sonny Liston and take the heavyweight title in 1964. *Left:* Right on. Despite such classic rights as this one, Thomas Hearns *(on the right)* lost his 1981 welterweight showdown with Sugar Ray Leonard. Leonard fought back to stop the Hit Man in the fourteenth round.

Courtesy Boxing Illustrated

© AP/Wide World Photos

the one with which Rocky Marciano knocked out Jersey Joe Walcott in 1952 to win the heavyweight championship. Marciano's "Suzie-Q," described by several members of the ringside press as a "roundhouse" right—who, in the days before instant replay all too often missed the key moments of fights—was in fact anything but a roundhouse right. With Walcott backed against the ropes, Marciano threw a straight right lead that landed flush on the champion's jaw. Walcott, as A. J. Liebling described it after viewing the fight film, "flowed down like flour out of a chute."

Such is the effect of a good right hand.

The Left Hook

Ernest Hemingway once wrote, "If you fight a good left hooker, sooner or later he will knock you on your deletion. He will get the left out where you can't see it, and in it comes like a brick. Life is the greatest left hooker so far, although many say it was Charley White of Chicago…"

A good left hook is a thing of beauty—short, crisp, a matter of balance and timing more than brute force. The movement is a difficult one to learn, awkward at first, with its pivot and shift of weight. But once a fighter masters the move, the hook often becomes a favorite punch. Sugar Ray Robinson used to hook once, off the jab, and if he landed, just keep hooking—more often than not as his opponent went down. (The single hook with which Robinson kayoed Gene Fullmer in their return bout in 1957, by the way, should be preserved somehow in a glass museum case—it was as perfect a punch as was ever thrown.) The left hook is a cornerstone punch. Cus D'Amato used to advise his charges always to finish a combination with a left hook, as it leaves a fighter in position to come right back with more blows.

The left hook can be just as effective to the body as to the head. Bob Fitzsimmons knocked out Corbett with the blow. Their fight, held in Carson City, Nevada, on St. Patrick's Day 1897,

Ccurtesy Boxing Illustrated

was the first heavyweight title match recorded on film, and the devastating effect of Fitzsimmons's short, sharp shot to Corbett's belly is clearly visible in the grainy black and white. The punch lands, and Corbett sinks to the canvas, reaching for his side, gasping for air, in his eyes a look of disbelief. Gentleman Jim failed to beat the count, and Fitzsimmons took the title. The blow became known as the solar-plexus punch, but it was merely a classic left hook to the body.

For a seminar in the use of the left hook, study the first Ali-Frazier fight. It is 1971, and Frazier, a product of the tough Philadelphia gyms where the left hook was everything, has carved a swath through the heavyweight ranks with the punch. From the opening bell he sets out to do the same against Ali, bobbing, weaving, and hooking, always hooking. In the eleventh round Frazier drives Ali to a corner. He drops the left in a short arc over Ali's lowered right glove. Ali sags as if shot. The ropes keep him up and he fights desperately to survive the round. For the rest of the fight Ali is never the same. In the fifteenth and final round, another Frazier hook, this one slower and wider, but just as powerful, crashes

against Ali's jaw. Ali goes straight down on his back. Though he rises and finishes the round, the hook has won Frazier the fight. Ali, his right cheek ballooning, shakes his head and says, "Never trade hooks with a hooker."

Sooner or later the hook will get you.

Body Punching

"Kill the body and the head will die," goes the old adage. Ask any unfortunate fighter who has spent a few rounds absorbing left hooks to the ribs and rights to the belly and felt his arms slowly lowering to his sides and his legs turning to stone, and he'll tell you it's sound advice.

Good body punching is a sign of maturity in a fighter. Most young boxers, in the impatience of

Leonard again, this time bouncing a textbook left hook off the bald, bobbing head of Marvin Hagler in their 1987 match. Leonard scored a tremendous upset when he beat Hagler on a twelve-round decision.

their youth, confine their attacks to their opponent's head, often with inefficient and wasteful results. Steady body punching, by contrast, builds a foundation.

June 22, 1938. After waiting two years for a rematch, Joe Louis *(on the right)* wasted little time in destroying former conqueror—and former heavyweight champ—Max Schmeling. Louis's assault began with body shots, including this right that ringside observers said caused Schmeling to scream in pain.

When asked once why he focused so much of his attack on his opponent's body, the great old heavyweight Sam Langford said, "Because the head got eyes."

Study the list of the sport's great punchers and you'll find that each was a great body puncher as well. Jack Dempsey always claimed that it was a right hand "under the heart" that started his destruction of the huge Jess Willard in their 1919 match. Ali, after his first bout with Frazier, went home with bruises on his hips, the overflow of Frazier's thudding body attack. Archie Moore, who held the light heavyweight championship from 1952 to 1962 and whose career total of 145 knockouts still stands as the all-time record, was a master at picking apart his opponents with well-placed body shots, "like a mechanic working a car," A. J. Liebling once wrote, "a tap here, a yank there." Those taps and yanks add up.

Putting Them Together

"The ol' one-two." It is a term used in every walk of life. It comes, of course, from boxing and refers to the classic combination: the left jab followed by the right cross. Set 'em up and knock 'em down.

Combination punching is what we think of when we think of the difference between the early prize ring and the fighters of today. Modern boxers put punches together. In so doing they dramatically increase their offensive effectiveness. Study videotapes of Mike Tyson in action. In his knockout wins over Larry Holmes and Michael Spinks, Tyson's blows came in tight murderous sequences. In his loss to Buster Douglas, they came one at a time, with plenty of breathing room in between. It was Douglas who threw the combinations—and Tyson who wound up on the canvas for the first time in his career.

Former light heavyweight champion of the world Jose Torres—like Tyson, a one-time pupil of the late Cus D'Amato—speaks of throwing punches in predetermined sequences to predetermined spots.

"That's when a fighter is most effective," says Torres. "that's when you know you're on and when you do the most damage."

D'Amato had his fighters practice those predetermined sequences in the gym. He assigned a number to each specific punch—a left to the liver, for example, or a right to the jaw. Then D'Amato would call out a string of numbers and the fighter would whomp the heavy bag with the intended series of blows.

Among heavyweights, the greatest combination puncher was Ali, with Louis a close second. Ali was never a real banger, but then a fighter doesn't have to be when he can land a half

Ducking a right lead at head and
countering with right at body.

The cross-parry.

Defense

When James J. Corbett challenged the already legendary John L. Sullivan for the world's heavyweight championship in 1892, Corbett was considered something of a dandy by the fight crowd, a dancer who wouldn't stand and make a fight of it. And he was just that. He also knocked Sullivan out in twenty-one rounds.

Corbett, outweighed by the Boston Strong Boy 212 pounds (96 kg) to 178 pounds (81 kg), knew that if he wanted to win the title, he would have to concentrate on avoiding the champion's punches. Corbett would land his own in time. But he would need to be standing to do so. Sullivan, who wanted only to hit, never found the prancing, parrying Corbett. While it is difficult to imagine Gentleman Jim offering much opposition to any modern boxer, they all owe him a debt of thanks. Corbett showed them you don't have to stand and take it.

Obviously, the best defense would be to turn and run, perhaps execute a headlong dive through the ropes. Boxing asks of its practitioners, however, not merely self-preservation, but retaliation as well. A superior defense allows a boxer to avoid punishment while retaining position for his own attack or counterattack. The fighter slips punches, blocks them with his glove or forearm, ducks them, all while remaining within striking range.

Willie Pep, the great featherweight champion of the forties, once won a round on all three judges' cards without throwing a punch. It was against Jackie Graves in Minneapolis in 1946. Pep moved, feinted, slipped Graves's punches, spun Graves around, but never landed a blow. "I might have thrown a jab or two," says Pep, "but I don't think so." They called Pep the "Will o' the Wisp."

Not all defenses are as flamboyant or as graceful as Pep's. The wise old champion Moore had his crossed-arms "Armadillo" defense, from which he peered out over his gloves. D'Amato's champions, Floyd Patterson, Jose Torres, and Mike Tyson, all used the "peek-a-boo" stance, gloves together in front of their faces, bobbing and weaving. Ali, in contempt of established wisdom, pulled back at the waist from punches, hands at his sides. Of course, what the classicists failed to notice was Ali's footwork. He was always in position.

As Corbett knew, defensive skills often go unappreciated by the average boxing fan, who has little patience for a boxer who refuses, as the phrase goes, to fight like a man. But defense does not always mean turning a championship fight into a track meet. Roberto Duran, usually thought of as one of the purest offensive fighters ever, was, at his best, nearly impossible to hit. Dempsey, with his crouch and his bobbing and weaving, was also an extremely difficult target. Both fighters were so effective offensively in large part because their defenses allowed them to stay so close to their opponents. After all, the point of the whole thing is to hit and not get hit.

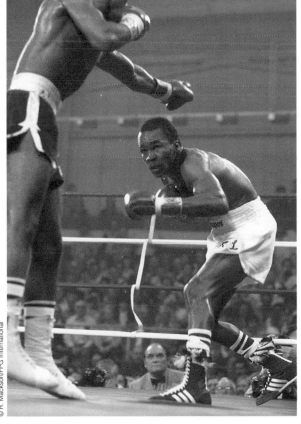

dozen punches at will. Ali's November 1966 destruction of Cleveland Williams (a pretty fair puncher himself) in the Houston Astrodome remains a classic display of combination punching. In the third round, Ali's fists seemed less to hit than to dance—a thudding, bloody dance—across poor William's face. The fight ended in that round with Williams flat on his back.

The difference between just throwing punches and throwing combinations is like the difference between knowing a few phrases of French and being truly fluent. The first is just enough to get you in trouble in Paris; with the second, the city is yours.

Throughout his long career, Sugar Ray Leonard made it clear that the point of boxing is to hit—and not get hit.

© Cheryl Dunn/Courtesy Sports Auctions of New York

© R. Mackson/FPG International

The Referee

On St. Patrick's Day 1990, Richard Steele made the kind of move that gets referees noticed. Ordinarily a boxing referee, like a good second base umpire, remains invisible. Fans recognize the top refs, of course, even call their names during the prefight instructions. But once the bell rings a good referee is expected more or less to disappear. If he is noticed at all, it should be because he is gliding around the periphery of the action, sliding in and breaking up the fighters with a touch and a sharp command. If

there's a knockdown he counts for a while and then wipes the fighter's gloves on his shirt.

On that St. Patrick's Day, Steele reminded the boxing world why that third man is in the ring. Overseeing the junior welterweight match between WBC champion Julio Cesar Chavez and IBF title holder Meldrick Taylor, Steele stopped the fight with just two seconds remaining in the twelfth and final round. Taylor, ahead (it turned out) on the judges' cards, had taken a terrific series of punches from Chavez and had gone down in a neutral corner. He got to his feet, but never raised his gloves and when Steele

asked him twice, "Are you okay?" Taylor said nothing. Steele waved the fight over—and immediately brought a storm of criticism down

---

Referee Arthur Donovan counts out Joe Louis in the twelfth round of Louis's 1936 fight against Max Schmeling. Donovan performed the same rites for ten Louis opponents (including Schmeling in 1938) during the Brown Bomber's twelve-year reign as heavyweight champion.

---

on his head. Surely he knew Taylor was ahead? That there were only two seconds left? That Taylor had been distracted from answering by a cornerman climbing into the ring?

What Steele knew was what every good referee knows: The safety of the fighters is in his hands alone. How much time is left, who is ahead—none of that matters. Just ask Ruby Goldstein, referee for the Emile Griffith–Benny (Kid) Paret fight on March 26, 1962, at Madison Square Garden. In the twelfth round Griffith pinned Paret in a corner and landed twenty-one unanswered punches before Goldstein stopped the fight. Paret never regained conciousness and died eight days later. Goldstein took his own beating in the press for his delay in going to Paret's aid. He never refereed again. It should be pointed out, though, that Goldstein (a former top featherweight and one of the sport's premier officials) had already taken a great deal of criticism for his judgement a decade earlier. Goldstein was the ref in the second Sugar Ray Robinson–Randy Turpin fight. In the tenth round, Robinson, bleeding badly from a butt, landed thirty-one straight shots before Goldstein, supporting the limp Turpin in his arms, stopped the bout. That time they'd said Goldstein stopped it too soon.

"There's one person in the position to know," said Steele after the Chavez fight. "That's the referee."

In the early years of the sport the referee for a bout was often a hand-picked representative of one of the principals, there to insure "fair treatment"—to guard against fouls, real or imagined. The position has evolved, thankfully, into one of a more impartial, even-handed nature. And despite the generally low profile of the job, there have been some famous refs. One wonders if any fighters or handlers ever dared protest the officiating of Bat Masterson or Wyatt Earp, two early lawmen of the ring. (One active ref firmly in the Masterson-Earp mold is Mills Lane of Nevada, a Las Vegas prosecuter by pro-

fession.) A great many top fighters went on to do some refereeing, perhaps welcoming the chance simply to tell people what to do in the ring. The list includes such all-time greats as Jim Corbett, Jim Jeffries, Benny Leonard, Jack Dempsey, Joe Louis, and Jersey Joe Walcott. Some proved better at the job than others. Dempsey never was a great referee, but his popularity was such that he was often a bigger draw than the competing boxers.

When Joe Louis fought Arturo Godoy in Santiago, Chile, in 1947, the referee was Luis Angel Firpo, the old Wild Bull of the Pampas. Godoy, a wild-swinger, drew a warning from Firpo and, angered, promptly knocked Firpo down. Louis knocked Godoy out before things got out of hand.

Say, Who are Those Two Guys in the Ring with Harry?

Longtime referee Harry Kessler (Kessler handled the Marciano–Moore fight, among others, and continued refereeing until he was seventy-eight), liked to refer to himself as "Mr. Unobtrusive." In fact, he liked it so much much that he wrote a 371-page autobiography entitled *The Millionaire Referee.*

Probably few fight fans could identify Dave Barry, but it's likely he is the most famous referee in boxing history. Barry was in the ring for the second Dempsey–Tunney fight in Chicago in 1927, the famous Battle of the Long Count. In the seventh round of that fight, Dempsey caught Tunney with a seven-punch barrage that left him dazed on the canvas. Barry delayed the start of his count until he had finally maneuvered the

homicidal Dempsey to a neutral corner (as the rules clearly demanded), thus giving Tunney an estimated fourteen seconds to recover. It was enough. Tunney got up and went on to win the ten-round decision, retaining his title. And people have been arguing about Barry's action ever since.

At Barry's next assignment, the Mickey Walker–Mike McTigue fight held a month later, the crowd greeted the ref's introduction by chanting slowly from one to fourteen.

Who says referees don't pay their dues?

What They Don't Teach You in Referee School

Billy Joh was the official in the ring for the Willie Harris–Sailor Burke fight on August 13, 1909, a scheduled ten-rounder, and he more than earned his wages. In the first round Burke dropped Harris for a six count. In the second round Harris floored the Sailor for nine. But they were just warming up. In the third round, with a pair of identical right hooks, Harris and Burke knocked each other down at the same time. Faced with the two fighters lying on top of each other in the center of the ring, the crowd roaring in amazement, Joh did what any ref would do, he started counting. The bell sounded with both fighters still on the canvas, saving Joh from having to make an almost Solomonic decision. "I would have continued the count," Joh later told Nat Fleischer of *Ring Magazine,* "The man who got to his feet first would have been the winner."

The Corner

For the first time in his career Mike Tyson was losing a fistfight. The scene was Tokyo, Japan, February 11, 1990, and Buster Douglas was making Tyson look foolish. Nothing the champion tried seemed to work against Douglas.

"What," viewers wondered, "are Tyson's handlers telling him between rounds? What are they doing for the champ?"

The answer, to judge by the videotapes of Tyson's corner, was nothing. Tyson's corner crew whispered and implored, but there was no clear voice of authority. They fussed over his injuries, but used an ice bag on his eye, not the accepted instrument for such emergencies, an Enswell. And in the end, they sent Tyson out alone to take his beating.

Of course, all fighters are alone in the ring. There are no tag-team partners to jump in, no pinch hitters. But a good corner can make a difference. During those sixty seconds between rounds (thanks to the Marquess of Queensberry) a fighter gets whatever help he is going to get, whatever companionship and encouragement there is to be found in this arena into which he has gotten himself. The bell rings and the fighter, his head buzzing, his arms aching, his breath coming in gasps, goes back to his corner. There's a stool, there's water (splashed in his face or maybe poured down his trunks), there's tactical advice (shouted or mumbled or whispered; coherent or not, cogent or otherwise), and there's medical attention (the flow of blood is dammed). For that minute, his trainer, along with maybe his conditioner or just a buddy with a bucket, and a cutman are all there just for him. They are, as the phrase goes, "in his corner." And then the bell sounds again and somebody yanks away the stool.

"The best corners are the ones that are noticed the least," trainer Eddie Futch once said. Futch should know. He was the man in Joe Frazier's corner when Frazier beat Ali, and he's been in countless other winning corners in his

The Seated Boxer, revisited. While Roberto Duran sometimes behaved as if he never wanted to stop punching, let alone sit down, even he benefitted from the ministrations and advice of his corner crew.

career. "Control, that's the word," Futch said. "Control of the fighter. Control of yourself."

Originally a fighter's seconds served much the same function as the seconds of a man fighting a duel. They helped choose a site for the bout, handled the side wagers, got their hero there on time and, presumably, ready. They were even responsible for dragging him back for the start of a new round—whether he was in shape to continue or not. After all, their money was riding on the fight.

In the days of the English Prize Ring, a second's duties went even further. Pierce Egan tells of Tom Johnson, a former champion serving as a second for Richard Humphries in the latter's 1788 battle with Daniel Mendoza. In this fight, Johnson leapt onto the stage to catch a particularly powerful blow of Mendoza's.

In more modern times, boxers have come to expect less violent, but no less dedicated support from their corners. Philadelphia Jack O'Brien, the great light heavyweight champion, once wrote a pamphlet of instructions for the seconds in Jack Dempsey's corner. Throughout the pamphlet O'Brien referred to Dempsey as Big Boy, or B. B. "Chief second should have B. B. ready for next round ten seconds ere the gong strikes so that B. B. may look keenly at foe to endeavour to discern next move of opposition."

Of course one's corner is not always a safe haven. Victor McLaglen, the big gruff Hollywood actor, was once a professional fighter. One hopes he got better support from his cameramen than he did from his cornermen. According to Nat Fleischer, McLaglen was fight-

Between a Rock and a Hard Place

When former heavyweight champion Max Baer faced Joe Louis in 1935, none other than Jack Dempsey was in his corner. As Dempsey told it, Baer was terrified of Louis's power. After the first round, Baer came back to his stool and told Dempsey he couldn't go on.

"He told me he couldn't breathe," said Dempsey. "I told him I'd kill him right there with the water bottle if he didn't go back out there and get knocked out."

ing Phil Schlossberg in 1908 when he received a badly cut lip. The blood was flowing down McLaglen's throat when he returned to his stool between the third and fourth rounds. His chief second produced a "healing potion" and ordered McLaglen to open up and throw back his head. He did, and the man poured a bottle of ammonia in McLaglen's mouth.

In a 1989 bout against Prince Charles Williams, light heavyweight Bobby Czyz took a fearful battering. By the end of the tenth round, his left eye was swollen shut. Czyz returned to his corner. "That's it," he said in obvious despair. "I can't see. My eye." "You've got this eye, here" said his trainer, pointing at Czyz's right eye. Czyz might have fared better in Williams's corner.

Sometimes an inspired cornerman can work a little magic. Muhammad Ali, then still known as Cassius Clay, took on British Empire champion Henry Cooper in London's Wembley Stadium on June 18, 1963. It would be the young Clay's last fight before facing Sonny Liston for the title the following year. Clay was dominating Cooper until the fourth round when one of Cooper's big left hooks dropped him on the seat of his pants. Clay wobblingly rose as the bell sounded, ending the round. He had a minute to recover—or would have, had his trainer Angelo Dundee not noticed (and some say enlarged) a tear in the leather of one of Clay's gloves. The ensuing delay, during which a replacement glove was fetched and laced on, gave Clay more than enough time to clear his head. Fresh again, he cut Cooper up in the fifth round for a TKO.

Sometimes a fighter can help his corner. When Joe Louis defended his title against Buddy Baer in 1942, Louis's trainer, Jack Blackburn, was ill. "Chappie," said Blackburn in the dressing room, calling Louis by their mutual nickname, "I don't think I can make it up them stairs tonight."

"You'll only have to go up those stairs once, Chappie," said Louis. Louis knocked Baer out in 2:56 of the first round.

The Cutmen

Eddie Aliano has a distinctive nickname. They call Eddie "The Clot". A big man with an honest wiseguy's battered face topped with an old slouch cap, Aliano could play a boxing cornerman in the next *Rocky* movie—except he's too busy. Aliano is a freelance professional cutman. He crisscrosses the country each week, preventing fighters from bleeding to death—or worse, losing on a TKO.

Aliano comes from a long and distinguished line of cutmen. Together with his contemporaries, Ralph Citro and Angelo Dundee, Aliano practices a craft that has been in existence since the earliest days of the prize ring. The great cutmen are remembered like great wizards, their formulas for the stemming of blood handed down like potions. The great ones have included Ray Arcel, Whitey Bimstein, Freddie Brown (charged with patching up Rocky Marciano, a fighter who, for all his toughness, cut alarmingly easily), and Charley Goldman.

Whatever the secret ingredients, though, the basic formula remains the same: Adrenalin, pressure, and some coagulant paste. And then watch your handiwork get chopped open again in the next round.

Equipment

We have come a long way since the days of the Greeks, with their fists bound in leather, not to mention the Romans, with their iron-studded *caestus*. The tools of the Sweet Science, like those of every other worthy trade, have evolved over the years. Boxing, however, is not a complicated sport. There is nothing remotely high-tech about it. Unlike, say, track and field, where the hand-held stopwatch has given way to sophisticated electronic timing systems, or baseball, where rickety old ball parks have bowed to climate-controlled domes, and grass is rolled under by the green plastic of Astroturf, boxing has retained much of its old shape and feel. The gloves are still leather, the surface of the ring still canvas (though there is likely to be a beer company logo emblazoned across it now), and the bell still rings with its stirring sound of steel.

Tools of the Trade

Gloves, of course, have been around since the days of Jack Broughton, when, known as mufflers, they preserved the features of the young aristocrats then dabbling in the sport. The first recorded prize fight with gloves was a match between two unknown British fighters at Aix-la-Chapelle, in Germany, on October 8, 1818. Still, bare-knuckle bouts prevailed for at least another sixty years until the new Queensberry rules specified the use of gloves. The 1889 battle between John L. Sullivan and Jake Kilrain was history's last bare-knuckle heavyweight championship match. Sullivan himself preferred fighting with the gloves—perhaps because he hit so hard. The standard eight- or ten-ounce (227- or 283-g) boxing glove, it should be noted, does far more to protect the fist than it does to cushion a blow (training gloves on the other hand, with fourteen or sixteen ounces [370 or 454 g] of padding, are more like Broughton's mufflers). In fact, a fighter with a well-padded fist can afford to land many more punches than he could with

A small price to pay for protection. Boxing equipment like gloves *(left)* and headguards *(above)* remains pretty much unchanged from the earliest days of the sport.

bare knuckles. Recently, thumbless or attached-thumb gloves have been introduced in an attempt to reduce the danger of eye-gougings. Fighters, dedicated traditionalists—even with their own safety at stake—have been slow to accept the innovation.

There are two other principal items of safety equipment used by professional boxers (amateurs, of course, use head protectors, as do the pros in training). The mouthpiece, or gumshield, was originally devised by a London dentist named Jack Marles in 1902. According to boxing historian Ian Morrison, the first fighter regularly to use the device was Ted (Kid) Lewis, the great English welterweight of the teens. The other crucial safety item was the protective cup.

The ring itself has evolved from a mere circle of spectators to the classic elevated, roped-off square. Current rules allow a ring to be anywhere from 18- to 22- feet (5.5- to 6.7-m). A smaller ring favors the slugger, who can more easily trap his opponent in its tighter confines, while the boxer is more effective in the larger square. There have been experiments. One promoter unveiled a circular ring (in a San Francisco shipyard on May 26, 1944; the ropes were made of tubular aluminum), another a hectagonal ring; both were created with the intention of minimizing the risk of a fighter getting trapped in a corner. Neither design caught on. The boxing ring remains, in the sportswriter's tired phrase, "the squared circle."

Apparel

The most dramatic changes through the years have come in what fighters wear into the ring. Photographs of even obscure bouts can be dated to within a decade just by an examination of the fighters' apparel. There is John L. Sullivan in long white tights, high stockings, and black boots; Corbett and Fitzsimmons in tight, diaperlike shorts; Joe Louis in trim, dark trunks and low black shoes; any number of fighters in the seventies and eighties, bedecked in sequins and neon lettering. The only constant in professional boxing, it seems, has been the bare chest, necessary, one imagines to better show the effects of body blows. That touch of nakedness, the hero stripped for action (unseen in any sport—with the exception, of course, of swimming), probably helps preserve boxing's "savage" image.

As a rule, boxers are vain men. Maybe because their faces are so often rearranged, usually in less than flattering fashion, they become acutely sensitive to their appearance. Most are natty dressers out of the ring. In it, they seem to select their attire not only on the basis of function, but also, and more important, really, on the basis of image. Why else would Hector Camacho, the gifted lightweight champion of the 1980s, step into the ring in a multicolored, feathered loincloth and

Ring attire has evolved through the ages. Some looks remain classic, though. Just ask Mike Tyson (above).

fringed boots? And why did Joe Frazier wear those spectacularly baggy trunks in the midseventies, the ones that looked as if they'd been cut from his living room draperies? Beside such excess is Mike Tyson, who during his heavyweight reign of terror carved out his own image based on a kind of retro-Spartanism. Tyson, with his executioner's black trunks, his low black shoes worn without socks, and disdain for robes, was a welcome throwback, a man come to fight.

Training

After he retired from the ring, Philadelphia Jack O'Brien opened a gymnasium on Broadway in New York City. Jack's slogan was "Boxing Taught Without Punishment." Most devotees of the sport would tell you that it doesn't work that way. To be fair, as A. J. Liebling pointed out in a *New Yorker* article he once wrote on O'Brien, "Philadelphia Jack doesn't say that boxing can be learned without punishment—just taught."

The training of boxers, like the making of good champagne, is a process that has changed very little over the past century; indeed, over the past twenty centuries. Today's fighters shadowbox, spar, and punch the bag much like Ancient Greek boxers did. The equipment used evolves slowly and fitfully, and specific techniques come in and out of vogue, but the basic formula remains the same, made up of equal parts sweat, repetition, concentration—and punishment.

For every minute he spends in actual competition, a boxer spends more than one hundred in the gym and on the road. The conditioning demanded of a professional boxer is astonishing, and there is no room for compromise; no room for faking it.

"I found out that the harder you work in training, the easier the fights are," Thomas Hearns, one of the greatest fighters of the seventies and eighties, has said. "I *wanted* to work."

Hearns's labor, like that of most boxers, is prescribed by tradition. It starts with roadwork. Few fighters will say they actually enjoy running, but they all do it. All those miles build endurance, put something into the legs and the heart that will be there in the late rounds of a tough fight. The young Muhammad Ali had a habit of shirking his roadwork—until he learned that Sugar Ray Robinson, his idol at the time, ran five miles (8 km) a day. Ali hit the road. Tradition says a boxer should rise before dawn to do his roadwork. It makes no difference to the body, of course, when it runs, but tradition carries a punch in this sport, and long before the fun-runners and triathletes ever laced on a pair of Nikes, the fighters were there every morning, slogging their miles in heavy sweats and old Army boots.

In the afternoon, it's into the gym. A club or preliminary fighter, one whose ring earnings are still such that he must hold down a day job, will drag himself in after work. A champion might rouse himself from an afternoon nap, or hurry over from taping a television commercial or closing some new real estate deal. Once in the gym, though, the routines of the fighter and the champ are the same.

After warming up with a few rounds of shadow boxing—shuffling, bobbing, snapping short quick punches, the fighter watching himself in the mirrors on the wall, looking for rhythm, grooving his muscles for the task ahead —he moves on, the sweat rolling, to skipping rope. This exercise develops both stamina and footwork. And it's no little kid's game. The glowering Sonny Liston skipping away to "Night Train" was a fearsome sight. Of course, the greatest with a rope was Robinson, whose skipping was so spectacular he included it in a dance act on stage.

Now it's on to the bags. The heavy bag, made from leather or canvas and suspended from the ceiling, is where the fighter learns his punches and builds his power. Watch George Foreman, the former heavyweight champion now trying to make a comeback, work the big bag, and you'll see power. The speed bag develops timing, hand speed, and rhythm. It also provides the timeless rat-a-tat background music of every gym.

At any given moment in a respectable boxing gym you can find fighters counting out sit-ups, push-ups, or leg raises, absorbing blows to the ribs with a medicine ball, or performing tortuous-looking neck bridges. These exercises —these punishments, if Philadelphia Jack will allow—steel the body for the assaults it will take in the ring. Watch the straining neck muscles of a fighter doing bridges and then think of the impact of a hard left hook. As quaint and

For every round of fighting, a boxer spends countless hours in the gym. Roberto Duran *(opposite page, on the left),* though known to let himself go between bouts, was a fearsome worker in the gym. Here he hardens those hands of stone in a sparring session.

esoteric as some of these exercises seem, everything that's done in the gym has a reason.

And every trainer has his favorite drills—exercises for teaching footwork or combination punching or defense. Charlie Goldman, the trainer who molded Rocky Marciano into a champion, taught him balance by tying a length of rope between his ankles and having him shadow box, the rope insuring that the fighter's feet never got too far apart. Emanuel Steward, Hearns's longtime trainer/manager and once a national amateur champion himself, has kept in shape over the years working the punch mitts with Hearns, bobbing and weaving and sliding around the ring while Hearns slammed combination after combination against Steward's thickly padded palms.

Finally, the real work of training is done in the ring—with gloves and headgear and another boxer in there throwing punches at you. Most boxers spar every day, going anywhere from two to ten rounds, often against different opponents. If you're a champion or a contender, your manager hires your sparring partners for you, guys who can mimic the style of your upcoming opponent. If you're a novice or a club fighter, you work with whomever is in the gym that day—and you hope he's in your weight class.

All fighters approach sparring differently. For some—Ali was a prime example—those rounds in the gym are an opportunity to relax, play around, and showboat a little. Ali worked hard in the gym, but there was never any doubt about what was sparring and what was fighting. For

---

All good gyms are the same: Enough room to move around, shadow box, skip some rope; maybe a mirror or two; big bags, speed bags; a ring for sparring; a few posters on the wall—and plenty of sweat. For the boxer, this is where the hard work is done.

Having a ball. Rocky Graziano, middleweight champion from 1947 to 1948, demonstrates the accepted medicine ball catch—against the belly. Rocky was training for his third fight with Tony Zale when this photo was taken.

other fighters, that sense of relaxation was impossible. Jack Dempsey was incapable of taking it easy ("He's got a grudge against anybody with gloves on," Mickey Walker once said, explaining why he refused to spar with Dempsey). For the up-and-comer trying to make a name for himself, the performance he puts on in the gym can often make more of an impression with the people who count—trainers, managers, and promoters—than any four-round preliminary bout. Several generations of Philadelphia fighters have left their greatest battles in that city's notorious gyms.

The young boxer, fighting once a month, is constantly in shape. There is an honored tradition among champions, however, for whom fights are much fewer and farther between, of letting oneself go. For them, the training camp was invented. A place where the fighter can get away from all distractions and all excuses and concentrate fully on getting in shape, the camp also provides a focus during the build-up for a big fight. In the old days, sports writers filed daily dispatches from each camp, discussing what the fighters ate, how much they weighed, how they looked in sparring. Reading these old columns, one is struck by the timeless, bucolic images: Nat Fleischer's tales of Stanley Ketchel dispatching some greenhorn reporter on a midnight snipe hunt; Joe Louis sitting on the porch in his training camp at Pompton Lakes, New Jersey chatting with a group of New York writers up from the city for the day; Rocky Marciano, swaddled in blankets, walking from the makeshift gym to his little cabin at Grossinger's; even Ali, chopping wood and running the dirt roads around his Deer Lake, Pennsylvania, camp. Trainer Whitey Bimstein put it well when he told Liebling, "I like the country. It's a great spot."

These days, the top fighters pitch their training camps in converted ballrooms at the big casino hotels, their rings set up under dripping chandeliers. The atmosphere is not the same.

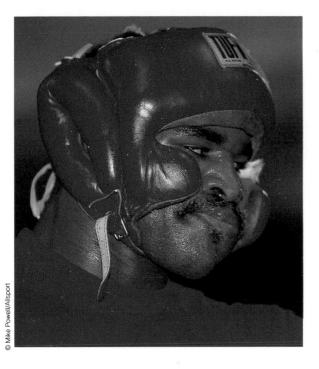

Heavyweight champion Evander Holyfield has a good head on his shoulders. In training, he makes sure he protects it.

Finally, training is not all physical. The most important element is preparing the boxer mentally. A trainer must provide his charge not only with the tools to win, but also with the belief that he can win—as well as the motivation to do so. Always in the back of a fighter's mind is the image of his opponent, a symbol of what all this work and punishment is for. It raises a healthy resentment against the man who will be standing across the ring come fight time. Floyd Patterson, who lost the heavyweight championship on a knockout to Ingemar Johansson in 1959, spoke of the fury he built up against Johansson while training for their rematch in 1960. "I don't ever want to hate like that again," Floyd said. He flattened Johansson in the fifth round.

Boxing is never taught without punishment.

The Trainer

While most young boxers start off simply fighting—fighting for survival or for fun, at home or on the streets—the real learning starts only with a trainer. A boy goes into a gym somewhere, anywhere, and there is a man (in the movies, he is a wizened little man with baggy pants and a garbage-disposal voice; he often is in real life, too) who teaches him, shows him how to stand and punch and move his head. If he is a good trainer, he shows him a great deal more than that. The following are some of the very best; call it a Trainers' Hall of Fame:

James Figg. He started it all.

Jack Blackburn. A clever and gifted lightweight in his day, Chappie Blackburn was the architect of Joe Louis' career.

Charlie Goldman. Straight from Central Casting, Goldman, himself a former bantamweight who fought four hundred fights, trained a dozen fighters at a time for more than three decades. He also transformed Rocky Marciano from a crude brawler into a relatively less crude brawler who was also one of the most destructive heavyweights of all time.

Whitey Bimstein and **Freddy Brown.** Bimstein—once described as looking like a choirboy who'd spent forty years in bad company—and Brown trained hundreds of fighters out of old Stillman's Gym, among them Rocky Graziano.

Cus D'Amato. A prophet in the wilderness, D'Amato has been called a genius and a paranoid madman. He was probably both. There have been few trainers as creative as D'Amato, few as committed to the sport and to his own way of doing things. He created Floyd Patterson, Jose Torres, and Mike Tyson.

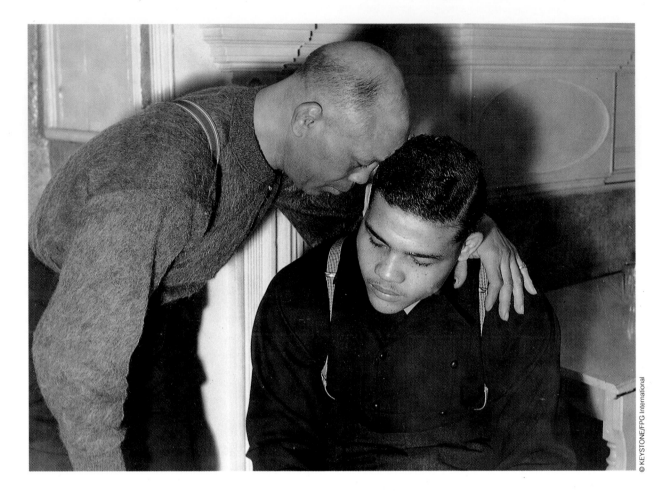

Gil Clancy. For thirty years, a consistent producer of top talent (including Jerry Quarry and, most famously, welterweight champion Emile Griffith), the gruff Clancy remains one of the best boxing minds in the business.

Angelo Dundee. Angelo is included just for putting up with Ali for all those years. He is also a great strategist, an inspired cornerman, and the best cheerleader in boxing. If you're going up those stairs, Angelo's the guy you want coming up behind you.

Ray Arcel. Arcel was among the best. From the thirties and forties, when he trained several of Joe Louis's challengers to the eighties, when he worked with Roberto Duran.

Emanuel Steward. The boss of Detroit's Kronk gym, Steward produced several world champions in the seventies and eighties, including all-time great Thomas Hearns. After spending several years concentrating on the managerial and business aspects of the sport, Steward has announced his intention of getting back into the gym to work with young amateur fighters. The nineties should see some more Kronk champions.

Eddie Futch. Futch may be the last of the great ones. Through the years, he has trained or managed sixteen world champions, including Larry Holmes, Joe Frazier, Michael Spinks, and Alexis Arguello. With Frazier, and then with Ken Norton, Futch figured out how to beat Ali. The quiet, gentle Mr. Futch could probably figure out how to beat anybody.

The Gyms

There was a time when the center of the fistic world was on Eighth Avenue in New York City, between 49th and 55th Streets. Madison Square Garden was there—the old Garden, between 49th and 50th—but the real heart of the fight scene was Stillman's Gym, just up the street. Liebling called it the University of Eighth Avenue, and Stillman's was, indeed, the pre-eminent institution of higher learning for the Sweet Science.

Opened in 1921, Stillman's quickly acquired a patina of grime and sweat that made it seem somehow timeless. There were two boxing rings on the main floor of Stillman's and a balcony above where the light and the heavy bags hung. At one time some 375 fighters trained regularly at Stillman's. Out-of-towners, in the city for a Garden bout or a card at the old St. Nick's Arena, worked out there during their stay. Trainers worked with several boxers at once, and managers, on the lookout for new fighters, or bouts for those they already had, hung out in the gym all afternoon. Those were the days when boxers stood in line for their chance to get into the ring to spar—and spectators stood in line to watch them train. This activity was presided over by Lou Stillman (born Lou Ingber; he changed his name when he took over the gym) from his tall stool near the rings, and the whole place moved to the eternal three-minute, one-minute, three-minute rhythm of round and rest. Stillman's closed in 1959, but it remains a kind of Platonic ideal of what a boxing gym should be.

Great trainers make great fighters. Jack Blackburn (*opposite page,* with his charge, Joe Louis) was one of the best. *Right:* For many years the center of the fistic universe was Stillman's Gym, the place A. J. Liebling called the "University of Eighth Avenue."

Sex and the Single Boxer

Traditionally, fight trainers have approached the subject of sex with the same open-minded attitude they bring to weight lifting: It's perfectly acceptable—just not for boxers. At least not those in training. Francis Dowling, author of the remarkable 1841 boxing manual, *Fistiana, or the Oracle of the Ring,* wrote that "indulgence with women...[can] enfeeble, undermine, and at last prostrate the constitution." That view has changed very little over the ensuing century and a half. Sex is said to "ruin legs," whatever that means. Trainers are notorious for their watchdog tactics. Jerry Quarry, a top heavyweight contender of the sixties and seventies, got married during preparation for a major bout and brought his bride with him to his training camp. Horrified at this potentially ruinous situation, Quarry's trainer, Gil Clancy, promptly moved his bed into the room next to the newlyweds. "Anytime we made a sound," recalled Quarry, "there was Gil, pounding on the wall and shouting, 'What's going on in there?'"

Boxing taught without punishment?

All the great gyms, though, have their own distinct character. Miami's famous Fifth Street Gym—Angelo Dundee's base—with its scuffed wood floor and bright Florida light, will always be the home of the young Ali, the backdrop for those newsreel interviews in which we first heard, "I am the Greatest." There's Johnny Toc-

co's Ringside Gym in Las Vegas, with its iron gates across the open doors. Here's where Marvin Hagler used to train for his Vegas fights, scorning the glittery ballrooms of the casinos. There's the Kronk, a close, sweltering room in the basement of a city recreation building on Detroit's raw west side. The Kronk's ring has seen some wars—and produced some champions, including Thomas Hearns, Michael Moorer, and Milton McCrory.

There are others, of course—the big ones where the champs train, and the little ones, the basement Police Athletic League gyms in cities around the country—and they all move to the same pulse that quickened Stillman's.

The New Wave

To suggest to a classically minded fight trainer that there might be a better way to prepare a man for the rigors of boxing than by, say, dropping a medicine ball on his belly one hundred times a day, is to invite scorn. Boxers do what boxers have done, and that's it. Still, in this era of fitness institutes (that's something no one ever called Stillman's), when every high-school gym teacher has a Ph.D. in exercise science and every executive has a personal trainer, a new breed of physical conditioner is making inroads in the sport. These men and women disregard the inherited fistic wisdom by insisting that boxers could improve their conditioning and thus their performance by adopting the modern, scientifically based training methods used in virtually every other sport today.

Mackie Shilstone, a New Orleans nutritionist, built former light heavyweight champion Michael Spinks into a genuine heavyweight through a program that shocked the old guard. Instead of steak and eggs, Shilstone had Spinks eating measured amounts of pasta and chicken. Instead of long, plodding runs along the roads, Spinks performed 880-yard (805-m) intervals on a track. And instead of pitching

around a medicine ball, the fighter lifted weights, long a taboo in boxing (weights make you muscle-bound, is the accepted theory). On September 22, 1985, Spinks weighed in at a solid 200 pounds (90 kg), then went out and took the heavyweight title from Larry Holmes on a fifteen-round decision—becoming the first light heavyweight champ ever to step up to win the heavyweight title.

Yeah, But How Long Would He Last in a Philly Gym?

In 1987, East German sports scientists developed Der Boxroboter, an expensive computerized robotic sparring partner that can be programmed to assume any fighting style.

Evander Holyfield is another example of the efficacy of the new methods. When Holyfield, the 1984 Olympic light heavyweight bronze medalist, first turned pro he weighed less than 190 pounds (86 kg) and was huffing and puffing at the end of eight-round bouts. With the help of trainer Tim Hallmark (who normally worked with professional basketball players), Holyfield embarked on a scientifically monitored conditioning program involving a battery of aerobic-training devices, as well as a full weightlifting circuit. Holyfield emerged as not only a body beautiful, but as a full-fledged heavyweight as well.

The success of athletes such as Spinks and Holyfield might be expected to have changed the face of boxing training overnight. It hasn't. Yet clearly there is room for even greater experimentation—in the fields of nutrition, sports psychology, and biomechanics, particularly. In the meantime, medicine ball sales remain steady.

Training Ideas Whose Times Have Come ...and Gone

- In his 1841 boxing manual, *Fistiana,* Francis Dowling advised that should the weather prove too damp or windy for roadwork, the boxer should "spar at home, grind the meal, rub down a horse, or play at ninepins, leap frog or any manly exercise."
- Jack Dempsey was famous for soaking his face in brine to toughen it.
- Tony Galento, the cigar-smoking New Jersey saloon-keeper who once floored Joe Louis, sparred with a bear, a kangaroo, and an octopus.
- Muhammad Ali, in a September 8, 1961 article in *LIFE* magazine, demonstrated his unique underwater training technique, throwing punches in the deep end of a swimming pool.
- The ancient Greek writer Antyllus set down careful instructions for the use of the punch-ball (a kind of Greek heavy bag filled with millet or sand): "Punch it away beyond arm's reach so that as it returns it falls with greater violence on the body...take it on the chest...[or] turn round and receive it on the broad of the back."

Master of the Universe. Evander Holyfield began his professional career as a cruiserweight, but a team of experts and the most modern training and nutrition techniques available have transformed him into the heavyweight champion.

© E. Doris Lee

The Ten Greatest Fighters of All Time

When comparing fighters, statistics don't mean much. It's all a matter of style. Still, the true fan invariably finds himself imposing rankings upon the fighters he has seen or read so much about. He can't help it: "Jimmy Wilde was the greatest flyweight who ever lived." "Primo Carnera, Jess Willard, and Tommy Burns stand one-two-three as the most useless heavyweight champs of all time." And so on. It's the sort of talk that can provide countless hours of entertainment—and argument. In other sports, baseball for instance, you can look it up, it's all there in the record book. In boxing, it's all there too—but in the heart.

So, how does the educated fight fan compare? First, forget the numbers. In boxing, they don't matter—at least not that much. Fight people pay attention to wins and losses—and of course knockouts—and that's about it. Even then, one win may be far from the equal of another. One fighter's 25-0 record can mean a lot less than another's 20-4-1 record.

Different eras change things as well. Today, a heavyweight with a respectable record of 32-6 would be lucky to get even an undercard slot on television. Yet that is exactly the record (plus seven no-decisions) that about-to-be-heavyweight-champion Bob Fitzsimmons

brought in with him against Jim Corbett in 1897. Then there is the question of size. Is former heavyweight champion Buster Douglas a greater boxer than light flyweight title holder Michael Carbajal just because (one is reasonably certain) Douglas would knock out Carbajal every time they fought? Was Gerry Cooney greater than Sandy Saddler? No and no, right?

The question then becomes not who would win a hypothetical match, but a more subtle and more interesting one: Who brought the most into the ring—given his era, his size, his opponents? The answer comes not only from the record book, but also from watching how a fighter moves; noticing what he looks like in the corner between rounds; what his opponent's legs do when the fighter's punch lands; how the fighter reacts when he's hit. In the case of the old timers, a big part of the answer is found in what his contemporaries said and wrote about him. It is a wonderfully subjective and passionate exercise, and the arguments can go on forever. Which of course, is why the sport goes on.

In that spirit, then, here is one fan's list of the ten greatest fighters ever to put on a pair of gloves and slide through the ropes into the light of the ring.

The Greatest. For twenty years, Muhammad Ali was the most exciting—as well as the most colorful, the most outrageous, the most controversial, and the most beautiful—figure in sports. His one-round, one-punch knockout of Sonny Liston *(opposite page)* in Lewiston, Maine, in 1965, was called a "fix" by some, a "perfect" punch by others. Either way, it finished Liston—and left Ali shouting.

T H E **1** T E N
G R E A T E S T
F I G H T E R S

Muhammad Ali

He told us. From the day he danced onto the world's stage as an eighteen-year-old light heavyweight in the Rome Olympics, Muhammad Ali said he was the Greatest. As it turns out, he was.

Ali's professional career extended from 1960 to 1981, and for those twenty-one years Ali WAS boxing. Born Cassius Marcellus Clay, the son of a Louisville sign painter, Ali began boxing at the age of twelve. Another boy had stolen his bicycle and young Cassius went for help to a local gym run by a Louisville cop. "If I catch that boy, I'm gonna whip him good," said Cassius. He joined the gym the next day. By the time he was eighteen, he was an Olympic gold medalist and was commanding the world's attention in a way no athlete before him had. In or out of the ring, he was fast, fresh, and inventive, in absolute command of his world.

Clay turned pro in October of 1960, managed by a syndicate of white Louisville businessmen and trained by the redoubtable Angelo Dundee. In those first two years Ali was regarded as little more than a curiosity—the handsome, brash, poetry-spouting ("Jones likes to mix/He must go in six/If he starts talking jive/I'll cut it to five...") Louisville Lip. The purists complained that he held his hands too low, that he pulled away from punches rather than block them, that he didn't know how to go to the body. They were right, of course, but

none of that mattered. Ali was the fastest heavyweight of all time. And he was the most inventive and resourceful.

How wild were those times! In his 1964 title shot against Sonny Liston—a scowling thug of a man, one of the most feared heavyweights in history—Clay, a 7-1 underdog, went wild at the weigh-in on the morning of the fight. Eyes popping, surrounded by his entourage, he railed at Liston. The commission fined Clay $2,500, and the doctor pronounced the young fighter, "scared to death." Thirty minutes later, back in his dressing room, he was perfectly calm. "Shook him up," he says of Liston. That night he humbled Liston, cutting him up with the jab and making him look old. Liston quit on his stool before the seventh round. Cassius Clay was the new heavyweight champ. The next day, he announced that he had become a Black Muslim and that he had changed his name to Cassius X.

Soon he would change his name again, to Muhammad Ali, though many in the sporting press and the public—and several of his opponents, in misguided attempts to gain a psychological edge—continued to call him Clay. It is hard to realize now how fresh Ali must have seemed—a revolution in boxing gloves—and, to some, how threatening.

Like all great artists, Ali went through many periods in his career. As a fighter he probably was most brilliant during his late-Clay period, in 1966 and 1967, when he was carving his way through challengers. That period, of course, was cut short when Ali was stripped of his title and his license to box following his refusal to be inducted into the armed services (and his infamous, "I ain't got no quarrel with them Viet Cong" line). Ali lost three and a half years of his prime.

But he came back. Remember the glittering black-tie turnout, the joy, in Atlanta in 1970 when he sliced up Jerry Quarry. The rolling cheers of "Ali! Ali!" That fight, and a subse-

quent last-round stoppage of the lumbering Argentine, Oscar Bonavena, set up the first Frazier fight. That bout, held in Madison Square Garden on March 8, 1971, remains, amid all the Fights of the Century, the quintessential Big Fight. Here were two undefeated heavyweight champions. The boxer, Ali, against the puncher, Frazier. Subversive Black Muslim draft dodger against the Establishment's honest workman. They were fighting for the richest purse in history (at that point), $2.5 million each, and the entire country watched.

The fight lived up to its billing, fifteen of the busiest, most stubborn rounds ever fought by heavyweights. In the end, Frazier's relentless, remorseless pressure exposed the rust of Ali's gifts, and Joe's big left hook put Ali down. He got up, but he had lost. Still, in getting up, he earned a grudging respect. Ali can take it, they said.

The loss to Frazier signaled the beginning of yet another period for Ali, the era of the People's Champion. He fought all over, in Tokyo, Dublin, and Jakarta. In 1974 he beat Frazier (who in the meantime had lost his title to George Foreman) in a twelve-round rematch. Then Ali signed to fight the new champion Foreman in Zaire. The Rumble in the Jungle, he called it. Ali saw it as a mission and never faltered. When he came out flat-footed against Foreman, when he slid passively to the ropes and began to absorb the champion's thudding blows, the calls came, shrill and desperate—from his corner, from the stands, from closed-

---

Nineteen years old and still called Cassius Clay. A young Ali shows the speed and grace he brought to the ring, here stopping a reeling Alex Miteff in the sixth round in Louisville, Kentucky, on October 7, 1961. It was Ali's ninth pro fight.

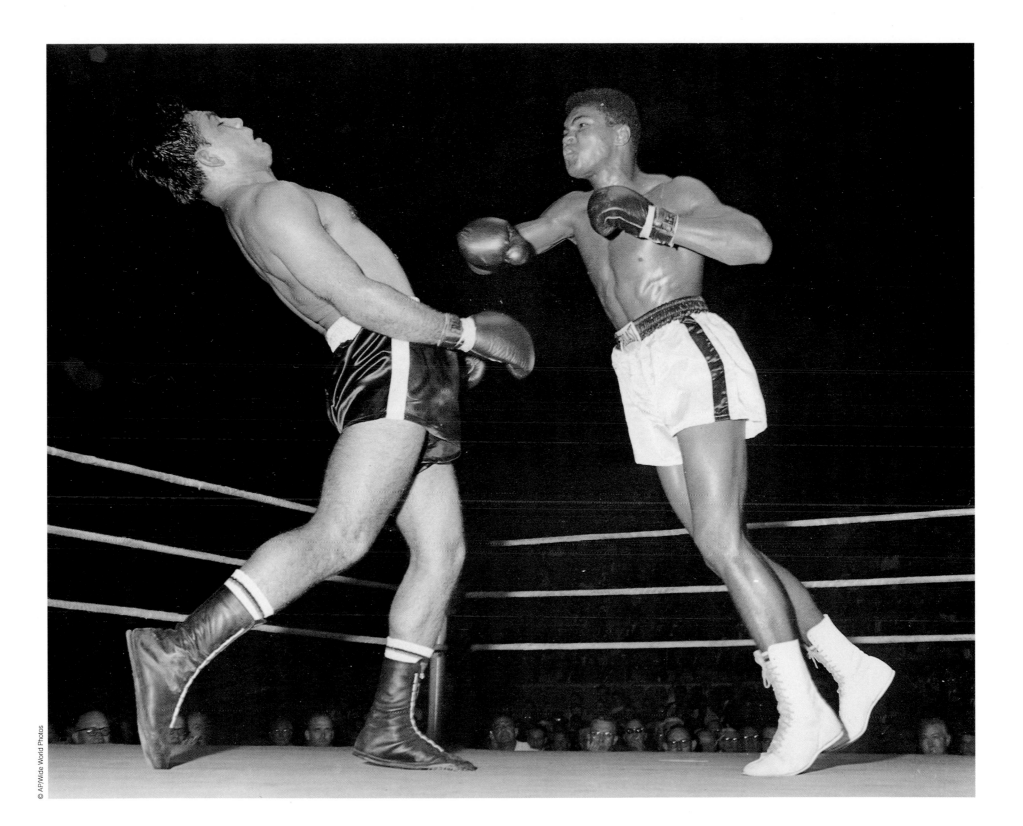

circuit theatres around the world: "Dance, Ali! Dance!" But Ali had called a different tune for this night. When he came off the ropes in the closing seconds of the fifth round and sent the sweat flying from Foreman's head with a quick combination, those watching began to catch on. And when Foreman toppled, spinning to the canvas in the eighth round, they believed. Ali was champion again.

There would be a final peak with the third Frazier fight in 1975, but the last years were hard to watch. Yet we, like the fighter himself, did not want to let go. In 1978 Ali lost to Leon Spinks, a marginal little heavyweight in his eighth pro fight. Eight months later, he beat Spinks in a rematch. "The triple-greatest of all-time!" said Ali.

Those final fights, even the losses to Larry Holmes and Trevor Berbick, added the final element to Ali's greatness. The butterfly, once thought to be so frivolous, had proved himself one of the sport's great survivors.

But don't dwell on those late, puffy-faced, years. Remember him, instead, after the first Liston fight: Young, wide-eyed, riding the pandemonium in the crowded ring and calling out, "I shocked the world! I shocked the world!" He did. He also changed it.

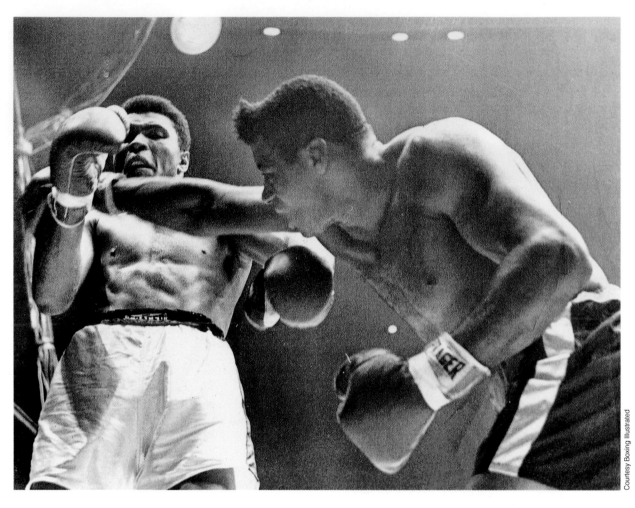

Courtesy Boxing Illustrated

Ali, shown above slipping a right thrown by Floyd Patterson in their 1965 bout, was a master showman both in and out of the ring. His three fights with Joe Frazier (right) took on nearly mythical proportions in the eyes of the sporting public.

Record

Born (Cassius Marcellus Clay) in Louisville, Kentucky, January 17, 1942; 6 foot, 3 inches (190 cm). 186–230 pounds (84–104 kg). 1960 Olympic Light Heavyweight Champion.
PRO DEBUT: October 29, 1960; W6 Tunney Hunsaker.
LAST FIGHT: December 11, 1981; L10 to Trevor Berbick.
Won Heavyweight Championship February 25, 1964; KO7 Sonny Liston. Stripped of title for refusing induction to armed services; inactive from March 22, 1967 to October 26, 1970.

Regained Heavyweight Championship October 30, 1974; KO8 George Foreman.
Lost title February 15, 1978; L15 Leon Spinks.
Won Third Heavyweight Championship September 15, 1978; W15 Leon Spinks.
CAREER RECORD: 56-5, with 37 knockouts.
PEAK MOMENT: Against Cleveland Williams, November 14, 1966.
NICKNAMES: The Louisville Lip, The Greatest.

DIRECT FROM RINGSIDE · EVERY THRILLING MOMENT
POPULAR PRICES
FIGHT PICTURES
ROUND BY ROUND · BLOW BY BLOW
BATTLE OF THE CHAMPIONS
IN COLOR
JOE FRAZIER
VS.
MUHAMMAD ALI
CASSIUS CLAY   JOE FRAZIER
WILL NOT BE SHOWN ON HOME TV FOR 6 MONTHS!

© Cheryl Dunn/Courtesy Sports Auctions of New York

Sugar Ray Robinson

The phrase has become a part of his name, repeated in every obituary column when he died in 1989, spoken with reverence whenever the talk turns to boxing history: "The greatest ever, pound-for-pound." That is how Sugar Ray Robinson is remembered, and it is hard to argue.

In the beginning, he was Walker Smith. Born in Detroit, in 1921, he started boxing when he was seven, at the Brewster Recreation Center. The hero of the gym at the time was a big kid named Joe Barrow. Barrow, of course, would go on to more widespread acclaim as Joe Louis. Walker Smith's name change came later, after he and his family packed up and moved to New York. There Smitty, as he was known, resumed boxing under trainer George Gainford in Gainford's Salem-Crescent Athletic Club in Harlem. Those were the days of bootleg fights—supposedly amateur bouts in which the winner was given a watch. But you never saw a boxer who could tell you the time. They all sold their watches right back to the promoter for ten dollars apiece. It was good money in the Depression, and Smitty wanted into the bootlegs.

One night in Kingston, New York, Gainford signed him up—using another kid's amateur registration card. The kid's name was Ray Robinson. (The "Sugar" came later, and quite naturally, when a sportswriter told Gainsford, "That's a sweet fighter you got there." "Sweet as sugar," said Gainsford.)

The young Ray Robinson was a revelation, as complete a boxer as ever fought. His work in the ring seemed almost effortless, flashy only in its pure, technical perfection. He was fast. He could hit with either hand. His footwork was impeccable, his ring sense unequalled. After turning pro in 1940, Robinson won forty straight fights before he lost a ten-rounder to Jake LaMotta in 1943. He didn't lose again for eight years. Along the way, he whipped LaMotta five times for good measure, including the fight in which Robinson first won the middleweight crown. That bout, held in Chicago on February 14, 1951, was called the Valentine's Day Massacre. Robinson stopped LaMotta in the thirteenth round.

All told, Robinson won the middleweight championship five times, a record unmatched by any other fighter in any other weight class. Of course, that meant he also lost the title four times. Robinson, even in his greatness, could be a little careless. He was stopped only once in his career, one that spanned twenty-five years and 201 fights. On June 25, 1951, Robinson—already the former welterweight champion and current middleweight title holder—took on Joey Maxim in a bid for the light heavyweight crown. It was the hottest June 25 in the history of the New York Weather Bureau, 104 degrees F (40°C) ringside in Yankee Stadium. Referee Ruby Goldstein collapsed at the end of the tenth round and had to be replaced. Robinson, who dominated what fighting there was, built up an insurmountable lead on Maxim, but the cost was too great. He'd been pushing and shoving and hauling around a man fifteen and a half pounds (6.8 kg) heavier than himself and after thirteen rounds Robinson had nothing left. It went into the books as a fourteenth-round knockout by Maxim. Robinson retired.

He spent nearly two years touring as a dancer before various business dealings went sour and the need for money brought him back to the ring in October of 1954. Robinson

Throughout his twenty-five-year career, Sugar Ray Robinson fought the best in boxing. Here he hangs on as Carmen Basilio bears in. Basilio beat Robinson in this 1957 bout, but Ray, as he did so often, won the rematch.

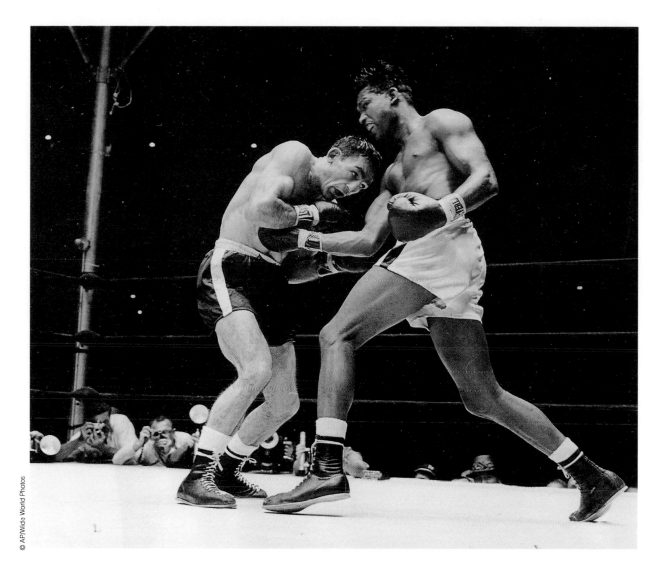

© AP/Wide World Photos

Record

Born (Walker Smith Jr.) in Detroit, Michigan, on May 3, 1921. 5 feet, 11½ inches (181 cm); 145–157 pounds (66½–71 kg).

PRO DEBUT: October 4, 1940; KO2 Joe Escheverria.

LAST FIGHT: November 10, 1965; L10 Joey Archer.

Won Welterweight Championship December 20, 1946; W15 Tommy Bell.

Won Middlweight Championship February 14, 1951; KO13 Jake LaMotta. Lost Middlweight title July 10, 1951; L15 Randy Turpin.

Regained Middleweight Championship September 12, 1951; KO10 Randy Turpin.

Announced retirement December 18, 1952.

Announced return October 20, 1954.

Won Middleweight Championship December 9, 1955; KO2 Bobo Olsen. Lost title January 2, 1957; L15 Gene Fullmer.

Regained Middleweight Championship May 1, 1957; KO5 Gene Fullmer. Lost title September 23, 1957; L15 Carmen Basilio.

Won fifth Middlweight Championship March 25, 1958; W15 Carmen Basilio. Lost title January 22, 1960; L15 Paul Pender.

CAREER RECORD: 174-19-6 (2 no-contest), with 109 knockouts.

PEAK MOMENT: Against Randy Turpin, September 12, 1951.

NICKNAME: Didn't need one.

---

still had three of his middleweight reigns to come, along with some of his most thrilling fights, but he would never again be as great as he was in the early years, when he was, indeed, as sweet as sugar.

Sugar Ray Robinson will be remembered not only for his spectacular ring record, but even more for the style and flair he brought to the role of champion. In the days before celebrity was bestowed on any athlete who ever hit a baseball or dunked a basketball for pay, Robinson—with his pink Cadillac, his Harlem nightclub, and his unmatched personal grace—was the real thing.

© PHOTOWORLD/FPG International

■The two Robinson–Basilio fights produced thirty rounds of brutal action—and two split decisions. *Above:* Despite punches like this one, Basilio took the middleweight crown from Ray in 1957. *Opposite page:* He regained the title from Basilio six months later. Late in his career, Robinson, who once went eight years and ninety-one bouts without losing, found himself beaten by the likes of Terry Downes *(left).*

Roberto Duran

*F*orget the puffy middleweight of the 1980s, the man they came to call Jelly of Belly instead of Hands of Stone. Forget the lethargic third fight against Ray Leonard that closed out the decade. Forget the earlier losses to Kirkland Laing and Wilfred Benitez, and the devastating knockout by Thomas Hearns. Forget even *"No mas."* Remember instead the pure, savage lightweight of the 1970s. *Manos de Piedra.* There has never been a purer fistfighter.

Duran had just turned twenty-two—lean, scruffy, and feral, a product of the streets of Panama City—when he met Ken Buchanan of Scotland for the lightweight championship of the world in New York's Madison Square Garden in 1972. Buchanan, a gifted boxer of the classic school, never had a chance. The sneering, snarling Duran seemed to have a different understanding of what the sport was about. He battered Buchanan from the opening bell until, in the thirteenth round, referee John LoBianco pulled him off the helpless Scot. Buchanan complained afterward that he'd been fouled at the finish, which was rather like a man who had just been run over by a train griping that the conductor had been rude to him. Duran had the title.

He would hold it—with fury and arrogance—for the next seven years before relinquishing the belt to move up in weight. As a lightweight Duran lost just once in sixty-eight bouts—a ten-round non-title match to Esteban DeJesus

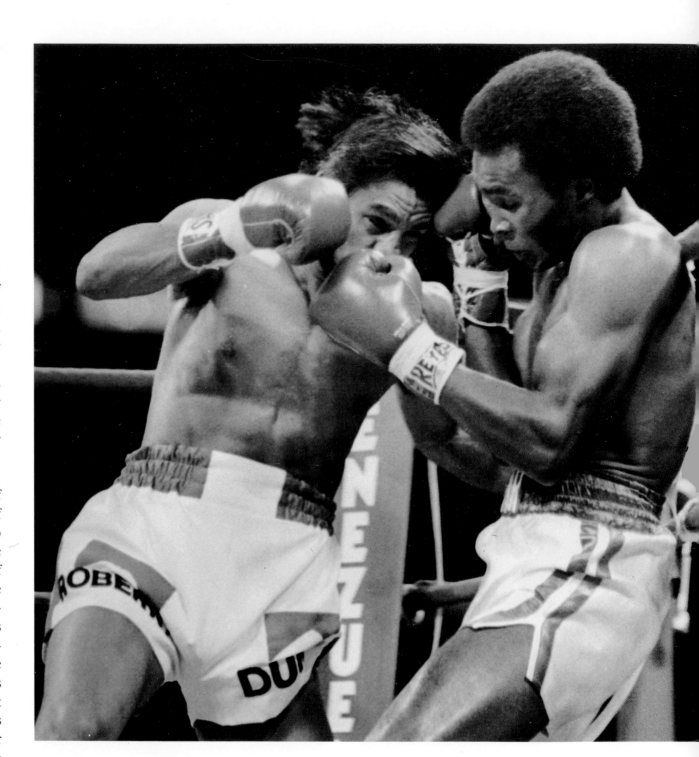

*M*anos de Piedra. An inspired Roberto Duran *(on the left)* mauled Sugar Ray Leonard to take the WBC welterweight title on June 20, 1980.

in late 1972. He knocked DeJesus out twice in return. Duran was at his best in that third DeJesus fight (held in Las Vegas in 1978), outboxing the slick DeJesus the whole way before catching up to him in the twelfth round.

All told, Duran defended his lightweight title twelve times, scoring eleven knockouts. After one of those kayos a television commentator asked Duran if he was aware that his opponent had been taken to the hospital.

"I did not hit him quite right," said a sweating but calm Duran, "If I hit him right, he would be in the morgue, not the hospital."

Duran brought his fury with him to the heavier weights, but not his all-conquering punch. His finest moment after leaving the lightweight ranks came in June of 1980 when he overwhelmed Sugar Ray Leonard to win the welterweight title. His darkest moment came five months later, when, in the eighth round of the rematch, Duran, frustrated and angry, threw up a glove and quit. *No mas.* The phrase has since become a sports cliché, and many have never forgiven Duran for uttering it.

Overweight and uninspired, Duran lurched through a series of comeback fights (waging his toughest battle along the way against the IRS) before knocking out Davey Moore in 1983 to win the WBA junior middleweight title. Later that year Duran further redeemed himself in a losing but hard-fought challenge to Marvin Hagler for the middleweight championship. Five more lackluster, almost aimless, years followed before the old champion's last stand. In February of 1989, Duran, thirty-seven, outboxed, outfoxed, outbanged, and outgutted twenty-nine-year-old Iran Barkley to win a split decision and the WBC middleweight title. Ten months later Duran got his third shot at Leonard. Leonard, boxing brilliantly, made Duran look old and, worse, like he didn't care. People went home calling it No Mas II. They were wrong. Leonard took sixty stitches in his face from the two clean punches Duran landed. Old Stone Hands cared. He just couldn't do it anymore. Not like he used to.

Record
Born in Guarare, Panama, June 16, 1951.
5 feet, 7 inches (170 cm); 130–160 pounds (59–72 kg).
PRO DEBUT: March 8, 1967; W4 Carlos Mendoza.
LAST FIGHT: December 7, 1989; L12 Ray Leonard.
Won Lightweight Championship June 26, 1972; KO13 Ken Buchanan. Relinquished title February 1, 1979.
Won Welterweight Championship June 20, 1980; W15 Ray Leonard. Lost title November 25; KOby8 Ray Leonard.
Won WBA Junior Middleweight Championship June 16, 1983; KO8 Davey Moore.
Won WBC Middleweight Championship February 24, 1989; W12 Iran Barkley.
CAREER RECORD: 85-8, with 61 knockouts.
PEAK MOMENT: Against Esteban DeJesus, January 21, 1978.
NICKNAME: *Manos*  *de Piedra.*

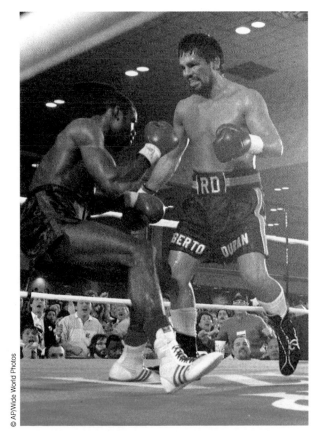

Duran, a product of the mean streets of Panama City, moved to his own viscious rhythm in the ring. As a lightweight, he was unbeatable, a crushing puncher. Moving up to welterweight, he overwhelmed Leonard with his rage and his ring savvy—his sheer will to fight. To many, it was Duran at his best.

THE TEN
GREATEST
FIGHTERS

Benny Leonard

*T*he old-timers liked to say that Benny Leonard was so slick in the ring that no opponent could so much as muss his hair. That may have been an exaggeration, but not by much. Leonard, who held the lightweight championship of the world from 1917 until he retired undefeated in 1925, was the consummate ring artist. With his classic stance, his precise, economical footwork, his speed, his remarkable punching power, and his smooth, brilliantined hair, he remains the ideal image of the boxer. In the ring, Benny Leonard was in control.

They also said that Leonard was the original mama's boy. There are almost more pictures of Benny posing with his mother than there are of him in the ring. Mama Leonard never wanted her son to be a fighter. Born Benjamin Leiner on the Lower East Side of New York in 1896, Leonard started boxing in local clubs at the age of fifteen. To keep his parents, especially his mother, from finding out what he was up to, he took the name Leonard—after the famous minstrel performer Eddie Leonard.

One night early in his career Leonard came home from a fight to find Mama crying. "She had found out," Leonard told interviewer Bud Greenspan. "My father came in and started shouting at me. 'Viper, tramp,' he yelled. 'Fighting, fighting, fighting—for what?'" Benny pulled out the five dollars he had

earned and handed it to his father. "When's your next fight?" said his father.

Leonard began to make a name for himself in 1916. On March 31 of that year, he outclassed then lightweight champion Freddie Welsh in a ten-round no-decision contest. A year later, on May 28, 1917, at the Manhattan Casino in New York, Leonard left Welsh hanging over the ropes in the ninth round and took the title. Even Mama had to agree her boy had made good.

Leonard became one of the most popular figures in the sport during the early twenties. As friendly and well-spoken out of the ring as he was efficient in it, he was a refreshing contrast to scowling heavyweight champ, Jack Dempsey. And then there were all those pictures of Mama.

Leonard's reign marked a golden era for the lightweight division. Despite his sheer mastery of his craft, Leonard was given all he could handle by a crop of challengers that included the likes of Charley White, Richie Mitchell, Rocky Kansas, Jack Britton, and Lew Tendler. Many of his title defenses have become the stuff of legend.

In 1920, Leonard was knocked clear out of the ring by the master left hooker Charley White in Benton Harbor, Michigan. He clambered back through the ropes just in time and then bluffed White long enough to clear his head. He knocked White out in the ninth round. Leonard prided himself on his psychological tactics as much as on his physical skills. Before his 1921 defense against Mitchell, Leonard stood in the ring directly in front of his opponent as referee Johnny Haukaup explained the new boxing commission rule requiring a boxer to go to a neutral corner after scoring a knockdown.

"Let me get this straight," said Leonard, with an open, innocent look of interest. "Every time I knock him down…" He pointed to Mitchell, "I have to go to a neutral corner?" Mitchell's jaw tightened perceptibly.

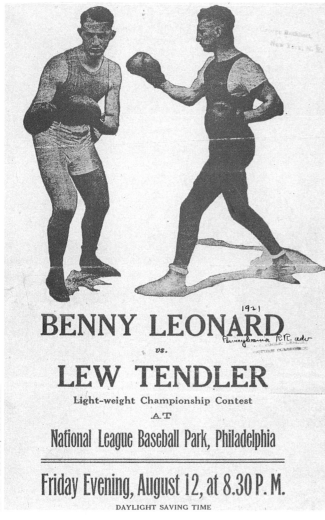

BENNY LEONARD
vs.
LEW TENDLER
Light-weight Championship Contest
AT
National League Baseball Park, Philadelphia
Friday Evening, August 12, at 8.30 P. M.
DAYLIGHT SAVING TIME

Benny Leonard *(opposite page)* was so slick in the ring that it was said no opponent ever mussed his hair. In fact, the Professor, as Leonard was known, survived several hair-raising bouts against some of the best lightweights of all time, including *(above)* Lew Tendler.

Leonard had good reason to start to work on Mitchell early that night. He'd knocked Mitchell out four years before and, confident of his abilities, had told a gambling friend named Arnold Rothstein that he thought he could do it in one this time. Rothstein, taking the champion at his word, told Leonard he would bet $25,000 on a one-round kayo. The bell rang. Leonard, working carefully, not rushing, put Mitchell down three times in the first two minutes. Each time, Mitchell struggled up at nine. Now Leonard measured his man, moving him around, setting him up for the certain kill. Out of nowhere, like a drowning man grabbing a piece of driftwood, Mitchell threw a left hook that landed in the pit of Leonard's stomach. Leonard stiffened, momentarily paralyzed, and Mitchell landed a right to the chin that dropped Leonard.

"The atmosphere was tense with utter astonishment," wrote Nat Fleischer. "Benny Leonard, the idol of New York, out on the canvas!"

On instinct, Leonard rose at the count of seven and, with his manager, Billy Gibson, screaming from the corner, and every fan in the old Madison Square Garden on his feet, he hung on desperately. Then, in the words of Fleischer, "Benny fiddled about and kidded Richie into doing nothing until the bell rang." He'd survived. Working even more methodically than usual, he knocked Mitchell out in the sixth round. His friend Rothstein showed up in the dressing room after the bout to tell Benny he never did get the chance to get the bet down.

The Mitchell fight, Leonard always said, was his toughest.

Leonard survived two more tough outings—against Lew Tendler in 1922 and 1923—before announcing his retirement on January 15, 1925. The papers ran a picture of Leonard, slick and dapper in a three-piece suit, raising his smiling mother's left arm, as a referee raises the glove of the victorious boxer. Mama had won.

Leonard's seven-and-a-half-year reign as lightweight champion remains the longest in history. It should have ended there. Unfortunately, after the stock market crash, Leonard, needing money, made a brief comeback as a welterweight. Pudgy, his un-mussable hair almost gone, he went undefeated in nineteen straight fights before being knocked out by Jimmy McLarnin on October 7, 1932.

Fifteen years later, Benny Leonard died in the ring. He was refereeing a bout between Julio Jiminez and Eddie Giosa at the St. Nicholas Arena in New York when he collapsed from a stroke.

Record

Born (Benjamin Leiner) in New York City, New York, April 7, 1896. 5 feet, 5 inches (165 cm); 123–153 pounds (56–69 kg).
PRO DEBUT: 1911; TKOby3 Mickey Finnegan.
LAST FIGHT: October 7, 1932; KOby6 Jimmy McLarnin.
Won Lightweight Championship May 28, 1917; KO9 Freddie Welsh.
Announced retirement January 15, 1925.
Returned to ring October 6, 1931.
CAREER RECORD: 179-20-4 (8 no-decision), with 69 knockouts.
PEAK MOMENT: Against Lew Tendler, July 27, 1922.
NICKNAME: The Professor.

THE **5** TEN
GREATEST
FIGHTERS

Sam Langford

"*I*n November 1901," Nat Fleischer once wrote, "Joe Woodman was running a small drugstore in Boston and, as a side issue, staging boxing bouts at the Lenox Athletic Club. Into this drug emporium one chilly morning drifted a slim Negro youth, with a yellow dog of uncertain parentage at his heels."

The eventual fate of the dog is unrecorded. The youth, however, was to leave his mark. He landed a job as janitor at Lenox A.C., filled out —in the end no one would ever call him slim— and went on to become one of the greatest fighters of all time. His name was Sam Langford.

Langford never won a world championship. Then again, he was never given a chance to fight for one. In twenty-four years as a professional boxer he beat the best in six weight classes, from featherweight to heavyweight. But as a black boxer in the era of the color line, he found himself shut out of the big-money championship bouts. Even Jack Johnson, after he'd won the heavyweight title, ducked Langford. Johnson had beaten Sam once, in a tough fifteen-rounder in 1906, when Jack weighed 185 pounds (84 kg) and Sam just 156 pounds (71 kg). Johnson, once champion, saw no reason to expose himself to a bigger, stronger Langford. Often through his career, in order to get a match—and thus money to eat—Langford had to agree to carry an opponent. Not that Langford ever took a dive. It was enough that he let his man finish the fight on his feet. That's the way it was in the days when

© Syndication International

Stocky Sam Langford, the greatest fighter never to hold a world championship, fought and beat the best in every weight class, from welterweight to heavyweight. In 1909 *(above),* he traveled to London to kayo Iron Hague in the fourth round at the National Sport Club.

a black fighter could be given a nickname like "Boston Tar Baby" without anyone questioning such blatant racism.

Still, as Fleischer put it (his style getting away from him this time): "You never hear Sam Langford being lambasted as a false alarm whenever a fistic talkfest is on the tapis." That is, everyone who saw him agreed that Sam Langford could fight a little.

Langford was born in Weymouth, Nova Scotia, on March 4, 1886. Like many boxers of the era, he spent his early years riding the rails, learning to fight in the hobo jungles. He was just fifteen when he showed up in Woodman's drugstore, but within weeks he was making a name for himself on the Lenox's weekly amateur cards. In January of 1902, under Woodman's guidance, Langford turned pro. The record book says he had 291 fights. In all likelihood he had more. Langford always insisted that many of his early fights went unrecorded.

In Langford's day, there was no coddling a

young fighter, no careful matchmaking to build up an impressive record. Within two years, Langford was meeting the likes of Joe Gans and Jack Blackburn. He fought Gans, the reigning lightweight champion and already a legend, in an over-the-weight bout on December 8, 1903. Both fighters weighed in at about 140 pounds (63 kg). Gans dominated the early rounds, but as the bout wore on young Langford's confidence grew. The Old Master wasn't hurting him. Langford began to attack. Though Gans held him off, the referee's decision went to Langford. Two weeks later he took on Blackburn, a welterweight and one of the cleverest boxers of his day. Blackburn won a twelve-round decision, but the fight further increased Langford's belief that he could hold his own with anybody.

That confidence never wavered. In 1907, Langford sailed to London to fight Tiger Smith at the National Sporting Club. When the question of the referee arose during prefight discussions, the British organizers were puzzled at Langford's apparent lack of interest in the matter. Sam set them straight. "I brought my own referee," he said, raising his right fist in the air. He flattened Smith in four.

Besides the prejudice of the times, Langford's main problem was his weight. He outgrew every weight class, all the way up to heavyweight. At five-foot-six (168 cm), Langford was thick and squat—but all muscle. His chest and shoulders were huge, his head was set on a columnlike neck. He had a seventy-three-inch (185 cm) reach, just an inch (2.5 cm) shorter than the much taller Johnson's. Langford could hit hard with either hand and, in the wake of the Gans and Blackburn bouts, he became one of the smartest fighters of all time. Langford's motto was, Don't let the other man do what he wants. He very seldom did.

Langford met most of the great names of his era—though never with a championship at stake, and often with his "hands tied." He

Courtesy Boxing Illustrated

fought a six-round no-decision bout against middleweight champion Stanley Ketchel. Most at ringside thought Ketchel, great as he was, got off easy in that one. He knocked out Jack O'Brien in five rounds in New York in 1911. Of Langford, O'Brien once told A. J. Liebling, "When he appeared upon the scene of combat you knew you were cooked." Indeed. So sure of himself was Langford that he could

afford to play around in the ring. He was fond of talking to his opponents. He told Liebling of his 1917 bout with one Battling Norfolk. At the beginning of the second round, Langford gestured for Norfolk to shake hands. "Why?" said Norfolk. "This ain't the last round." "Oh, yes it is," said Langford, and he knocked Norfolk out a moment later. There was always the impression with Sam that he could end a fight whenever he chose. On the way to his dressing room before his 1908 fight with Fireman Jim Flynn, Langford noticed one of Flynn's cornermen slicing up oranges. Langford watched and finally asked the man what he was doing. "Jim likes to suck on oranges between rounds," said the cornerman. "You're wasting money," said Langford. "He won't be needing all that fruit." He kayoed Flynn in the first round.

Sam Langford spent the last two decades of his life, blind and poor, working as a watchman at a city-run lodging house in Harlem—a charitable position created by New York City Mayor Fiorello La Guardia. He died in 1956. Never a champion. Forever a champion.

Record

Born in Weymouth, Nova Scotia, March 4, 1883. 5 feet, 6½ inches (169 cm); 150–200 pounds (68–91 kg).

PRO DEBUT: 1902; KO6 Jack McVicker.

LAST FIGHT: 1926; TKOby1 Brad Simmons. Never given chance at any World Championship.

CAREER RECORD: 187-50-47 (3 no-contest, 4 no-decision), with 102 knockouts.

PEAK MOMENT: Against Iron Hague, May 24, 1909.

NICKNAME: The Boston Tar Baby.

Mickey Walker

Mickey Walker's most famous fight is one he probably didn't even have. On July 2, 1925, Walker, the reigning welterweight champion of the world, challenged Harry Greb for the middleweight crown. Greb, known as the Pittsburgh Windmill—and as a walking encyclopedia for dirty tactics—won a decision over the smaller Walker at the end of fifteen savage rounds. (That bout is in the record books.) According to legend, Walker and Greb ran into each other much later that same evening at the Silver Slipper saloon. After a few drinks, Walker turned to Greb and, in the expansive spirit of new friendship, said, "You know, Harry, you never would have licked me if you hadn't had your thumb in my eye all night." Greb froze. "Why, you Irish bum," he said, "I'll whip you again any day of the week!" A moment later, the story goes, the two were slugging it out again on the sidewalk.

"I lost the first fight to Greb," Mickey wrote in his autobiography. "But I always thought I won the second one."

True or not, it's the perfect Mickey Walker story: brawling, bright lights, and booze. Those were the Roaring Twenties, and Walker, along with his manager Doc Kearns, was ready to roar louder than anyone. In his twenty-year career, Walker took on anyone and everyone, from welterweight to heavyweight, and fought them all the same way—with an all-out savage attack. In between he trained on gin and partied with mobsters and stars. He was married seven times to four different women.

© AP/Wide World Photos

"I not only fight return bouts," Walker once said. "I fight return weddings."

Walker was born in Elizabeth, New Jersey, in 1901. His father wanted him to be an architect, and Mickey spent three years as a draughtsman at the firm of Post and Company on Park Avenue before he was fired—for fighting. In 1919, Walker had his first professional bout, a four-round no-decision affair against Joe Orsini in Elizabeth. The evening was enlivened when Mickey's mother crashed the gate—literally. Unlike her husband, Liz Walker was an ardent supporter of her son's boxing ambitions. Determined to see her son's debut—though women were barred from the match—Liz climbed onto the roof of the auditorium and watched through a skylight until, caught up in the action, she swung a fist against the glass and shattered it. "The cops had to [get] Mom off the roof," wrote Mickey.

That Walker determination—he was known as the Toy Bulldog—carried Mickey throughout his career. He was a relentless body puncher and he never quit, whether winning or losing. Walker captured his first title on November 1, 1922, when he decisioned Jack Britton in fifteen rounds in the old Madison Square Garden. Liz Walker's son was twenty-

one years old and welterweight champion of the world.

The following year Walker's original manager, Jack Bulger, died, and Walker, at the suggestion of Damon Runyon, hooked up with Kearns. The Doc was on the outs with his other champion, Jack Dempsey, and the pairing with Walker was a natural. Together they set out to conquer the world.

Walker lost the welterweight crown to Pete Latzo in May of 1926. Kearns barely noticed. He had his eye on bigger game. The year before, Walker, still 149 pounds (68 kg), had outboxed light heavyweight champion Mike McTigue, but came away with only a no-decision. Kearns knew the big money was in the heavier weights.

On December 10, 1926, Walker pounded out a ten-round win over Tiger Flowers to take the middleweight title. Within the year, Kearns had the Toy Bulldog yapping after the big boys. In 1927, Walker knocked out his old adversary McTigue—now fighting as a heavyweight—in one round. He followed that with a win over Paul Berlenbach. Over the next three years Mickey fought twenty-five times, though only two of those bouts were in defense of his middleweight title. Finally, in 1931, after two impressive wins over heavyweight contender Johnny Risko, Walker relinquished his crown. Three days later, at Ebbets Field in Brooklyn, Walker took on Jack Sharkey. The year before Sharkey had seen his chance for the vacant heavyweight title dissolve on the canvas in front of him after he fouled Max Schmeling, but he was still the best heavyweight in the world.

Though outweighed by twenty-nine pounds (13 kg), and five inches (13 cm) shorter than Sharkey, Walker took the fight to the bigger man, pressing him all the way. Walker banged away at Sharkey's body and bulled him to the ropes, never giving him a chance to set or even to breathe. At the end of fifteen rounds they called it a draw. The thirty-five thousands fans sent their boos rolling down over the ring. The

The Toy Bulldog bites. Mickey Walker, welterweight and middleweight champ in the Roaring Twenties, lived for the ring and bright lights of Broadway and Hollywood. *Opposite page:* He is shown here flattening 223 pound (101 kg) Arthur Dekuh in 1932, as movie queen Lupe Velez cheers at ringside.

next day, columnist Paul Gallico wrote, "Walker won the Sharkey fight but didn't get it."

Walker never reached that peak again. A year later Schmeling stopped him in the eighth round. As Walker, bloody and battered, sat on his stool after that one, Kearns said, "I guess this was one we couldn't win."

"Speak for yourself, Kearns," said Walker. "You're the one who threw in the towel, not me."

In his retirement, Walker quit drinking and took up painting. He had several one-man shows. One critic heralded his work, referring to him as "a primitive."

"A few years ago, if you'd have called me that," said the old Toy Bulldog, "I'd have knocked you flat."

Record

Born Edward Patrick Walker in Elizabeth, New Jersey, July 13, 1901. 5 feet, 7 inches (170 cm); 147–170 pounds (67–77 kg).

PRO DEBUT: February 10, 1919; No-Decision 4 Young Orsini.

LAST FIGHT: June 22, 1939; KO2 Red Bush.

Won Welterweight Championship November 1, 1922; W15 Jack Britton. Lost title May 20, 1926; L10 Peter Latzo.

Won Middleweight Championship December 3, 1926; W10 Tiger Flowers. Relinquished title June 19, 1931.

CAREER RECORD: 94-19-4 (1 no-contest, 45 no-decision), with 61 knockouts.

PEAK MOMENT: Against Jack Sharkey, July 22, 1931.

NICKNAME: The Toy Bulldog.

THE 7 TEN GREATEST FIGHTERS

Joe Gans

When he was heavyweight champion of the world and the self-proclaimed "baddest man on the planet," Mike Tyson used to prepare for his multimillion-dollar title defenses by taping old fight photographs on the walls of his Atlantic City or Las Vegas training quarters—classic shots to get him in the mood and to inspire his sense of heritage. Tyson's favorite subject was a little man named Joe Gans, a man who died fifty-six years before Tyson was born.

"The Old Master," Tyson would say, the reverence clear in his high, soft voice. "The Old Master."

That nickname was coined by fight cartoonist Tad Dorgan, and its worth noting that no one has ever come up with a better one for the man who held the lightweight title from 1902 to 1904 and again from 1906 to 1908.

Gans, a one-time oyster shucker in a Baltimore fish market, started his career in the rough-and-tumble Battle Royales held in those days in the back rooms of saloons. A dozen men in the ring at once, and Gans, often the smallest, was always the one left standing. His obvious natural ability drew the attention of Baltimore restaurateur and boxing manager Al Herford. Herford signed the young Gans to a contract and soon had him fighting steadily.

The early records are spotty, but Gans's rise clearly was spectacular. From 1891 through September of 1896, reports show, he fought thirty-two times, winning twenty-nine and drawing three. He scored twenty-four knockouts. His victims included such stars of the day as George Siddons and Walter Edgerton, the Kentucky Rosebud. Gans's first loss came on October 6, 1896, when Dal Hawkins beat him on points in New York. Gans would avenge that setback four years later with a two-round kayo. Few men ever got the best of Joe Gans for good.

What set Gans apart right from the start was not so much his physical superiority (at five-foot-six [168 cm], he was compact and muscular, with dazzling speed; he could put a man down with either hand—with a punch to the head or to the body), but his intelligence. Gans, the Old Master, was a tireless student of the game. He would study other boxers in the gym and experiment endlessly with moves and countermoves, defense and footwork. Through analysis and application he made himself into the most complete and efficient fighter of his day.

The only knock on Gans was that under a misguided sense of obligation and loyalty to the shady Herford and associates he occasionally failed to fight to the best of his ability. A great fighter, Gans was a lousy actor. His second-round "knockout" at the hands of featherweight Terry McGovern in Chicago drew such a stink that the City Council promptly banned boxing.

Still, by 1900, with wins over Billy Ernst, Kid McPartland, and George McFadden (the last avenging an earlier twenty-three-round knockout loss and twenty-round draw), Gans had raised himself to the position of leading contender for Frank Erne's lightweight title. Gans was matched with the champion on March 23, 1900, at the Broadway Athletic Club in New York City. The result was a shock. Eighty years before Roberto Duran, Gans pulled his own *"No mas."* He had built a substantial lead through the first eleven rounds, but in the twelfth, Erne rocked him with a right and then accidentally butted him, open-

© KEYSTONE/FPG International

Joe Gans *(opposite page)* emerged from a Baltimore fish market to become a fistic work of art. The Old Master, as Gans was known, moved with classic grace and style—and carried a nasty wallop, scoring eighty-five knockouts in his eighteen-year career. His statue *(left)* stands in Madison Square Garden, a reminder of his greatness.

ing a deep cut over Gans's left eye. "I quit," Gans told referee Johnny White.

A rematch was held on May 12, 1901, in Fort Erie, Ontario. With the appeal of the Horton Law in September of 1900, boxing was no longer permitted in New York. Determined to wipe away the stain of the first bout, Gans went right to work. A right hand halfway through the first round rocked Erne. A left and another right put him down and out. The time was 1:40 of the first round, and Gans was lightweight champion.

He defended the crown successfully nine times over the following three years before relinquishing it to move up to welterweight— where, on January 19, 1906, he stopped Mike (Twin) Sullivan to stake a claim to the vacant title. In the meantime, Battling Nelson had knocked out Jimmy Britt to take the light-

weight title. Gans decided he wanted it back. The first Gans-Nelson fight, held on September 3, 1906, in Goldfield, Nevada, remains one of the classic battles in ring history. Gans, though badly weakened by having to make 133 pounds (60 kg), outboxed and battered Nelson round after round. Finally Nelson, wobbly and frustrated, deliberately began to foul Gans. A blatant low blow in the forty-third round ended the fight. Gans was champion again—on a foul. The new champion wired his mother, "Am bringing home the bacon!"

Though Gans would fight for another two and a half years, he would never be the same after the Goldfield bout. The training grind had badly undermined his constitution. In 1908, suffering from tuberculosis, he was knocked out twice by Nelson. Gans died in Baltimore on August 10, 1910.

Record

Born (Joseph Gaines) in Baltimore, November 25, 1874. 5 feet, 6 inches (168 cm); 122–134 pounds (55–61 kg).

PRO DEBUT: 1891; KO12 Dave Armstrong.
LAST FIGHT: March 12, 1909; W10 Jabez White.
Won Lightweight Championship May 12, 1902; KO1 Frank Erne. Relinquished title November, 1904.
Won Welterweight Championship January 19, 1906; KO15 Twin Sullivan.
Regained Lightweight Championship September 3, 1906; W-foul Battling Nelson.
Lost lightweight title July 4, 1908; KOby17 Battling Nelson.
CAREER RECORD: 132-9-15, with 85 knockouts.
PEAK MOMENT: Against Battling Nelson, September 3, 1906.
NICKNAME: The Old Master.

THE TEN GREATEST FIGHTERS

Henry Armstrong

Henry Armstrong lost his first professional fight. That was in North Braddock, Pennsylvania, in 1931. Somebody named Al Iovino knocked Henry out in three rounds. Armstrong won his second fight, then lost two more. Fighting mostly in Los Angeles, in the hard early days of the Depression, Armstrong lost one or two fights a year. He had no direction, no management. He was fighting merely to eat, taking bouts when and where he could get them.

Things began to turn around for Henry in 1934, when manager Eddie Meade, at the urgings of his friends George Raft and Al Jolson (who helped put up the money), bought out Armstrong's contract. Under Meade's direction, Armstrong began to progress to bigger purses and better opponents. But it didn't happen overnight. Armstrong's biggest success of 1936, for example, was a ten-round decision over fight immortal Baby Arizmendi.

That victory earned Armstrong his first title, something called the California-Mexican world featherweight championship.

And then Henry Armstrong became unbeatable. In 1937, he fought twenty-seven times and won twenty-seven times. Only one opponent, Aldo Spoldi, lasted to the final bell. On October 29 of that year Armstrong won the world featherweight title when he stopped Petey Sarron in six rounds in Madison Square Garden.

It was Meade's—and Jolson's—grand scheme that Armstrong, in order to compete with new heavyweight king Joe Louis for the public's fight dollar, do something extraordinary. "I had to get super-popular, colossal. They had those words in Hollywood," Armstrong once told writer Peter Heller. The plan called for Armstrong to win championships in three weight divisions, something no fighter had done.

Meade and Jolson had picked the right man for the job. Armstrong, born in Mississippi and raised on the hard streets of St. Louis, Missouri, had been fighting since he was a boy. Over the years he had developed a blazing, irresistible style, a perpetual-motion attack that allowed him to swarm over his opponents, even men bigger than himself. The second step in the plan came on May 31, 1938, when Armstrong took on Barney Ross for the welterweight championship. Ross, a masterful boxer and one of the greatest welterweights of all time, was still only twenty-nine when he took on Armstrong. But he learned that night in the Madison Square Garden Bowl in Long Island City, New York, that he was past his prime. By the twelfth round, the crowd was screaming for referee Arthur Donovan to stop the mugging, and twice Armstrong himself stopped punching and turned to Donovan as if to ask, "What more do I need to do?" But Barney Ross had never been off his feet in eighty previous fights and he'd never been stopped. For fifteen rounds Armstrong battered and mauled Ross, but he finished, standing, against Armstrong. Henry had his second title; Ross would never fight again.

Three months later, Armstrong completed his quest with a fifteen-round decision over Lou Ambers for the lightweight title. That was the peak. Armstrong immediately relinquished the featherweight crown. He successfully defended the welterweight title six times before paring down to lightweight again for the first time since winning that title. The fight, on August 22, 1939, was a rematch with Ambers and it developed into an ugly brawl. Armstrong, penalized for hitting low, lost the title on points. Now he was merely a single world champ. He defended his welterweight title eight more times, before challenging Ceferino Garcia of the Phillipines for the middleweight championship at Gilmore Stadium in Los Angeles on March 1, 1940. Armstrong, who came in at 142 pounds (64 kg) to Garcia's 153½ (70 kg), should have won his fourth title.

© AP/Wide World Photos

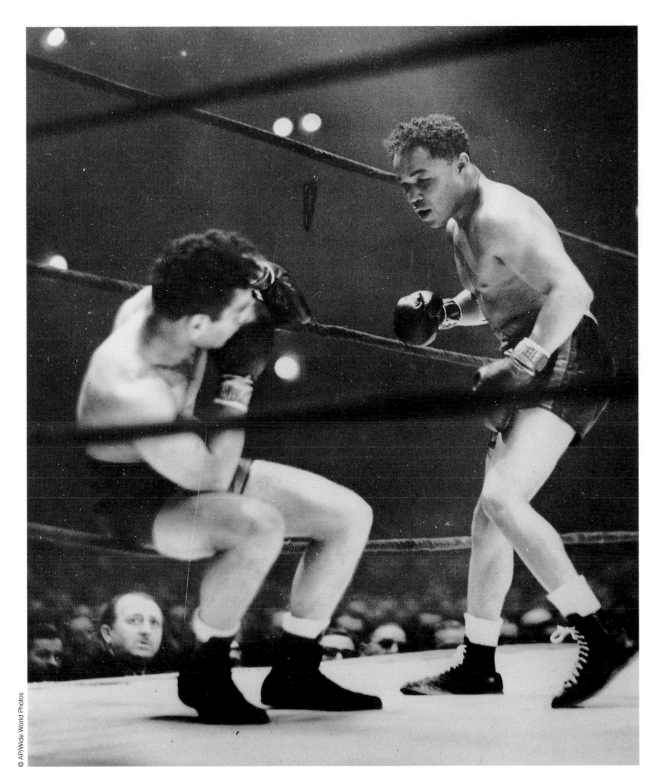

Poetry in perpetual motion. Henry Armstrong, shown above stopping welterweight challenger Pedro Montanez in the ninth round in 1940, simultaneously held the featherweight, lightweight, and welterweight titles.

Queensberry rules," "the master of unholy tactics," or "the most vicious fighter of all time." He was all of those things and more. Gouging, butting, thumbing, holding, and hitting low, Zivic decisioned a tired Armstrong. In a rematch three months later, Zivic stopped Henry in twelve.

Though he would fight forty-nine more times—including a ten-round non-title win over Zivic and a sad ten-round loss to Ray Robinson in 1943 (Robinson, a friend of Armstrong's, carried the former champion) —Armstrong would never again challenge for a title. His last fight came on Valentine's Day, 1945.

Armstrong made more than a million dollars in the ring, but most of it was gone by the time he retired. In 1951, Hammerin' Henry became an ordained Baptist minister and returned to St. Louis to preach.

Instead, the fight was called a draw, although many thought Armstrong had won.

The end of Armstrong's great run came in October of 1940, when, in his nineteenth defense of the welterweight crown, he ran into Fritzie Zivic. Zivic's name never seems to appear in print without being linked to such phrases as, "dirtiest fighter in the history of the

Record

Born (Henry Jackson) in Columbus, Mississippi, December 12, 1912. 5 feet, 5½ inches (166 cm); 124–146 pounds (56–66 kg).
Pro Debut: July 27, 1931; KOby3 Al Iovino.
Last Fight: February 14, 1945; L10 Chester Slider.
Won Featherweight Championship October 29, 1937; KO6 Petey Sarron.
Won Welterweight Championship May 31, 1938; W15 Barney Ross. Lost welterweight title October 4, 1940; L15 Fritzie Zivic.
Won Lightweight Championship August 17, 1938; W15 Lou Ambers. Lost lightweight title August 22, 1939; L15 Lou Ambers.
Career Record: 145-20-9, with 98 knockouts.
Peak Moment: Against Barney Ross, May 31, 1938.
Nicknames: Hammerin' Henry, Homicide Hank, Little Perpetual Motion.

THE **9** TEN GREATEST FIGHTERS

Jack Dempsey

When Jess Willard defended his heavyweight title against Jack Dempsey on July 4, 1919, it seemed a mismatch of near criminal proportions. Willard, the man who had knocked out Jack Johnson in twenty-six rounds in Havana four years before, the man they called the Pottawatomie Giant, stood 6 feet, 6¼ inches (199 cm) and weighed 245 pounds (111 kg). Dempsey, a shade over six feet (182 cm), weighed 187 pounds (85 kg). As the two fighters posed for prefight photographs under a scorching sun in the ring at Toledo (the temperature that day was a reported 110 degrees F [43°C]), Willard nodded and beamed. Dempsey stared at the canvas, pawing nervously with his feet. The tableaux suggested a man about to spank a boy.

But look closer. Willard's huge chest is white, his belly above his trunks is soft. Dempsey is lean and hard all over, his arms and neck burnished from the sun. The sides of his head are shaved clean and he shows a two-day shadow of beard. Dempsey scowls, glances up at Willard, and suddenly here is a different picture. Suddenly here is an angry butcher sizing up a side of beef.

Later, they called the fight the Massacre at Toledo. Seven times in the first round the crouching, slashing Dempsey punched Willard to the canvas. The big man's jaw was broken, his ribs and cheekbone smashed. There was a scramble at ringside, they say, for his teeth. At the end of the round, Willard sat in a

heap in a corner, his arm hooked on a rope, his bloody head laid on his chest. The bell had saved him and somehow he lurched through two more rounds before the fight finally was stopped. The world had a new heavyweight champion—one perfectly suited for the wild, exciting years to come. In the Roaring Twenties, Dempsey would fill the role of Champ the way Babe Ruth filled the role of ballplayer and Al Capone filled the role of mobster.

William Harrison Dempsey was born in Manassa, Colorado, and came of age in the deadly rough hobo jungles and mining camps of the west. It was there he perfected his fighting style—in countless unsanctioned bouts for money to eat and in countless other battles for simple survival. Dempsey's method was pure attack. He fought out of a crouch, bobbing and weaving, his fists held low. His hand speed startling, and his punch as good as any heavyweight's who ever lived. On his way to the title he knocked out Fred Fulton in eighteen seconds in July of 1918 and Jim Morris in fourteen seconds five months later. All told, Dempsey would score twenty five one-round knockouts in his career.

And then there was what the newspapers liked to call "the killer instinct." Dempsey was in the ring for just one thing: to destroy his opponent. Just ask Jess Willard.

Or Paul Gallico. In 1923 Gallico, then a young reporter with no boxing experience, arranged to spar with Dempsey during Dempsey's preparation for Firpo. Gallico hoped to write a column about what it felt like to go a round with the champ. Dempsey simply flattened him.

Dempsey defended his title only six times in seven years, yet his reign as champion remains the stuff of legend. Together with his manager, the legendary Doc Kearns, and promoter Tex Rickard, Dempsey was involved in some of the greatest events in boxing history. His fight against French light heavyweight champion Georges Carpentier on July 2, 1921,

drew the first million-dollar gate in history. Rickard begged Dempsey, for the sake of the promotion, to carry his opponent—at least past the opening round. Dempsey left Carpentier—invariably referred to as "the gallant Frenchman," or by his less-than-blood-stirring nickname of the Orchid Man—quivering on his side in the center of the ring a minute and sixteen seconds into the fourth.

After a break of two years spent touring on the stage and making movies in Hollywood, Dempsey outpointed Tom Gibbons in Shelby, Montana, in a promotional disaster that left the town bankrupt, but made Kearns several thousand dollars richer. Dempsey's next opponent was Luis Angel Firpo. Another million-dollar gate, and the wildest, most spectacular opening round in heavyweight history. Dempsey put Firpo down seven times in the first round, before the huge "Wild Bull of the Pampas" stormed back and knocked Dempsey through the ropes. With some helping hands pushing from press row, Dempsey climbed back in before referee Johnny Gallagher could count him out. Dempsey finished Firpo fifty-seven seconds into the second round.

More than three years would pass before Dempsey fought again. Thirty-one years old, ring-rusty, he lost his crown on a ten-round decision to the smooth-boxing former Marine, Gene Tunney. "What happened, Ginsberg," asked Dempsey's wife, Estelle Taylor, using

■Jack Dempsey emerged from the hobo jungles of the American West to become the greatest figure in the Golden Age of Sports—and the most ferocious heavyweight champion ever.

Courtesy Boxing Illustrated

her pet-name for Dempsey. "Honey," said Jack, "I forgot to duck."

In defeat Dempsey became even more popular than he had been as champion. The public never forgave Tunney—vaguely suspicious anyway for his literary friends and admitted fondness for Shakespeare—for upsetting Dempsey.

The rematch, held on September 22, 1927, at Soldier's Field in Chicago, drew 104,943 spectators and a gate of $2,658,660. The fight itself, the Battle of the Long Count, remains a kind of touchstone, the peak moment in what has come to be known as the Golden Age of Sport. Once again, Tunney dominated, completely outboxing an aging Dempsey—until the seventh round. In a sudden flash of his old destructiveness, Dempsey caught Tunney with a five-punch combination that even in the flickering black and white of old films is frightening in its power and accuracy. Tunney dropped glassy-eyed beside the ropes.

Before the fight it had been agreed that the neutral corner rule (a rule created with Dempsey in mind) would be in force. A fighter scoring a knockdown would be required to go to the farthest neutral corner before the count would begin. Dempsey, his mind back in Toledo or perhaps in the mining camps, stood over the fallen Tunney for several long sec-

onds until referee Dave Barry pushed him away. Tunney, down for as long as fourteen seconds, arose at the official count of nine, and went on to win the fight handily.

Could he have gotten up within ten seconds? Tunney always maintained he could have, but the debate has raged among boxing fans ever since.

Dempsey himself insisted that losing the rematch with Tunney was the best thing that ever happened to him.

"Not a day goes by when someone doesn't ask me about it," he said once, while signing autographs in his Broadway restaurant. "They remember."

They remember it all, Jack.

Record

Born (William Harrison Dempsey) in Manassa, Colorado, June 24, 1895. 6 feet, ¾ inch (185 cm); 180–190 pounds (82–86 kg).
PRO DEBUT: August 17, 1914; D6 Young Herman.
LAST FIGHT: September 22, 1927; L10 Gene Tunney.

Won Heavyweight Championship July 4, 1919; KO3 Jess Willard. Lost title September 23, 1926; L10 Gene Tunney.
CAREER RECORD: 62-6-10, with 49 knockouts.
PEAK MOMENT: Against Jess Willard, July 4, 1919.
NICKNAME: The Manassa Mauler.

THE **10** TEN
GREATEST
FIGHTERS

Stanley Ketchel

Mickey Walker, the story goes, was in a bar one afternoon (that part at least is easy to believe) when he was approached by another patron, clearly a fan. The man, who'd had a few, flung his arm around Walker's shoulder and exclaimed, "Mickey Walker! God-damn, you're the greatest middleweight who ever lived. And don't let anyone tell you different." "What about Ketchel?" said Walker. "Ketchel?!" roared the fan. "You bum, you couldn't lick one side of Stanley Ketchel on the best day you ever had!"

Stanley Ketchel, called Steve by his friends, invoked that sort of passion in those who saw him fight. He was called "savage," "reckless," "a demon of the roped square," "supremely confident," "a killer"—and "the greatest middleweight who ever lived." In Ernest Hemingway's story "The Light of the World," a peroxide-blonde prostitute proclaims, "Steve Ketchel was the finest and most beautiful man that ever lived." The object of all this devotion was born on a farm in Michigan, the son of Polish parents. By the time he was fifteen he was headed west, riding the rails and sleeping in hobo camps. The legend says Ketchel had more than 250 unsanctioned bar fights before turning pro in 1903 in Butte, Montana. Officially, Ketchel ran up a record of 42-2-5, with forty-one knockouts, before flattening Jack (Twin) Sullivan in San Francisco for the vacant middleweight title in 1908.

(A footnote question: Whatever became of Maurice Thompson? Thompson, of Butte, fought Ketchel three times in 1904 and came away with two wins and a draw.)

Virtually every fight in Ketchel's all-too-brief career was memorable. Even his losses. In a great upset, Ketchel was knocked out by Billy Papke on September 7, 1908 (in a bout refereed by former heavyweight champion James Jeffries). Ketchel had beaten Papke five

Colma, California, 1909: Stanley Ketchel has heavyweight champion Jack Johnson on the canvas. A moment later, Johnson got up and flattened Ketchel, but no one has ever kayoed the Ketchel legend. The Michigan Assassin was among the fiercest and most exciting fighters of all time.

months before in his first defense of the title, and Papke clearly wanted revenge. At the opening bell of the rematch, when Ketchel extended his glove to shake hands, Papke fetched him a tremendous right to the windpipe. Ketchel went down spitting blood. He got up, but he never recovered. Papke gave him a brutal beating, though it took him until the fourteenth round to finish the game against Ketchel. (Since that bout, the referee's instructions have included the phrase, "Shake hands and come out fighting.") Eighty days later Ketchel knocked Papke out in eleven rounds.

Ketchel's 1909 bout with Philadelphia Jack O'Brien (whose description of Ketchel vies with all the others: "An example of tumultuous ferocity") remains one of the most celebrated encounters in boxing history. O'Brien, who dominated the early rounds with his jab and ring generalship, finished the bout unconscious, his head resting ingloriously in the resin box. Ketchel's left hook had come in the closing seconds of the tenth round, and the bell sounded before O'Brien could be counted out. The fight was a no-decision contest, and Ketchel's fans insisted Stanley had won by kayo. O'Brien's backers maintained that their man had earned the verdict. What most people forget is that the two fought again ten weeks later and Ketchel finished Philadelphia Jack in three rounds.

Ketchel's most famous bout was one he lost, his October 16, 1909 meeting with Jack Johnson in Colma, California. Though Ketchel, at 170 pounds (77 kg), was greatly overmatched against the 205-pound (93-kg) heavyweight champion (Johnson always insisted he toyed with Ketchel for the benefit of ringside movie cameras), he did knock Johnson down in the twelfth round. At least that's what the legend says. In the film it looks more like Ketchel's long right catches Johnson behind the head and half-pulls, half-clubs the champion to the canvas. What is clear is that Johnson gets up, grin on his face, and meets the onrushing Ketchel with a right uppercut that flattens the smaller man, shearing off several of Ketchel's front teeth in the process. Still, there are those pictures of Johnson on the canvas, and the Ketchel legend grows.

With the exception of the ill-advised challenge of Johnson, though, Ketchel remained unbeatable, a raging, irresistible force in the ring—and, it seems, out of it as well. Alexander Johnson, in his fine book *Ten…and Out,* wrote of Ketchel, "he would have been a leader in any walk of life…a great general or an admiral, if his path of life had lead him into those comparatively peaceful lines." But peace, as all who saw him in action knew, was never a part of Stanley Ketchel.

Ketchel was shot and killed by a man named Walter Dipley in Conway, Missouri, on October 15, 1910. While Dipley's bullet robbed the world of one of its greatest fighters, it did provide one of the classic leads in sporting journalism, John Lardner's famous, "Stanley Ketchel was twenty-four years old when he was fatally shot in the back by the common-law husband of the lady who was cooking his breakfast." Even in death, the Ketchel legend continued.

Record

Born (Stanislaus Kiecal) in Grand Rapids, Michigan, September 14, 1886. 5 feet, 9 inches (175 cm); 150–160 pounds (68–72 kg). PRO DEBUT: May 2, 1903; KO1 Kid Tracy. LAST FIGHT: June 10, 1910; KO5 Jim Smith. Won Middleweight Championship May 9, 1908; KO20 Twin Sullivan. Lost title September 7, 1908; KOby12 Billy Papke. Regained Middleweight Championship November 26, 1908; KO11 Billy Papke. CAREER RECORD: 53-4-5 (4 no-decision), with 50 knockouts. PEAK MOMENT: Against Billy Papke, November 26, 1908. NICKNAME: The Michigan Assassin.

Honorable Mention

Harry Greb, Jack Johnson, Sugar Ray Leonard, Joe Louis, Archie Moore, Willie Pep

Most Underrated

1. Ezzard Charles
2. Gene Tunney
3. Carlos Monzon
4. Larry Holmes
5. Bob Foster

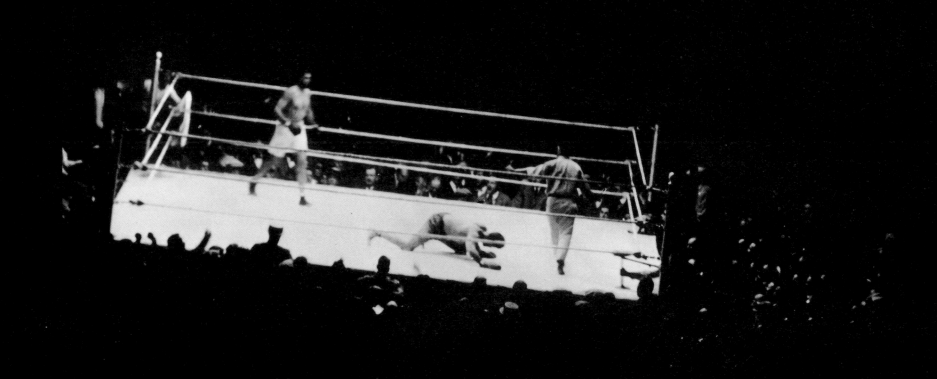

The Ten Greatest Fights of All Time

Jack Dempsey

VS

Luis Angel Firpo

New York, New York. September 14, 1923.

© AP/Wide World Photos

In perhaps the greatest single moment in boxing history, Luis Angel Firpo, the Wild Bull of the Pampas *(above)*, knocks heavyweight champion Jack Dempsey out of the ring in the first round of their epic battle. Dempsey, who had already knocked Firpo down seven times, crawled back through the ropes in time to avoid a knockout, then finished Firpo in the second *(opposite page)*.

Jack Dempsey and Luis Angel Firpo first met in 1922, when Dempsey, the heavyweight champion, was about to set sail for Europe on a promotional tour. Firpo, an Argentine heavyweight just brought to the United States by promoter Tex Rickard, showed up at the pier as Dempsey was about to embark. There, he introduced himself to the champion, called out "Bon voyage!" and promptly kissed Dempsey on both cheeks.

From such a cordial beginning was born the most savage and spectacular fight in boxing history.

Dempsey was never a fighting champion. He'd fought too often and too hard on his way up, and there were too many distractions for the heavyweight champion of the world during the heady Golden Age of Sport. After winning the title from Willard in 1919, Jack had defended it twice in 1920 and once in 1921 (the last was history's first million-dollar gate, against Georges Carpentier). He'd then spent two years touring and fighting exhibitions, before returning to action against Tommy Gibbons in a financially disastrous fight in Shelby, Montana. By the late summer of 1923, Rickard was ready to match the champion in what he called "a Big One." The opponent Rickard had selected, like Carpentier two years before, was a foreign fighter, a relative unknown whom Rickard could tout into a fearsome opponent for Dempsey. The opponent was Firpo.

Known as the Wild Bull of the Pampas, Firpo was a true original in the ring. He was six foot, three inches (190 cm) and a brutish 215 pounds (98 kg), with shaggy black hair and a handsome, brooding face. Possessed of absolutely no ring science, he had nonetheless beaten Bill Brennan and Jess Willard. By the time Rickard announced the fight, the public was convinced that Firpo was a man who would give Dempsey the fight of his life. The public was right, and Rickard had his second million-dollar gate. Just as he had before the Carpentier fight, Rickard came to Dempsey's dressing room and begged the champion to take it easy on his opponent, at least for a while. He didn't want the crowd going home disappointed after an early knockout. Dempsey, however, had no interest in Tex's plan this time.

"Listen," he told Rickard. "There's one difference between Carpentier and Firpo: Firpo is liable to kill me with one blow!"

Rickard insisted, assuring Jack that Firpo would never hit him.

"Go to hell," said Dempsey.

There were eighty-two thousand spectators in the Polo Grounds on the night of September 14, 1923. Despite Dempsey's refusal to play along with Rickard's crowd-pleasing battle plan, not one went home disappointed.

Trying to describe the first round is like trying to describe a series of explosions. James Crusinberry of the Chicago *Tribune* called it "the greatest round of battling seen since the Silurian Age." At the bell Dempsey came out in his patented crouch, bobbing and weaving and driving in on the challenger. Firpo, planting his feet and swinging, caught Dempsey with a right and knocked him down. The crowd was stunned. Jack jumped to his feet without a count from referee Jack Gallagher and tore back into Firpo. Seconds later a crashing left sent the challenger to the canvas.

Dempsey, in his fury, stood over the fallen Firpo, just waiting for him to rise. When Firpo stood, Dempsey drove him down again with a crushing series of blows. Again and again Firpo went down. Once Dempsey stepped over his crouching body to get a better angle of attack. Seven times in all Firpo went down, and seven times, amazingly, he got up to face the snarling Dempsey.

"He wouldn't stay down," Dempsey wrote in his autobiography. "The lust to kill was burning in his eyes, and nothing was going to stop him."

With the round drawing to a close, the wounded Firpo charged Dempsey to the ropes with a tremendous, clubbing, right hand, knocked the champion through the ropes and completely out of the ring. Call it the greatest moment in boxing. Go to the Whitney Museum and look at the painting by George Bellows. Or better yet, just look at the old black and white photos. In any view, it is a moment of myth. The heavyweight champion of the world sprawled across press row.

Dempsey claims he landed on Hype Igoe, saying, "Through the years it has amused me to hear this or that person take credit for breaking my fall and throwing me back as if I were a prized baseball. Igoe was the only one who said nothing."

Whomever he landed on, Dempsey received a push from several hands and somehow clambered back through the ropes by the count of seven. Firpo's inexperienced seconds missed the chance to call for a disqualification and Firpo missed the chance to finish Dempsey. He charged the champion wildly

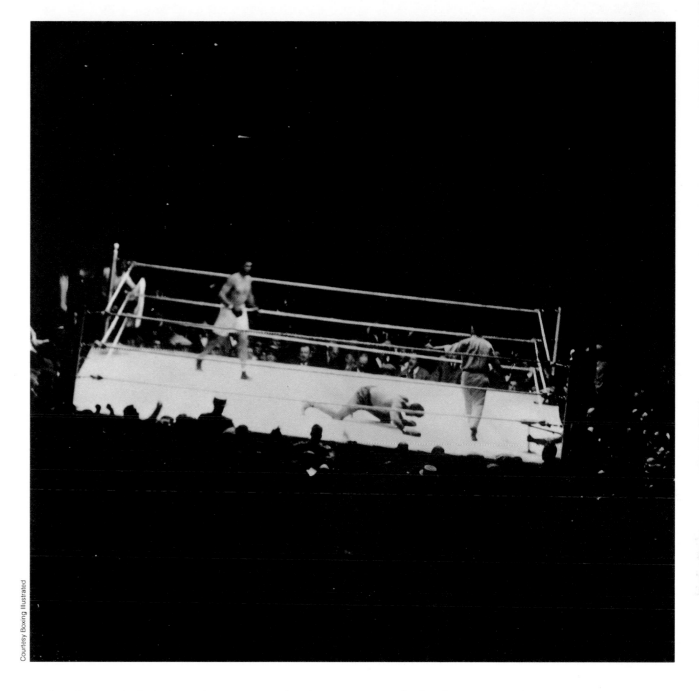

and Jack, nearly helpless, dove into a clinch and hung on until the round ended.

Back in his corner a still-dazed Dempsey asked his manager, Doc Kearns, what round he'd been knocked out in.

"You son-of-a-bitch," bellowed Kearns. "You weren't knocked out. Get out there and box this guy carefully. Let him think you're still groggy and look for an opening."

The ruse worked perfectly. Firpo charged in and Dempsey exploded. A left hook dropped the challenger to the mat. One last time the astonishingly game Firpo got up. Dempsey

was ready for him. A crushing combination put Firpo down for the ninth and final time. Gallagher counted him out at fifty-seven seconds of the round.

After the bout Firpo protested that Dempsey had ignored the prefight instructions to go to a neutral corner after scoring a knockdown. As a result, a new rule was introduced requiring that any fighter scoring a knockdown must go to the farthest neutral corner before the referee can begin his count. That rule, of course, would come back to haunt Dempsey four years later in his second bout with Gene Tunney.

Aaron Pryor
VS
Alexis Arguello

Miami, Florida. November 12, 1982.

Alexis Arguello was trying to do what no boxer had ever done. He was trying to win a world championship in a fourth weight class. At thirty years old, the handsome and gentlemanly Arguello, a Nicaraguan exile living in Miami, already had won the WBA featherweight title, the WBC junior lightweight title, and the WBC lightweight title. An impressive list, but Arguello had barely stopped to notice. He'd given up the first two of those already, moving up in weight. Arguello was thinking four.

Standing in his way on this warm Friday night in the Orange Bowl was a man they called the Hawk. Aaron Pryor was twenty-seven years old, a brooding, angry fighter from Cincinnati. He had a 31-0 record, with twenty-nine knockouts. He also was the WBA junior welterweight champion. Pryor was less interested in titles than in respect. He saw the match against Arguello as a chance for some of the acclaim he felt had too long been denied him. Pryor was known as a reckless, fearless puncher. Arguello, four inches (10 cm) taller at 5 foot 10½ inches (179 cm), would be expected to box carefully, to pick Pryor apart from the outside and then to break him down with his renowned body attack.

Among the crowd of 23,800 that turned out for the fight was sixty-nine-year-old veteran boxer Henry Armstrong. Armstrong, of course, once held the featherweight, lightweight, and welterweight titles—simultaneously. Arguello dedicated his fight against Pryor to old Hammerin' Hank.

At the bell Arguello came out as expected, calm and unhurried. And then Pryor was on him. Arguello had no choice but to stand and fire. He landed a thudding right on Pryor's chin that barely fazed him. Pryor came right back with a barrage of his own rights. It was an extraordinary round. Films show that Arguello had thrown 108 punches, Pryor 130.

The two champions continued to fight at a torrid pace. Twice in the second round Arguello landed thunderous rights. Twice Pryor shook them off. "If there's a better chin in the world than Pryor's," wrote Pat Putnam in *Sports Illustrated,* "it has to be on Mount Rushmore." Pryor was taking the best that Arguello had and was surviving. More important, he was forcing Arguello to fight the fight that he, Pryor, wanted.

In the sixth round, Pryor, bobbing and weaving, punching constantly, opened a cut over Arguello's left eye. The blood hampered Arguello's vision, and his handlers worked steadily over him between rounds. Across the ring, Pryor's cornermen were dousing their fighter with peppermint schnapps.

Both men fought all-out, with no thought for defense. Midway through the thirteenth round, Arguello caught Pryor coming in with one more huge right hand. This time Pryor wobbled, but before Arguello could press the attack, Pryor came back with a stiff combina-

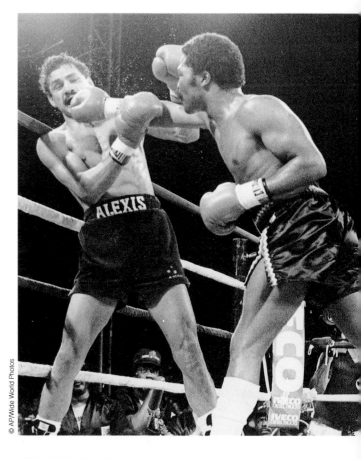

Alexis Arguello's *(above)* quest for a historic fourth title ended in a classic battle with WBA welterweight champ Aaron Pryor. After thirteen rounds of furious action, the Hawk left Arguello draped on the ropes *(opposite page)* in the fourteenth.

tion of his own. At the bell, Arguello went back to his corner in frustration. Still, with two rounds to go, the fight was up for grabs.

In the fourteenth round, Pryor grabbed it. He caught Arguello early with a savage left-hook/right-hand combination and drove him to the ropes. Arguello tried to set himself to fire back, as he had done all night, but now the Hawk's assault was overwhelming. Ten straight right hands slammed against Arguello's head. A right uppercut, two left hooks, and another right.

Take a look at the films again and count. Twenty-three unanswered punches. Referee Stanley Christodoulou finally stopped it at 1:06 of the fourteenth round. The gallant Arguello stood for a moment longer and then crumpled to the canvas. He would remain unconscious for four minutes.

"Do I feel like I stopped history?" said Pryor after the fight. "I can't say that, because the man is a three-time champion. He's already made history."

On November 12, 1982 in Miami, both Pryor and Arguello made history.

Muhammad Ali
vs
Joe Frazier

Manila, the Philippines. October 1, 1975.

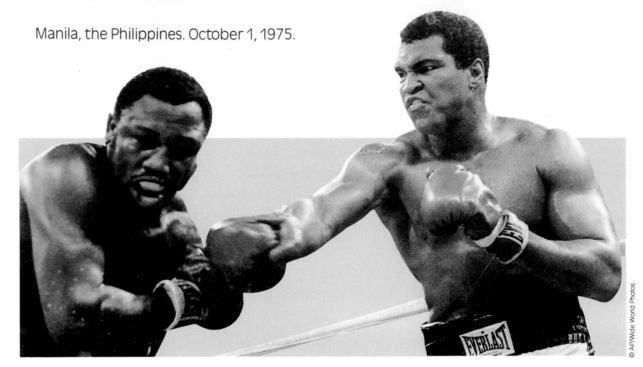

*T*he first time these two met, back in 1971, they were both undefeated. Frazier was the recognized champion; Ali, the champion in exile. They fought fifteen glorious, stubborn, bruising rounds that time and when it was over Frazier was still undefeated and still the champion.

Since then things had changed. In 1973, George Foreman bounced Frazier all over the ring in Jamaica to take the title. Ken Norton broke Ali's jaw. Ali came back, beat Norton—beat Frazier, too, over twelve less dramatic rounds full of holding and jabbing. Late in 1974, Ali beat Foreman, hammered him, unbelieving, to the canvas in Zaire. Now, suddenly, it was Ali and Joe again. Older, wearier, but made for each other, needing each other.

"It's gonna be a chilla' and a killa' and a thrilla' when I beat the Gorilla in Manila," Ali told the press.

Ali was convinced Frazier had nothing left, said he'd stand and trade with Joe. But, for Ali—for that floating, taunting presence, the man who called him "too ugly to be champion," the man he still called Clay—Frazier would always have something left.

They brought the two together before twenty-eight thousand people in the Philippine Coliseum, 10:45 a.m. in Manila so that the millions watching back in the States on closed-circuit would see it at night. Ferdinand and Imelda Marcos sat at ringside.

Ali came out for the first round flat-footed, contemptuous. His prefight words had been no ruse. He meant to outpunch Frazier from the start. And he did, rocking Frazier again and again with straight, hard combinations to the head. Frazier's legs buckled more than once in those first three rounds. The sweat flew from his snapping head. By the end of the third Frazier seemed all but finished. But Joe kept coming, kept firing those slashing, hooking punches. He would show Ali no fear, no weakness.

As if annoyed at Frazier's determination—here was a man too dumb to be beaten—Ali went to the ropes in the fifth round and Frazier followed. The tide turned. Frazier was close to Ali now, just where he wanted to be, banging away—to the ribs, the chest, the hips, the kidneys. He ripped his big hooks to the head, and

now it was Ali's legs that were going. Ali came out for the seventh round. "Old Joe Frazier," he said to the rock of man before him, "I thought you was washed up." Frazier grinned a lumpy grin. "Somebody told you wrong, pretty boy," he said.

By the end of the tenth round it was an even fight. And it was Ali who was fading, Ali who slumped on his stool, his cornerman Bundini Brown crying, screaming at him. "Go to the well once more, Champ!"

In the eleventh round, Frazier pinned Ali in a corner, slamming hooks off his head, punching as if to drive this man not just out of the ring, but out of his life forever. In the face of that awful barrage, Ali went back to the well, dragged himself to the well. He began to fire back, catching Frazier with long right hands. The fight turned again. Frazier, his face

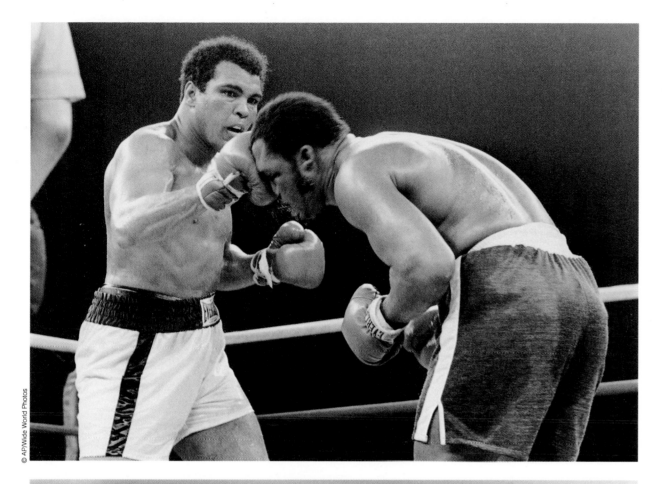

disappearing in lumps and bruises, began to lose strength. In the thirteenth round, Ali knocked Frazier's mouthpiece flying and nearly dropped him. Joe staggered blindly through the fourteenth round.

And then this most savage of fights ended, fittingly somehow, with a touch of compassion. Over the protests of his battered fighter, Frazier's trainer Eddie Futch stopped the bout. "Sit down, son," said Futch. "It's all over. No one will ever forget what you did here today."

Afterwards Ali said, "It was like death. Closest thing to dyin' that I know of."

"Lawdy, Lawdy, he's a great champion," said Frazier.

The Thrilla in Manila. Muhammad Ali and Joe Frazier brought out the best in each other, and their third fight was the best of the best. Ali rocked Frazier repeatedly in the opening rounds *(opposite page and above)* before Joe came back, hammering away at Ali's body *(left),* never stepping back. In the end, though, Ali prevailed. After going through what he called "the closest thing to dyin'" he knew of, Ali finally stopped his old foe.

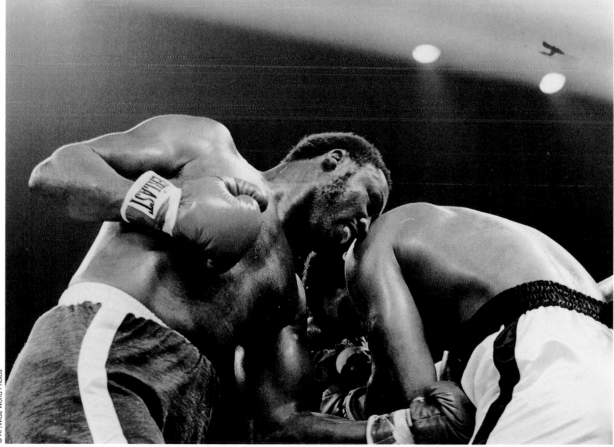

Marvelous Marvin Hagler

vs

Thomas Hearns

Las Vegas, Nevada. April 13, 1985.

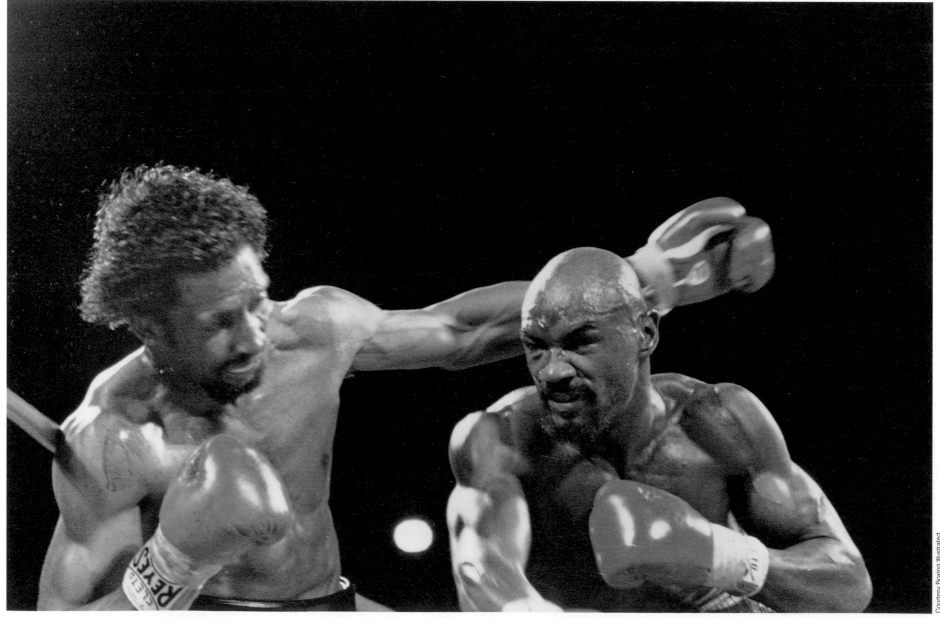

70

*I*n eight minutes and one second of savage combat in a ring set up on the tennis courts of Caesars Palace in Las Vegas, Marvin Hagler and Thomas Hearns cemented their place in ring history. This was a fight.

Hagler, the undisputed middleweight champion of the world, a man who had legally changed his name to "Marvelous" (what judge would dare refuse him?), seemed almost insulted at the prefight speculation that Hearns might actually have a shot at beating him. The southpaw Hagler, with his shaved head and chisled, superhero's body, had held the title since September 27, 1980, when he knocked out Alan Minter in London—and dodged a shower of bottles from outraged British fans afterward. He'd defended the crown ten times, scoring nine kayos. Only Roberto Duran had been able to last the distance against the relentless Hagler.

Now here was Tommy Hearns, a blown-up welterweight. Sure, Hearns was six-feet, two inches (188 cm) to Hagler's 5 feet, 9½ inches (176 cm). And, sure, he'd flattened thirty-four of the forty-one men he'd faced—including Duran, nailed to the canvas in two rounds. Only Ray Leonard had beaten Hearns. But Hagler wasn't impressed. Look at those spindly legs. "Hit man, my ass," was Hagler's prefight assessment of Hearns and his menacing nickname.

Hearns's longtime manager and trainer, Emanuel Steward, had promised ahead of time that Tommy would spend the early rounds sticking and moving, dissipating the champion's fury and strength. Then, in the later rounds, he would begin to put over the big right hand. "We'll go for the late knockout," promised Steward.

Hagler never gave them a chance. With the last notes of Doc Severinsen's trumpet version of the national anthem seemingly still lingering in the desert air, Hagler was on top of the challenger. Hagler threw no jabs, just bomb after bomb at Hearns's midsection and head. Hearns had no choice but to reply in kind. There would be no letup for the full three minutes, as the two men stood toe-to-toe, ignoring any hint of defense. Both were rocked repeatedly. That neither went down is astounding. Hagler was cut, a flash of red on his brow, and when the round ended, the ringside physician stepped in to examine the champion.

"Don't worry about the cut," growled Hagler. "You go to war, you're going to get wounded."

The doctor left the ring. In the other corner Steward was pleading with Hearns to box, to stay away from Hagler.

He couldn't. Though he shook Hagler with a powerful right halfway through the round, Hearns was fading in the face of Hagler's continued attack.

"He's ready to go," Hagler told his corner after the second.

Ready, maybe, but never willing, Hearns tried at last to box. On his toes, he snapped his jab at the onrushing Hagler. Hagler kept coming. One of Hearns's jabs widened the cut on Hagler's brow. Referee Richard Steele stopped the action and called the doctor back in. After a quick look at the snarling Hagler, the doctor signaled Steele that the fight could continue. Steele waved the two fighters together one last time.

Hagler charged in. He staggered Hearns with a left and right to the head. Hearns, those spindly legs going, lurched backwards. Hagler followed, landing a right, a left, and a final right, and Hearns went down.

He struggled up at the count of nine, but his eyes were glazed and gone. Steele stopped the fight. The bloody Hagler leaped into the air. Hearns, cradled in a handler's arms, was carried back to his corner.

A year later, Hagler and Hearns appeared again in the same Caesars' ring, but against different opponents. Hagler defended his title against John Mugabi, and Hearns faced James Shuler. Across the country, at the Beacon Theatre in New York City, a crowd had gathered for a closed-circuit telecast of the two bouts.

While they waited for the action to begin, the spectators were shown a videotape of the Hagler-Hearns match. When those eight minutes were over, the crowd stood and cheered. They knew that nothing they would see live that night could match what they had just seen on tape.

For eight stunning minutes in the Caesars Palace ring, Marvin Hagler *(opposite page, on the right)* and Thomas Hearns were carried along on the wave of their own furious violence. When it was over *(above)*, Hagler was borne aloft in victory, still the middleweight champion; Hearns was cradled in the arms of a friend.

Jersey Joe Walcott

vs

Rocky Marciano

Philadelphia, Pennsylvania. September 23, 1952.

When Jersey Joe Walcott signed to defend his heavyweight title against Rocky Marciano, there was little reason to suspect that their meeting would prove to be one of the greatest heavyweight fights of all time. Jersey Joe was thirty-eight years old and looked older. That he was even champion was a mild surprise. He'd taken the title a year and a half earlier, on July 18, 1951, with an upset knockout of Ezzard Charles. Four times before that he'd lost in championship bouts—twice to Charles and twice to Joe Louis. Walcott was considered something of a cutie, a fast, flashy defensive boxer, loathe to lead or even to stand and fight.

Marciano, on the other hand, was one of the most willing, but also one of the crudest boxers ever to challenge for the title. Observing Rocky in training before the match, A. J. Liebling would write, "His boxing had improved vastly—from terrible to mediocre." Still, the challenger was undefeated in forty-two fights, thirty-seven of his opponents having failed to go the distance. Marciano, for all his awkwardness, was a crushing puncher—as powerful, they were saying, as any heavyweight in history. He'd hammered Joe Louis into retirement in 1951, in a sad fight that many saw as a changing of the guard.

Walcott, though, figured to give Rocky little to hit. Old Jersey Joe was a master at sliding out of reach and at keeping an opponent off balance. Most fans expected the fight to develop into Rocky chasing Joe. Marciano's only hope would be to keep banging and pushing the older man around until Walcott tired enough for Rocky to start reaching him.

The fight was held in the Municipal Stadium in Philadelphia, just across the river from Walcott's hometown of Camden, New Jersey. The forty thousand fans who turned out were treated to, quite simply, the roughest, most hard-fought heavyweight fight in twenty-five years. From the opening bell, it was clear that the perceived notion of the fight and the reality would be very different. In the first place, old Jersey Joe, the fancy-dan, was bigger than Rocky, the slugger. Walcott, at six feet (183 cm) even, weighed 196 pounds (89 kg). Marciano, at a generous 5 feet, 10¼ inches (178 cm) weighed twelve pounds (5 kg) less. In the second place, Walcott wasn't running. He came right out from the start, moving in on Rocky, throwing punches and moving the challenger back. Marciano, unable to set himself, looked awkward, unsure. And then, with a perfect left hook, Walcott dumped Marciano on the seat of his black satin trunks.

It was the first time in his career that the Rock had been down. It was such a startlingly new experience that Marciano had no idea how to react. He scrambled back to his feet at the count of three—an act, it seemed, of reckless bravado. As Jack Blackburn once told Joe Louis, "If you get knocked down, take a full count. You can't get up fast enough they don't know you was down." Walcott couldn't get back to Marciano in time to capitalize, though he hit Rocky some solid shots throughout the remainder of the round.

In the second round, Walcott, showing no inclination to run, continued to press the challenger, banging him with lefts and rights. It seemed that he was reading from a different script than the one written in the public's expectations. Marciano, meanwhile, was settling into the original script just fine. If this man was going to speak new lines, Rocky would just go on saying his old lines—louder. Halfway through the third round, Marciano began to get to Walcott with thudding body blows and rough shots on the arms and head. Walcott began to back up—but not to run.

They fought like that through the fourth, fifth, and sixth rounds. In the sixth round Walcott was cut over the left eye, from either a Rocky right hand or a Rocky head. It seemed that the champion was fading. But the tide suddenly turned in the next two rounds. Marciano, his head brushing against Walcott's chest as they traded punches, got some liniment in his eye and began foundering. He too was cut, by a Walcott hook near the right eye. But Rocky kept coming, and by the ninth round he could see well enough to resume banging Walcott. Yet Walcott in turn refused to succumb. In the tenth round, the two fighters stood and traded, and at the bell the stadium roared.

That the fight had gone this far was a sur-

prise. That Jersey Joe was still there and, indeed, looking stronger by the round, was even more of a surprise. Walcott dominated the eleventh and the twelfth rounds, clipping Marciano with crisp lefts and rights. Rocky, still reading from the old script, was becoming less effective as the fight wore on, missing Joe with wild swings. Still, he kept coming, kept following, kept punching. It seemed a hopeless task. Jersey Joe—from right across the river, remember—was far enough ahead on the judges' cards that Rocky's only hope of taking the title lay in a knockout; a result that seemed increasingly unlikely with each passing round.

And then Rocky knocked him out. Less than a minute into the thirteenth round, Walcott, his back to the ropes, started a right hand for Marciano's head. Rocky beat him to the punch with his own right hand. Marciano's punch traveled less than a foot and landed flush on Walcott's jaw. It may have been the single hardest punch ever landed in a heavyweight title fight. Walcott went down as though shot through the heart. Referee Charlie Daggert counted to ten above him, though it was a mere formality, and Rocky Marciano, the shoemaker's son from Brockton, Massachusetts, was heavyweight champion of the world.

The end of one of the most stubborn heavyweight title fights in history: Jersey Joe Walcott, supposedly no match for the younger, stronger Rocky Marciano, had outboxed, outpunched, and out-maneuvered the challenger for twelve rounds—until Rocky caught him with the perfect right hand. In the photo at left, referee Daggert signals the end forty-three seconds into the thirteenth round, and Marciano became champ.

Stanley Ketchel

vs

Jack O'Brien

New York, New York. March 26, 1909.

Philadelphia Jack O'Brien was thirty-one and the light heavyweight champion of the world, a veteran of 170 professional fights and a favorite of New York society. But Philadelphia Jack was not quite satisfied.

Three and a half years before, O'Brien had knocked out old Bob Fitzsimmons in thirteen rounds to lay claim to the heavyweight title that had been vacated by James Jeffries. Jack's status as champion had never been accepted, though, and in 1906 he'd lost a controversial twenty rounder to the little Canadian Tommy Burns. Burns—five feet, seven inches (170 cm), became the heavyweight champ, and O'Brien was merely a light heavyweight who wasn't getting any younger.

Jack had a plan. Remember, this was the fighter who used to file his own accounts of his overseas bouts to the Associated Press, a fighter greeted on his return from Europe by ten thousand of his hometown fans chanting his name. O'Brien craved and understood publicity, and he figured that the best way to redeem himself in the eyes of the public was with a big win over middleweight sensation Stanley Ketchel.

Ketchel, known as the Michigan Assassin, was just twenty-one, but already he had a record of 47-3-5, with an astounding forty-five knockouts. He'd won the middleweight title in May of 1908, lost it in September of the same year to Billy Papke on a controversial knock-out, and then destroyed Papke two months later to reclaim the crown. He was a savage puncher and a handsome dramatic figure. But Ketchel had never fought east of Grand Rapids, Michigan. The O'Brien fight would be his New York debut. And, though Philadelphia Jack was one of the ring's most acclaimed artists, Ketchel and his handlers, including manager Willus Britt ("Known as the best eye-gouger and shin-kicker in America," wrote Liebling), must have figured O'Brien was over the hill—though still a big enough name to make an impact when Ketchel beat him.

It was just the sort of fight the public loves—the rough-and-tumble Ketchel against the highfalutin O'Brien.

"I had heard," said O'Brien, in his famous remark, "that Ketchel's dynamic onslaught was such it could not readily be withstood, but I figured I could jab his puss off."

The bout took place at the National Athletic Club, a "society" athletic club located in an old horse mart on East 23rd Street in Manhattan. The two thousand fans in attendance paid nearly a total of $20,000, an impressive gate for the time. They would not be disappointed.

"In my years of covering the fight beat," wrote Nat Fleischer, "I've witnessed many exciting bouts, but not many offered such a variety of bitter, tornadic milling.... The fight was so thrilling, it sputtered and sparked with moments so tense that I could feel my heart beating in my throat from start to finish."

Both fighters came into the ring at 160 pounds (72 kg), though O'Brien, reportedly, had been forced to sweat off the final two (0.9 kg) on the day of the bout. Ketchel went to O'Brien's corner to shake hands, but O'Brien, in an attempt at psychological warfare, ignored him.

Ketchel, of course, believed he could beat any man who lived, and he needed no snub to motivate him. But he had never faced a boxer as clever or as fast as O'Brien. For the first six rounds, Philadelphia Jack put on a virtuoso display of ringcraft, easily evading Ketchel's onrushes, all the while snapping his left into Stanley's face—indeed, "jabbing his puss off." Ketchel's face turned bloody. To ringside observers it appeared certain that the middleweight champion would go down at any minute. But Ketchel kept coming, absorbing everything that O'Brien threw. Finally, O'Brien began to slow. He still hit Ketchel, but without the same speed. Midway through the seventh round, Ketchel paused, took a visible breath and then stepped up his attack.

He was reaching O'Brien now, driving hard shots to his body. Just before the bell, Ketchel caught O'Brien with a right to the head that opened a cut over O'Brien's left eye.

In the corner after that round, Ketchel's handlers told him he was losing the fight, that his performance would have them leaving New York in disgrace. Ketchel came out for the eighth round in a fury. He battered O'Brien across the ring. O'Brien clinched, stalled, ducked. He was working now to survive. In the ninth round he went down for a count of nine, but pulled himself up and hung on until the bell.

Ketchel went all out in the tenth round, simply walking through O'Brien's desperate jabs. Twice he knocked the Philadelphian down. Twice O'Brien got up. With the round nearly over, he clung to Ketchel. The referee, Tim Hurst, separated the fighters, and Ketchel struck. He drove a left to the stomach and then a crashing right to the jaw. O'Brien fell like a tree, the back of his head landing in the resin box in Ketchel's corner.

Hurst began his count. O'Brien never stirred. Just as the referee reached six, the bell sounded. The fight was officially over, and under New York rules of the day, there could be no decision. That's how it would go into the books: A ten-round no-decision. There was pandemonium at ringside. Bets went unpaid. Arguments raged. Ketchel's supporters yelled that O'Brien had been kayoed. O'Brien's backers insisted their man had been saved by the bell and deserved the decision.

Ketchel died the following year, but O'Brien would be asked about the bout and its gaudy ending every day for the next thirty-three years.

Stanley Ketchel, the free-swinging "Michigan Assassin," seemed an ideal opponent for master boxer and showman Philadelphia Jack O'Brien. "I'll jab his puss off," predicted Jack. And he nearly did—before Ketchel, one of the fiercest champions ever, knocked O'Brien cold.

Joe Gans

VS

Battling Nelson

Goldfield, Nevada. September 3, 1906.

When Joe Gans and Battling Nelson entered the ring in Goldfield, Nevada, each man called himself the world light-weight champion. Gans, also called the Old Master, won the championship from Frank Erne in 1902—won it in no uncertain terms, too, knocking Erne out in a mere one-hundred seconds in Fort Erie, Ontario. Nelson, for his part, had beaten Jimmy Britt in Colma, California, in 1905—Britt having claimed the title the year before, when Gans relinquished it to move up to welterweight.

From such confusing, contradictory beginnings was born one of the most brutal and exciting prizefights in history. It took a while to make the match. Gans, campaigning as a 147-pounder (67 kg), knew how great the ordeal of making 133 pounds (60 kg)—the lightweight limit at the time—would be. He must have dreaded it. Yet, Gans also knew that the big money was not in the welterweight division, but back down among the light-weights. He had a wife and two children. Gans signed for the fight.

The Gans-Nelson showdown would be notable not only for the action in the ring, but for the fact that it was the first promotional effort of a man named George L. Rickard, known as Tex. Tex Rickard, of course, would go on to promote the first fight to earn a million-dollar gate, when he matched Jack Dempsey and Georges Carpentier at Jersey City in 1921. Rickard, after spending seven years following

the gold rush in Alaska, had headed down to Nevada when he heard that gold had been discovered there, in a town called Goldfield. Goldfield wanted a prize fight. Rickard's original plan called for a Jimmy Britt-Terry McGovern (former bantam- and featherweight champion) match and he wired both camps, offering a $20,000 purse, the largest guarantee ever. So incredible was the sum, that, thinking it was a hoax, neither fighter responded. Rickard shifted his attention to Nelson and Gans and eventually upped the ante.

Gans was the first to respond. Nearly broke, he agreed to the fight for a mere $11,000 from the purse. He also agreed to make weight—133 pounds (60 kg)—at ringside in full fighting gear. Gans drove himself unmercifully through the crushing training schedule. Nelson, knowing the deck was stacked in his favor, signed on for a whopping $24,000. The fight would be to the finish.

Gans's one consolation was that this time he would be free to fight all out, free to win. Too often in the past, he'd entered the ring with hands tied, under orders from his white management to "take it easy" on his opponent. Gans, a sensitive, diffident man, had been left humiliated by a couple of his most blatant acting jobs. This time, though, he was free to be himself—simply the best fighter in the world.

Under a broiling Nevada sun, Gans proved his greatness. Nelson, known as the durable Dane and renowned as a fearless, cold fighting

machine, rushed Gans from the start. But the Baltimore fighter remained cool and in perfect control, staving off Nelson's charges with stinging straight lefts and occasional well-placed rights. Nelson's face began to swell and bleed. But he, too, was doing some damage, banging away with both hands to Gans's mid-section. So telling were the punches that Gans reportedly vomited over the ropes several times between rounds.

The first fifteen rounds went by at a blister-ing pace, before the fight settled into a more on-again, off-again pattern. Gans continued to rock Nelson with crisp shots to the jaw. Nelson, frequently hurt, would fall into clinches until his head cleared, then rip loose and resume battering away at Gans's body. While Nelson was becoming increasingly desperate and increasingly rough and careless in his tactics, Gans was fighting a true gentleman's fight. Once, when he drove Nelson through the ropes with a punch, Joe helped the Dane back into the ring, then walked away until Nelson had a chance to compose himself and resume fighting.

That both men could continue for so many rounds was incredible. Nelson was taking a fearful beating, while Gans, already weakened by having to make weight, was throwing every-thing he had and also getting hit with repeated, stinging blows in return. The scorched crowd kept up a steady chorus of support.

The end of this brutal bout finally came in

the forty-second round (a figure almost hard to imagine on today's fight scene. Mike Tyson, by way of perspective, didn't fight forty-two rounds in his first nineteen bouts put together). Nelson, far behind on points, his eyes swollen shut, was fighting in a blind rage. Breaking from a clinch, he deliberately fouled Gans, fetching Joe a low blow that could have been heard on the outskirts of Goldfield. Gans fell to the canvas. Referee George Siler began to count, then waved the bout over. He declared Gans the winner on a foul. An old photo shows the wiry Gans seated on the mat, his gaze fixed on Siler, who appears momen-

tarily baffled. Nelson stands with his back to the camera, seemingly shaking a fist at Gans. The crowd is on its feet. It is Gans's face, though, that tells the story. He looks angry but collected as he watches the referee. Must he get up and resume thrashing this man? Or has he done enough?

Gans had done enough. His popularity was restored by the sensational victory over Nelson, but his health was ruined. He would fight just nine more times. Two of those bouts would be knockout losses to the relentless Nelson. Joe Gans, the Old Master, died less than four years later.

Joe Gans and Battling Nelson square off in San Francisco for their second fight. This one was won by Nelson in the seventeenth round. Two years before, though, the setting and the result were different. Their first fight took place in Goldfield, Nevada, marking the debut of promoter Tex Rickard, and was won by Gans in the forty-second round.

Joe Louis

VS

Billy Conn

New York, New York. June 18, 1941.

Joe Louis was in the middle of his Bum-of-the-Month parade. This time, however, he was about to meet a man who was anything but a bum.

Louis had won the title in 1937 with an eight-round kayo of Jimmy Braddock. He'd defended it seventeen times already—including his one-round annihilation of Max Schmeling in 1938—and had come to be viewed as invincible. No matter who it was they put in front of him, Joe belted his man out.

Billy Conn was a little different, though. A handsome, cocky Pittsburgh Irishman, Conn had won the light heavyweight title in 1939. He defended it three times before relinquishing the belt and moving up to take on the heavyweights. He'd already beaten Bob Pastor, Al McCoy, and Lee Savold. Louis, of course, was a different matter. But Conn figured he could lick anybody. Though never a heavy puncher, he was a gifted boxer with a slick left jab and unmatched enthusiasm for a fight. The irrepressible Conn once broke his hand on his own father-in-law's head during a free-for-all at a family christening.

Conn entered the ring on that warm June night—before 54,487 fans in the Polo Grounds —outweighed by 25½ pounds (11½ kg). Louis was 199½ (90½ kg), Conn 174 (79 kg). At that, the 4-1 odds favoring Louis seemed conservative.

Conn seemed atypically nervous in the opening round. Dodging a Louis right, he slipped to the canvas for an instant. Louis shuffled after him, patient and deadly. Joe landed some telling body shots to take the first and second rounds.

But soon Conn had the jab working, snapping with authority into Louis's face. The challenger was moving well, never letting Louis catch up or set himself. Late in the third round Conn began coming off the jab with quick, dazzling flurries that, while they didn't hurt Louis, left the champion looking befuddled. Conn was winning rounds.

Louis landed a crushing right to the body in the fifth round that nearly crumpled Conn, but the champion didn't, or couldn't, follow up and Conn went back to the jab. Over the next two rounds, he pulled himself together.

Boxing brilliantly, Conn took the eighth, ninth, and tenth rounds. Louis shuffled after him, increasingly frustrated.

"You got yourself a fight tonight, Joe," said Conn during a quick clinch.

"I know it," said Joe.

In the eleventh round, the crowd's rolling roar filling his ears, Conn began to open up. He slammed Louis with short hooks to the body and repeatedly nailed the champion with rights to the head. Conn's feet were planted to the canvas as he put all of his meager weight behind the blows. Louis winced, but couldn't counter.

The twelfth round was both Conn's finest and his undoing. Midway through, he landed a left hook flush on Louis's jaw that rocked the champion. Louis groped for a clinch to keep from going down as Conn kept hammering away.

At the end of the twelfth round, the fight was even on rounds on the judge's scorecards, with all the momentum on Conn's side.

"You're losing," Jack Blackburn told Joe in the corner. "You gotta knock him out."

Louis nodded.

"All I had to do," Billy would say later, "was stay away for the next three rounds and I would'a been champ."

What he said at the time—to his nearly hysterical cornermen—was: "I'm gonna knock this bum out."

He went out in the thirteenth round to do just that. For the first minute, Conn continued to land his punches, but he was working closer to Louis now, working within the range of Joe's big guns. Joe got him. First with a right and then with a left, and suddenly Billy was swaying. This was the moment that Louis had been chasing all night. Louis landed another combination, opening a cut under Conn's eye, rocking the challenger. Conn tried desperately to clinch, but Louis pushed him off, measured him, and again fired the right. It landed flush, and Conn flowed to the floor. He was on his way up when referee Eddie Josephs reached ten.

The press insisted afterward that Conn's Irish nature cost him the title. "What's the use of being Irish," replied a devastated Conn, "if you can't be stupid?"

So near and yet so far. On June 18, 1941, at the Polo Grounds, Billy Conn, outweighed by 25½ pounds (12 kg), put on a dazzling show, outboxing heavyweight champ Joe Louis round after round. After rocking Louis repeatedly in the twelfth, the cocky Conn told his corner he was going to "knock this bum out." The result of such rashness is clear, above; Louis kayoed the gallant Conn at 2:58 of the thirteenth round.

Benny Leonard
vs
Lew Tendler

Jersey City, New Jersey. July 27, 1922.

Courtesy Boxing Illustrated

Benny Leonard held the lightweight championship of the world at a time when there were more great challengers than ever before or since. As superb as Leonard was, he could never be certain of an easy match. After winning the title in 1917, the Professor, as Leonard was known, had survived harrowing fights against Charley White and Richie Mitchell. Now he was matched against Lew Tendler, a tough Philadelphia southpaw.

Leonard was favored against the brawling Tendler, but newspaper reports throughout the buildup for the bout focused less on the technical aspects of the match than on what was termed the bad blood between the two men. Whether such stories were mere hype or not, the fifty thousand fans who turned out at Boyle's Thirty Acres—the stadium in which Dempsey had flattened Carpentier the year before—were treated to one of the toughest, most bruising lightweight fights of all time. They were also treated to the spectacle of Benny Leonard at his most clever best.

Tendler's rough-charging style and left-handed stance quickly forced Leonard to abandon his usually classic boxing style. Tendler was awkward and unpredictable—and relentless. Leonard, the model boxer, had no choice but to slug with the challenger. Tendler kept the pressure on from the opening bell, driving rights and lefts to Leonard's body. Enough of these landed below the belt

that Leonard complained repeatedly to referee Harry Ertle. Tendler kept punching.

For the first five rounds Tendler dominated the scoring. In the fifth round, he knocked one of Leonard's teeth out with a vicious left. Leonard, who liked to boast that his hair was never mussed in a fight, was taking a licking. The crowd began to sense an upset in the making, and a sustained roar rolled back and forth across the huge wooden saucer. Finally, in the sixth round, Leonard began to find the range and to pick up his rhythm. He began to land his textbook jab and to make Tendler miss. In the seventh round Leonard took control, rocking Tendler with combinations. It appeared that once again the Professor was ready to dismiss another undergrad.

Then came the eighth round. As with all great ring moments from the days before instant replay, there are differing accounts of just what happened. What is certain is that the ever-resourceful Leonard saved himself once again from disaster. Tendler, bleeding from the nose and mouth, continued to press the champion. With Leonard's back to the ropes, Tendler drove a hard left to the champion's body. It landed solid, and Leonard sagged as if shot. Benny later said that the punch paralyzed his legs. He wobbled, helpless, before Tendler, who was setting himself for the kill. Unable to fight back, but still able to talk, Leonard suddenly dropped his hands and said to Tendler, "C'mon, Lew. Keep 'em up. Let's

make it look good." As the spectators, in their straw boaters and tightly knotted ties looked on in amazement, Tendler stopped in his tracks and turned to Ertle to protest. This time, he knew he had not hit low!

The break saved Leonard from an almost certain knockout. While Tendler argued, Benny was recovering. The feeling came back to his legs, and by the time Lew turned and began to punch, Leonard was moving away. He survived the round. It would be Tendler's last chance.

From the start of the ninth round through the final bell of the twelfth round, Leonard was at top form. Though Benny's left eye was cut and swollen, he was now the one in control. He shook Tendler repeatedly, but could never put him down. Leonard finished the fight with a flurry, saving his crown by a narrow margin. So close was the bout that many at ringside scored it six rounds apiece.

Leonard, who was paid $120,000 for the victory, said later he was lucky to survive. He fought Tendler again a year later in the Polo Grounds. This time the Professor had done his research. He dominated Lew for fifteen rounds to win the decision easily. Tendler, who went on to own a popular restaurant in Philadelphia, would say only, "I had my chance."

■The great Benny Leonard *(opposite page)* was pushed to the limit by Lew Tendler in their match at Boyle's Thirty Acres in Jersey City, New Jersey. Usually so in control that his hair was never mussed, this time Leonard had to survive a near-knockout in the eighth round to hammer out a decision over the extremely tough Tendler.

Rocky Graziano

vs

Tony Zale

Chicago, Illinois. July 16, 1947.

These days, when two boxers put on a particularly spirited fight, somebody in the crowd is bound to pay them the ultimate compliment: "Just like Zale and Graziano!"

Only there really never has been anything quite like Tony Zale and Rocky Graziano. Alone, neither was a truly exceptional champion. Together—in three fights, just fifteen rounds of savage fighting—they attained a kind of immortality. Red Smith once called the Zale-Graziano series, "the most two-sided fights" ever.

They first met on September 27, 1946, in Yankee Stadium. Zale, thirty-three years old, was the middleweight champion of the world, having won the vacant title in 1942 in a bout against Georgie Abrams. Yet this was the first defense for the Gary, Indiana, "Man of Steel". Zale, born Anthony Florian Zaleski, had spent nearly four years in the Army. After returning to the ring in early 1946, he had knocked out six straight. Rocky would be his first serious test.

Graziano, the original Dead End Kid, was born Thomas Rocco Barbella in Brooklyn on June 7, 1922. After bouncing in and out of reform school, prison, and the Army, he turned his energies full-time to the prize ring. A five foot, seven-inch (170 cm) straight-ahead brawler with a deadly right hand, Graziano had rung up a record of 43-6-5, with thirty-two kayos, by the time he faced Zale.

That first fight brought comparisons with Dempsey–Firpo. The pyrotechnics started in the first round when Zale dropped Graziano with a near-perfect left hook. Rocky got off the floor and by the end of the round was battering Zale across the ring. In the second round Graziano continued to club Zale with the right, knocking him down at the end of the round. Throughout the third round it seemed Rocky would put Zale away, but somehow the Man of Steel survived, and in the fourth round he began to turn the tide with a withering body attack. Still, Graziano roared back and he had Zale stumbling to the wrong corner after the fifth round. Then, in the sixth round it ended. A stunning right to the body, left hook to the head dropped Rocky to the canvas, where he was counted out by referee Ruby Goldstein.

The return match was set for July 16, 1947, in Chicago Stadium—Zale's turf. For fight fans everywhere, this was the match of the year. The gate was a record for an indoor bout. Graziano called the fight "a private war." Afterwards, he said, "If there hadn't been a referee one of us would have ended up dead."

Indeed. As brutal as the Yankee Stadium battle had been, the Chicago meeting topped it. The temperature in the stifling arena was close to 100 degrees F (38° C) when the fight started and it only got hotter. Rocky came out in a rush in the first, swinging hard rights and lefts to the head. He caught Zale with three of the rights, rocking the champion, but Zale meanwhile was scoring well to Graziano's mid-section. He was also clipping Rocky with jabs and short, solid left hooks. By the end of the round, Graziano's right eye was nearly closed and his left was badly cut. He stumbled, bleeding, back to his corner.

Despite his wounds, Graziano continued to attack in the second round, again staggering Zale. But Zale stood in and continued his workmanlike assault on Rocky's body and his eye. Both men were shaken. "Two rights and a left made Zale do a small wandering dance," wrote Jimmy Cannon of the closing seconds of the round.

The third round proved the greatness of both men. Zale came out fresh and eager and caught Graziano with a cracking right hand that dropped the New Yorker. As if determined to erase the shame of his knockout loss the previous year, Rocky bounced back up without a count, "smiling sheepishly through a crimson-smeared face," as the New York *Times* put it. For the rest of the round Zale hammered at Graziano, driving him to the ropes with thudding shots to the body and the head. Rocky, reeling, weary, and bleeding, continued to throw his haymakers. Still, it seemed he could not last much longer.

In the fourth round, it was Zale who appeared tired, and he seemed content to box Graziano in the crushing heat. Rocky, his eyes swelling dangerously, continued to try to find the range, throwing right after right at Zale. He was missing, but he was getting closer. And he

was getting his breath. In the fifth round Graziano leaped to the attack, and Zale could no longer hold him off. Rocky fought as if in a rage, clubbing at Zale repeatedly with the right, cursing, bellowing, and driving the champion back. Zale, his strength gone, tried to ride out the storm, but again and again he was rocked. The crowd, dripping with sweat, was on its feet and shouting at the bell.

It ended in the sixth round. Zale tried to jab, but Graziano caught him with a right, a big right, and Zale started to go. He wobbled backwards and Rocky charged in for the kill. Cannon reported counting thirty-six unanswered punches as Zale crumbled into the ropes. Referee Johnny Behr pulled Graziano off his helpless foe and waved the fight over at 2:10 of the sixth round. Rocky Graziano, the new middleweight champion of the world, remained in a blind rage for several moments, battering his own cornermen until he finally calmed down. Grabbing the ring microphone, Rocky blurted out, "Hey, Ma! Your bad boy done it."

The third bout, held in Newark eleven months later, was another brawl, though it paled in comparison to the first two. A crisp Zale hook knocked Rocky out in the third round.

Those two: They're a regular, well…Zale and Graziano.

Tony Zale and Rocky Graziano were clearly made for each other, their three bouts producing some of the most exciting moments in middleweight history. Here, Zale *(on the left)* tries to hold off a charging Graziano in the first round of their second, and greatest, fight. Though rocked and battered by Zale, Rocky continued to throw the right until it finally caught Zale, knocking him out in the sixth round.

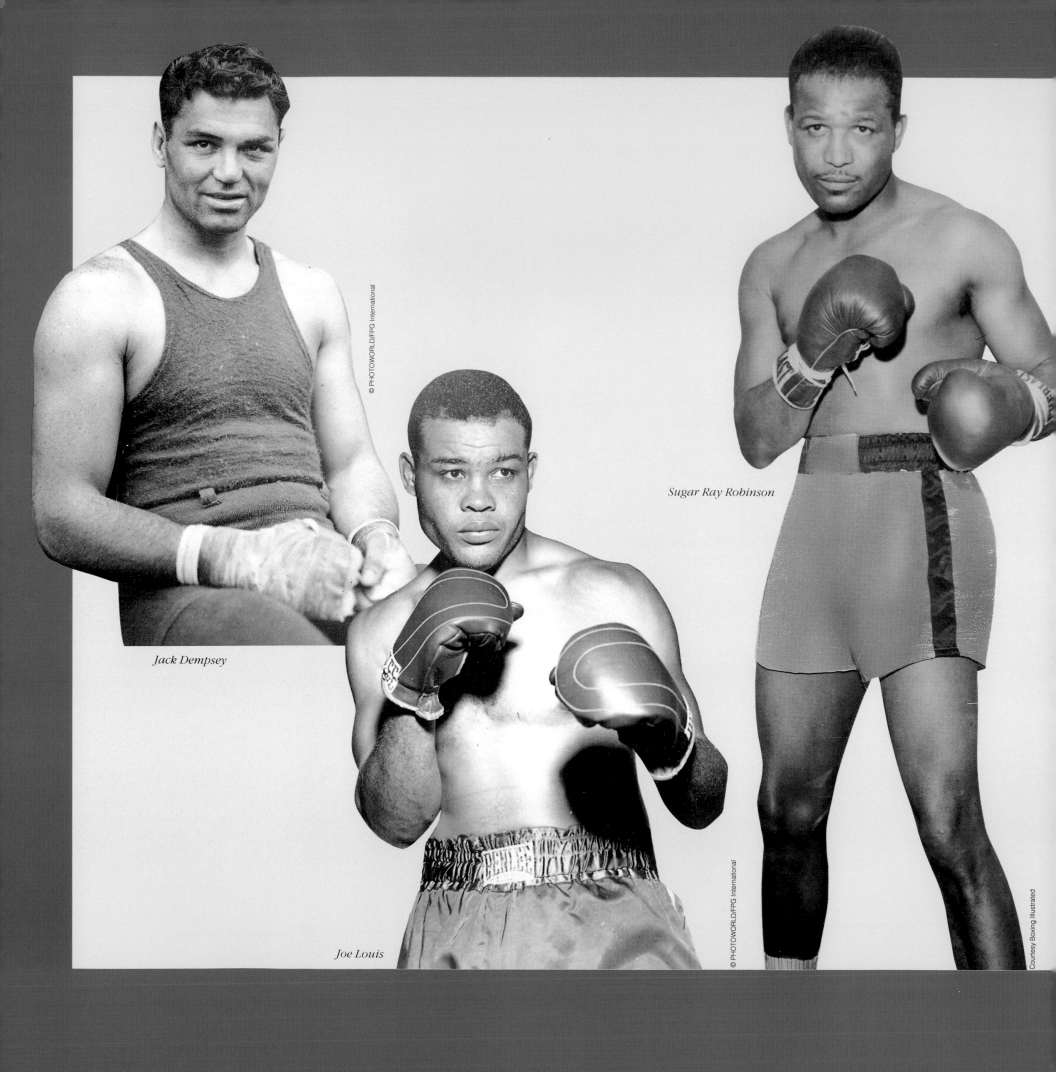

Jack Dempsey

Joe Louis

Sugar Ray Robinson

Ring of Dreams: Five Great Fantasy Fights

Every true fight fan has asked the question "What if?" What if Ali had not been forced to sit out three and half years of his prime following his refusal to be inducted? What if Dempsey had granted Harry Wills a fight? The list of possible *what ifs* is endless, limited only by the imagination and enthusiasm of the fan. The biggest *what ifs,* of course, are the purely hypothetical matchups, one fan's favorite hero against another's; the best of one era against his predecessor; the classic boxer against the pure puncher. *The Boxing Companion* invites you to sit back and imagine five such showdowns.

The rules here are simple: The fighters meet in their respective primes and fight at their peak weights. There are no handicaps given, no attempts to "even things up." The bouts are conducted under contemporary rules, at the classic championship distance of fifteen rounds. May the best men win.

Courtesy Boxing Illustrated

Rocky Marciano

Muhammad Ali
vs
Jack Johnson

Miami Convention Center, Miami, Florida

"Ghost in the house, ghost in the house!," Ali's cornerman-medicine man, Bundini Brown, shouted from ringside throughout Ali's first comeback fight against Jerry Quarry in Atlanta in October of 1970. "Jack Johnson's here! Ghost in the house."

And indeed the resurrected Ali, back in the ring at last after three years of exile—dancing and moving, carving up Quarry in three rounds—had conjured up images of the legendary Johnson. Of course Ali had established his own unique legend long before that fight in Atlanta. He needed no comparisons. The ghost that Bundini recognized was a similarity that went far beyond boxing styles. Both Johnson—who held the title from the day after Christmas, 1908, when he knocked out little Tommy Burns in fourteen rounds, until April 5, 1915, when he was stopped in the twenty-sixth round in Havana by Jess Willard —and Ali, the only three-time heavyweight champion, were figures of passion and controversy outside of the ring as well as in. Each had spent the better part of his career antagonizing a nation. Each had become, whether he wanted to or not, a symbol.

Johnson was the first black heavyweight champion. For that distinction alone he was hated and hounded. His own natural flamboyance and recklessness added fuel to the fire. As champion, Johnson fought, and beat, a suc-

cession of "white hopes" until Willard—and years of persecution—caught up with him in the heat of Havana.

Ali was the first black heavyweight champion to celebrate his race. The day after he won the title, he held a press conference to announce that he had embraced the Muslim faith. He changed his name from Cassius Marcellus Clay to Cassius X and then to Muhammad Ali. Later, he refused induction into the armed forces. "I got nothing against them Viet Cong," he said. "They never called me nigger." In the volatile early 60s, Ali was seen by many as a dangerous radical and he, too, faced a series of white hopes—many of whom were, in fact, black.

In action, Johnson was immensely stylish. He was very fast, a great defensive boxer, and maybe the best counterpuncher ever among heavyweights. He had a superb jab and, though he scored relatively few knockouts, was a dangerous puncher with both hands. Those who watched his career insisted that Johnson always fought with plenty in reserve. Nat Fleischer called Johnson the greatest of heavyweight champs.

Ali, of course, had his own ideas about just who was the greatest. Still, the match with Johnson will provide the biggest challenge of Ali's career. Always Ali has been the opposite —the butterfly against the ugly bear (Sonny Liston) and the clumsy mummy (George Foreman); beauty against—as he called Joe Frazier —the man "too ugly to be champ." Now here

Courtesy Boxing Illustrated

was an opponent with his own grace and beauty and style. During the prefight buildup Ali tries a series of nicknames—Old Baldy, Jack O'Lantern, the Nanny—before settling on an ironic "Mr. Johnson." It almost sounds like a term of respect. For his part, Johnson calls Ali "Son."

On the day of the bout, Johnson arrives first at the weigh-in. He drives up alone in a huge black Packard, sweeps through the crowd in a full-length fur coat. A moment later Ali comes in, accompanied by Bundini, a worried-looking Angelo Dundee, and several other attendants. For a moment it seems the wide-eyed Ali will recreate the mad scene he threw at the weigh-in for the Liston fight, but this Ali is all business. "This here is history," he says, posing for the photographers beside Johnson. "Me and Mr. Johnson gonna show some dignity." Ali weighs in at 211 pounds (96 kg), Johnson at 206 pounds (93 kg). At six feet, three inches (190 cm) Ali has an inch and a half (3.8 cm) on Johnson, though side-by-side near the scales they look nearly the same size.

That night in the ring, though, Ali looks bigger, all long arms and legs and smooth, supple muscles. Johnson appears squatter, more muscular. The crowd is curiously subdued. There are catcalls and boos for both fighters, though some cheers come from the upper decks.

Round one goes by without a serious punch being thrown. Ali circles, dancing around the perimeter of the ring. He mugs for the crowd, but his eyes are on Johnson. Johnson seems content to wait, shuffling along after Ali, his open gloves held out in front of him. Ali spins on his heel and heads back to his corner. Johnson grins.

Rounds two and three are more of the same, with the fighters talking to each other. Toward the end of the third, referee Arthur Mercante

Jr. waves the pair together. "Fight," says Mercante, but again the bell rings before any violence can transpire. Ali, on movement alone, has taken the first three rounds.

In the fourth round Johnson begins to press Ali, cutting the ring and stepping in behind his own long jab. Ali spins and bounces away to the sides. With thirty seconds left in the round, Johnson forces Ali to the ropes and lands a quick one-two and then another winging left hook. Ali sneers and wags his head and ties Johnson up. At the bell Bundini is up on the ring apron and yelling. "Work, Champ, work" he calls. Dundee looks like a man with a toothache.

For the next three rounds the only thing Ali works are the ropes, and Johnson, though he does not rush in as Foreman did in Zaire, is landing his punches. Ali covers up, then sets and tries to come back with his own combinations, but Johnson, in range now, picks off the blows. In the seventh round, Johnson lands a hard right uppercut, the best punch of the fight, and Ali sags. This time it is Dundee who is up and yelling at the bell. He crouches in front of his fighter during the minute rest.

"You're blowin' it," Dundee shouts. "This guy's the real thing. Don't give him nothin'."

Whether from Dundee's exhortations or from something inside, it is a reinspired Ali who comes out for the eighth round. For the next four rounds he makes Johnson look bad. Johnson has never seen a fighter this fast. Nor-

mally, he can parry his opponents' blows, shift around, and find an opening for a counter. But Ali's jab is reaching him now, popping off his forehead. Johnson can't get set to launch his own attack. Ali closes the eleventh round with a four-punch combination that rocks Johnson. At the bell Ali raises both hands above his head. From the upper tiers of the arena comes a rolling chant, "Ah-li, Ah-li."

But Johnson is not yet convinced. The fight takes another turn in the twelfth round as Jack, battered and tiring, starts firing right-hand counters over Ali's jab and then charging in with left hooks and uppercuts. Though Ali is still landing, so is Johnson, and for three minutes the Convention Center crowd is treated to a full-scale brawl. Ali returns to his corner with a puffy jaw.

It is as close as Johnson will get. Ali goes back onto his toes for the final three rounds, bouncing again, letting Johnson chase and giving Jack nothing to counter. With thirty seconds to go, Ali plants his feet and rips off a five-punch volley that sends Johnson's mouthpiece flying and brings the crowd to its feet. But Johnson comes back with a right flush on Ali's jaw and Ali immediately ties him up. The fight ends with the two men in ring's center staring at each other.

As the judges' verdict is announced—144–141, 145–140 and 145–141, all for Ali—Johnson raises Ali's arm. No one in the crowd is booing.

"Lawdy, he's smart," says Ali quietly in his dressing room. "He showed me things I never seen."

"He was just too fast," says Johnson.

Jack Johnson (*opposite page*) and Muhammad Ali (*above*) were two of the most flamboyant and controversial champions in boxing history. How would Johnson, a master counterpuncher, have coped with Ali's blinding speed?

Joe Louis

VS

Jack Dempsey

Polo Grounds, New York City

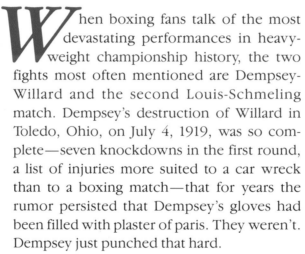

W hen boxing fans talk of the most devastating performances in heavy-weight championship history, the two fights most often mentioned are Dempsey-Willard and the second Louis-Schmeling match. Dempsey's destruction of Willard in Toledo, Ohio, on July 4, 1919, was so com-plete—seven knockdowns in the first round, a list of injuries more suited to a car wreck than to a boxing match—that for years the rumor persisted that Dempsey's gloves had been filled with plaster of paris. They weren't. Dempsey just punched that hard.

Louis lost his first fight against Schmeling. He was knocked out by the German on June 19, 1936. Though the defeat scarcely interrupted Louis's ascent—he won the heavyweight championship a year later, stopping Jim Brad-dock in eight rounds—it clearly galled Joe. "I won't be champion until I get that Schmeling," he said. On June 22, 1938, he got him. For much of the world, the rematch carried great political significance—Schmeling, represent-ing Hitler's Germany, against Louis, the black American—but for Louis it was purely per-sonal. He destroyed Schmeling in 2:04 of the first round. Ringside observers swore they heard Schmeling, draped on the ropes, scream as Louis's punches landed.

The Dempsey-Louis match is a promoter's dream, a showdown between the two greatest sluggers in boxing history. The Polo Grounds sell out in less than twenty-four hours. Co-promoters Tex Rickard and Mike Jacobs—who together outbid rivals Don King, Bob Arum, and Dan Duva for the rights to the bout—predict that this fight will outgross any fight to date. Dempsey, training in Saratoga, New York, seems edgier than ever, ripping into his sparring partners every afternoon. The rumor circulates that Jack's manager, the legendary Doc Kearns, has made a one-million-dollar bet on an early Dempsey kayo. When asked, the good doctor just smiles.

Louis, too, trains with unusual enthusiasm at his old Pompton Lakes, New Jersey, camp. "I never seen Joe work this hard," says his long-time trainer Jack Blackburn.

A week before the fight the Vegas sports books make Dempsey a 5–3 favorite. Louis, as heavy a puncher as ever held the title (James Braddock described the Louis left jab as, "like someone stuck a lightbulb in your face and then busted it") is a deadly finisher as well, but throughout his career, has been all-too-easy to hit. He was knocked down ten times. The feeling is that, against as fast and murderous a puncher as Dempsey, such a suspect chin will prove fatal.

On this warm June night Dempsey enters the ring first, to a thunderous ovation. The crowd continues to roar as Dempsey, his eyes fixed on the canvas, paces in his corner. The sides of his head are shaved to the skin, and his arms, neck, and face are a deep brown from the sun. Somehow the volume of the crowd increases when Louis appears, jogging down the aisle, a white towel draped over his head. He and Dempsey pose for photos in the center of the ring. Dempsey keeps his eyes on the mat, and Louis stares impassively at the camera. At 6 feet, ³/₄ inch (185 cm) and 187 pounds (85 kg), the raw-boned Dempsey is spotting the smoother Louis an inch (2.5 cm) and fifteen pounds (7 kg).

At the bell Dempsey charges across the ring, almost meeting Louis in his corner. Dempsey moves in a crouch, bobbing and weaving, fists

rolling at his waist. Louis, shuffling forward in his classic stance, chin tucked against his chest, misses with a jab at Dempsey's bobbing head. Dempsey steps in underneath with a left and a right to the body, driving Joe back toward the ropes. Louis, never a quick starter (with the exception of the second Schmeling bout), appears momentarily befuddled. He ties Dempsey up, but Jack rips his left hand free and bangs Joe twice on the cheek. Louis pushes Dempsey back and throws a hard left-right. Both punches catch the oncoming Dempsey, stopping him for a second in his tracks, and Louis slides away to the center of the ring.

Louis tried again to jab and again Dempsey weaves underneath. He rips another series of short lefts and rights to the body. Louis tries to back up, to set himself, and Dempsey, his head almost against Louis's chest, drives a hard right to the body and brings up a tight hook to the head. The punch lands flush on the jaw and Louis drops backward to the canvas like a man falling off a dock. Dempsey spins, fists still clenched at his waist, and heads for a neutral corner. There will be no count here. Louis is up at six. Referee Arthur Donovan wipes off his gloves and waves in the onrushing Dempsey.

Louis, back-peddling, jabs twice, snapping Dempsey's head back. But Jack has timed the blow. Louis jabs again and Dempsey throws a right over Joe's outstretched arm. It lands with a thud on Louis's cheek. Louis sags to the ropes and Dempsey leaps in, landing a right and two crashing lefts. Louis is down again. His gaze blank, his face slack and puffy, Louis is on his feet at nine. The crowd's roar drowns out the sound of the bell, and Donovan has to step between the fighters.

During the sixty seconds between rounds, Blackburn hunches over Louis, talking low and nonstop. He holds an icebag against the fighter's right eye. In the other corner Kearns dances in front of the scowling, quivering Dempsey.

Jack is out before the bell, and Donovan holds him off. The fighters meet in the center of the ring. Louis, abandoning the jab, meets the charging Dempsey with a jolting right uppercut. Shaken, Dempsey comes back with a combination to the body and a hard left-right to the head that rocks Louis. Both men have foresaken any attempt at defense and for the next ten seconds stand and trade punches. And then it is over. Dempsey lands a left hook, a short chopping right, and two more hooks and Louis drops to his knees and pitches forward on his face. He doesn't move as Donovan counts ten.

"I knew I had to go after him as fast as I could," says Dempsey after the bout. "I didn't want to lose him. Even after the knockdowns in the first, he nearly had me in the second with that uppercut. I don't even remember anything after that until he was on the ground."

A revived Louis is asked at a press conference to review a tape of the bout. He refuses. "I saw the fight already," he says.

Joe Louis (opposite page, left) and Jack Dempsey (opposite page, right) were the most celebrated sluggers in ring history—and the most feared fighters of their respective eras. Who would be left standing at the end of a fight between these two legendary destroyers?

Sugar Ray Leonard

VS

Sugar Ray Robinson

Caesars Palace, Las Vegas

The challenge is made when Leonard calls a press conference in Los Angeles. "Enough is enough," he tells the assembled media. "I want the name to myself. There's only room for one Sugar Ray."

The next day Robinson calls his own press conference at his restaurant in Harlem. He refers to Leonard as "that upstart." "Tell Mr. Leonard that if he has designs on my name, he can come and try to take it."

There is speculation that the two Sugar Rays, these two master showmen, engineered the whole feud together in perfect harmony in a Las Vegas hotel room. Certainly there have never been two fighters as aware of image and of the power of hype as these two. Nor have there been two better businessmen in ring history. Yet, throughout the five-week, twenty-five-city promotional tour for the bout—a fight dubbed the Sugar Ray Showdown—neither fighter will admit to any motivation other than pride.

"Money means nothing when a man's name is at stake," says Robinson (who was born Walker Smith).

"We'd be fighting even if it weren't for the money," says Leonard with the barest trace of a smirk.

Despite the glitz and hype, the bout promises to be a boxing fan's dream—two of the most complete fighters in ring history meeting in their primes. Robinson and Leonard, who each held titles at welterweight and middleweight, agree to meet as junior middleweights, at 154 pounds (70 kg). Robinson, at 5 feet, 11½ inches (182 cm) is 1½ inches (4 cm) taller than the dramatically muscular Leonard. Yet Robinson must be considered the more dangerous puncher, at least in terms of one-punch power. Both men are among the finest finishers in ring history. (The boyish Loenard, an adman's dream, turns into a cruel little demon when he has his opponent hurt.) Though Robinson and Leonard are rightly considered master boxers, both can be hit, and neither is afraid to stand and trade if he has to. Most important, both know how to win.

The outdoor arena at Caesars is jammed with high-rollers and celebrities. Billie Holliday sings the national anthem (this is a fantasy, right?). Leonard is first into the ring, accompanied by trainer Angelo Dundee. He removes his jet-black hooded robe to reveal black trunks with the word "SUGAR" in large letters across the front. He is sweating well and continues to dance and shadow box until Robinson slips through the ropes. Robinson wears white satin shorts with black stripes and short black boxing shoes. His hair is combed flat and he too is dripping in the desert air. The two fighters shake hands, and Leonard executes a neat little bow, before turning to go back to his corner.

The pace is fast from the opening bell, with Robinson, looking remarkably slender, jabbing and hooking, and Leonard, dancing and moving side-to-side, countering with fast, short-armed flurries. Leonard, with his intense, wide-eyes stare, seems jittery and a bit stiff. They split the first two rounds.

In the third round, Robinson, circling backwards to his left, fires a short straight right that catches Leonard on the jaw and drops him. Leonard is up at three. From ringside his face appears impassive as referee Richard Steele wipes off his gloves. Robinson moves in throwing hooks, but Leonard has clearly

© Christopher M. Farina

recovered quickly, and he hits Robinson with a couple of impressive combinations in the next thirty seconds. Robinson goes back to the jab. When the round ends, the fighters exchange words. Score the third round 10–8, Robinson.

The pattern continues over the next four rounds. Robinson is outboxing Leonard, but Leonard is giving him no chance to get set and is landing his share in return. There is a small mouse under Leonard's left eye. Robinson's hair has begun to spike up.

In the corner, Dundee is yelling at Leonard, but Leonard stares past him, still wide-eyed, boyish. In the eighth round, Leonard begins working closer to Robinson. He muscles the taller man around in the clinches. Halfway through the round Leonard lands a thudding left to the head that rocks Robinson. Leonard leaps in with another flurry and Robinson ties him up. Leonard rips free and steps back, flat-footed. He feints a jab and bangs Robinson with a right. Robinson misses a hook. Leonard comes back with two stiff jabs. Robinson slides away, and for the rest of the round Leonard is stalking. It is Leonard's first round.

The boyishness is gone from Leonard now. He looks hard and cold. Robinson in turn looks tired and a half a step slower. Leonard has yet to really hurt Robinson, but he's landing well to the body. Throughout the ninth and tenth rounds, Robinson continues to land the jab, but Leonard is pressuring him and he can't follow up as he did in the earlier rounds. In the eleventh round Leonard drives Robinson to the ropes and lands two good combinations. A hard left hook hurts Robinson, who tries to hang on. With a minute left in the round a scowling Leonard is throwing everything at Robinson, who—bobbing, weaving, picking off punches—is riding out the storm. Seconds before the bell, Leonard takes a step back, drops his hands and sticks out his chin. Robinson waits. Leonard smiles. He starts a jab and then steps in and throws a wide bolo

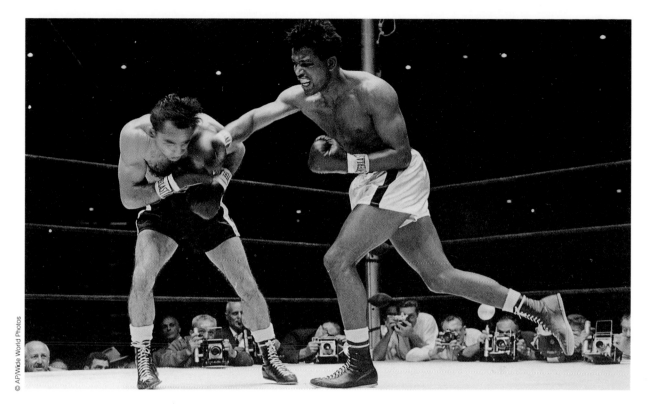

AP/Wide World Photos

punch. In that instant, simultaneous with the bell, Robinson fires a straight right that catches Leonard full in the face. Now it is Robinson who smiles.

The final four rounds are war, and in the end it's clear Robinson has brought the heavier weapons. There is no dog in Leonard. He never stops firing back, but his left eye is nearly shut, and his bottom lip is cut. Robinson, too, is showing some damage, with a cut beside his right eye. But Robinson is rocking Leonard. A left hook at the end of the fourteenth round leaves Leonard clutching the ropes at the bell.

Twice in the fifteenth round Leonard almost goes down from Robinson hooks, but each time he fights back. Both fighters are arm-weary, spent. Leonard stares fiercely at the gasping Robinson. And it is Leonard who lands the final punches of the fight, a soggy left-right as the bell sounds. The two fighters fall into each others arms.

The decision, when it comes, is unanimous—145-140, 144–139, and 146–141—for

■ In the sweetest match-up imaginable, two master showmen battle for the right to the name Sugar Ray.

Robinson. To the still-cheering crowd, it hardly matters.

The next morning Leonard and Robinson meet by chance in the hotel lobby. Both are wearing dark glasses and both are moving slowly. A young boy, maybe ten or eleven, detaches himself from his father's hand and runs across the lobby to where the two fighters stand. He stares up open-mouthed at this gaudy pair, his head turning from one to the other. This boy, he's a child of television. He's seen the soft drink commercials and he thrusts his paper and pen at Leonard. "Sugar Ray, man," he says. "You're the greatest, Sugar Ray."

"Just Ray," says Leonard, a thin, tight smile on his face. "Just call me Ray." Beside him, Walter Smith—Sugar Ray—grins.

Benny Leonard
vs
Roberto Duran

Madison Square Garden, New York

When it comes to prizefights, opposites attract. It is hard to imagine two more disparate champions than Benny Leonard and Roberto Duran. Leonard, the great Jewish hero of the 1920's—the master boxer whose motto was, "Hit and don't be hit," the gentleman champion who posed with his mother for publicity stills—against Duran, the swarming, savage guerilla fighter from the slums of Panama City, the man who talked of putting his opponents, "in the morgue," who ballooned to nearly two hundred pounds (91 kg) on food and booze between bouts. Now that would be a match, a match for the title of greatest lightweight of all time—as well as a match of fistic philosophies.

"I would be delighted to face him," said Leonard when the bout was first proposed. Duran, approached at his home in Panama City, said only, *"Si,"* but allowed a tight sneer to cross his face.

The match is a natural for the Garden. Leonard defended his title three times in the old Garden and was one of the most popular fighters in New York history. Duran won the lightweight championship in the new Garden and remains a hero to the city's large Latin population.

One man caught in the middle is Ray Arcel. Arcel trained Leonard late in the fighter's career and always considered him the greatest fighter of all time. Arcel also trained Duran. Both boxers approach their old trainer and ask him to help them prepare. In the end Arcel chooses his old champ Leonard.

"For me it's a chance to work with Benny in his prime," says Arcel. "In his prime!"

During the promotional build-up for the match, the differences between the fighters are underlined. Leonard is available for all functions, invariably polite and helpful to the press. He discusses strategy. He poses for more pictures with his mother. His sparring sessions are open to the public and he signs autographs. Duran, by contrast, is moody and unreliable. He misses press conferences. He snarls at reporters. He calls Leonard names in the Spanish press. His workouts are closed. There is an edge to Duran that has been missing for his past several fights. Arcel says, "He's hungry again. This one means redemption."

The Garden is sold out. Thousands of Panamanian flags beat the air, but the cheers for both fighters are equally loud. The sight of Duran, who enters the ring first, is both shocking and thrilling. It is the old Duran, *Manos de Piedra,* with his thick, blue-black hair and his wispy black beard. His body is as chiseled and hard as it has ever been. He struts and stamps around the ring, flashing punches in front of him, waving his fist in the air. The rafters ring. "Dooo-ran! Dooo-ran!"

In the face of this fierce passion, Leonard appears all business, with his slicked-down hair and his amused smile. He wears an old woolen coat over his black trunks. Leonard

The two greatest lightweights of all time, Benny Leonard *(above)* and Roberto Duran *(opposite page,* signaling the end against the other Leonard), offer a fascinating match-up of styles. Could the superb style and power of Leonard force Duran to pull another *no mas?*

and Arcel walk over to Duran and the two fighters shake hands quickly. Duran gives Arcel a tap on the shoulder.

With the opening bell, Duran charges out of his corner like a little bull, bobbing and weaving, banging his gloves together. He sneers at Leonard and his straight-up stance. But Leonard, deceptively fast and crisp, has Duran missing punches in the first minute. Leonard begins working his jab, catching Duran in the face. Duran brushes the jab away and lunges in with a hook. Leonard steps to the side and fires a crisp right that catches Duran flush on the jaw. Duran goes down, tumbling forward onto his knees and his face. He is up at five, shaking his head, stamping his feet as referee Carlos Padilla finishes the eight count. Padilla takes Duran's gloves to wipe them against his shirt and Duran wrenches them free. "That just made him mad," says somebody at ringside. Duran charges Leonard, forcing him back to the ropes. Benny breaks free, circles to the right, and jabs three more lefts into Duran's face. Duran, in a rage, catches Leonard with some glancing shots to the head, but Leonard keeps his balance and he hits Duran some telling blows. Though Duran stomps back to his corner at the end of the first round, waving derisively with his right glove, it is clear he has been hurt.

For the next four rounds, Duran keeps charging, and Leonard, the matador, keeps spinning and moving and sticking. Yet, as Leonard tells Arcel between rounds, Duran is not falling for Leonard's feints, and Leonard has not been able to land another clean right on the bobbing Duran. And, while Duran has yet to land a solid shot to Leonard's head, he is giving Benny a battering on the arms, ribs, and hips.

By the seventh round, the pace is beginning to tell on Leonard, who, though he is well ahead at this point, is still not dictating the tempo. The surprise is not how well Leonard is moving and boxing, but how well Duran is.

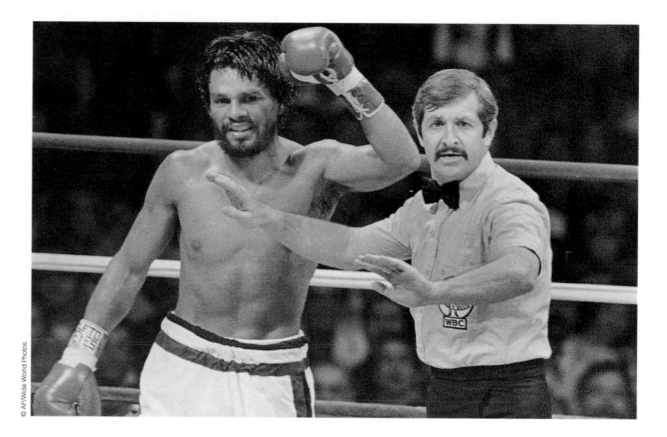

© AP/Wide World Photos

He is slipping and ducking punches now. No longer the uncontrolled would-be mauler, he is starting to pick his shots more carefully, and is still landing body punches. And he is still walking back to his corner with that sneer on his face.

In the ninth round, Duran catches Leonard on the ropes, and then, in an instant, the savagery is back. He batters Leonard to the body, several of the blows landing low. Before Leonard can complain, Duran brings his punches up, catching Leonard with two hard lefts and a right to the head. Leonard holds on. "Keep 'em up," he says, trying the trick he used on Lew Tendler. "Keep 'em up." But Duran is too busy to listen. And for good measure he digs another hook in below Leonard's belt. This time Padilla warns him, and with a shrug Duran reaches out to touch gloves. Leonard uses the moment to slide away to the center of the ring. Duran chases him and Leonard plants and rips two hard rights to

Duran's jaw. This time Duran walks through the punches. Just before the bell he rocks Leonard with his own right.

Over the next three rounds Leonard uses every trick in his extensive bag to keep Duran off of him. He slaps, he parries, he spins, he counters, and always he jabs. But he finds himself spending more time on the ropes—and taking more punches. In the thirteenth round, Duran drops Leonard with a short hard right. Leonard takes a nine-count and, when he rises, clinches desperately. Duran shakes free and, snarling, batters Leonard back to the canvas with a series of lefts and rights. Leonard rises once again, and tries to hold, but Duran brings up a right uppercut and follows it with a sweeping left hook. Leonard is counted out at 2:36 of the thirteenth round.

Duran, the savage, kneels down and helps Leonard to his feet. Later, he will say he has never faced a more gallant opponent. "This Leonard, he come to fight," says Duran.

Rocky Marciano

VS

Joe Frazier

Yankee Stadium, New York City

No opposites here. These two are the hardest-working heavyweight champions in history. Neither man was big for a heavyweight. Marciano at his peak weighed 185 pounds (84 kg). Frazier, who came along a generation later, 205 (93 kg). Marciano stood 5 feet, 10¼ inches (178 cm), Frazier, five feet, eleven inches (180 cm). Yet, against men much bigger than that, neither took a backward step. And neither cared to do anything but hit.

Marciano, of course, never lost a fight. He retired on April 27, 1956, with a record of 49-0, with forty-three knockouts. He'd held the title for three and a half years since his dramatic thirteenth-round knockout of Jersey Joe Walcott and he'd defended it six times. He was knocked down only twice, once by Walcott and once, in his last fight, by Archie Moore. No fighter ever trained harder than Rocky. He was an explosive puncher and incredibly strong for his size. What he lacked in finesse—and he lacked plenty—Rocky made up for in sheer power.

From 1968 through 1972 Joe Frazier was as formidable a heavyweight as ever fought. He never had the one-punch knockout capability that Marciano had, but he was just as deadly. A former butcher in a Philadelphia slaughterhouse, Frazier simply chopped his opponents down, more often than not with his big left hook. Born in Beaufort, South Carolina, reportedly Joe started training to lose weight. And never eased up. He was called Smokin' Joe for

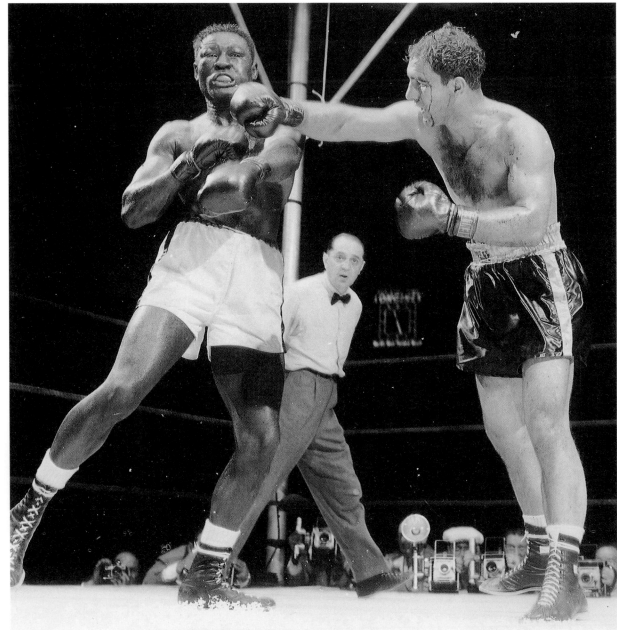

his relentless style. Though always coming at his opponent, Frazier, at his best, was remarkably hard to hit. He had a constant, bobbing, rolling style that, combined with the pressure he could create, made him a tough target.

From the day that they signed for the bout, it was clear that Rocky and Joe shared a quiet respect, even admiration, for each other. It is a matter of style perhaps. Both fighters train in upstate New York, in camps close to each other. Shuffling through their roadwork from opposite directions, they meet one morning on the road in the predawn darkness. Marciano runs with two sparring partners. Frazier with a half-dozen people, a car rolling along beside them, music blaring out the window. The fighters stop and exchange greetings. "I'm gonna smoke you, Rock," says Frazier, still bobbing slightly in time to the music, steam rising from his sweaty shoulders. Marciano, peering out from under his knit cap, grins, shrugs, and sticks out his thick right hand. The two fighters shake, then set off again in opposite directions along the roadway. "He sure likes that music loud," says Rocky.

The music is blasting again a week later as Frazier climbs first through the ropes of the eighteen-foot-square (5.5 m) ring set up on the spot in the stadium normally occupied by second base. Frazier's brocaded pink trunks reach almost to his knees. Marciano arrives a moment later, a towel draped over his head, a lopsided grin on his face.

Neither fighter is known as a fast starter, and indeed the opening round is uneventful. Though Frazier comes bobbing in throwing his left hook, he has not yet got the range. Rocky meanwhile is awkwardly trying to set up a right-hand counter.

"The other guy's a hooker," says Marciano's trainer, Charlie Goldman. "We figured we'd try to give Rock something to work on."

Everything changes in the second round, as both fighters, sufficiently warmed up, meet in the center of the ring and begin to trade punches at a furious pace. Both men bang

Courtesy Boxing Illustrated

away to the body. Frazier, as though still hooked up to his music, works faster than Marciano, throwing more punches and landing more, bouncing hooks off Rocky's head. Marciano seems to stumble to the side, but he never goes backwards. He lands his own thudding shots to Frazier's arms and ribs and then scores with two hard rights at the end of the round that rock Frazier. The old ballpark shakes with the noise of the crowd. It seems impossible that such ferocity can last.

Midway through the third round, a Frazier hook rips open the skin next to Marciano's right eye. Bleeding heavily, the Rock continues to throw his big right hands, but Frazier is bobbing under them now, banging back with that terrible hook. Joe goes back to his corner grinning, but so does Marciano—a big lopsided grin under the blood. He has tasted Frazier's best. Now, he seems to be saying, it's my turn.

For the first thirty seconds of the fourth round the two fighters stand toe-to-toe and throw everything. Though Frazier is still landing the hook, it's landing high. And then Marciano lands a hook of his own and Frazier is

hurt. He lurches sideways, a little stutter step, sets himself, and throws the left again. It is what he knows to do. This time Marciano gauges the right perfectly. It crashes against Frazier's jaw and Joe goes down in a heap. Marciano turns briskly, the blood flowing again down his face, and heads for a neutral corner.

Frazier is up at eight, his white mouthpiece jutting out between his lips. He is dazed. Marciano trots in on his thick legs to meet him. On instinct, Joe starts another hook, and Rocky intersects it with his right. The punch sends Frazier bouncing down into the ropes, where he lands stretched across the bottom strand. His mouthpiece is gone, and this time Joe does not make it up.

N either Rocky Marciano (*opposite page*, against Ezzard Charles) nor Joe Frazier (*above*, in his first fight against Ali) ever took a backward step. What would happen if history's two most relentless heavyweight champs met in the ring?

The Undercard

"I Coulda Been a Contender"

The history of boxing is written in the names of the titleholders. Through these names we recognize the sport's eras, its trends, its changing character. Yet, by definition, the champions are only the peak of the pyramid. The base is made up of all those fighters who never won a title—who, in most cases, never came close. For, without the George Chuvalos and the Doug Joneses there never could have been an Ali.

These days, with sixteen weight classes and with mushrooming governing bodies creating new "world" titles every week, it seems that a fighter who can't win at least one championship belt should consider retiring—in disgrace. Ah, but there was a time—a time with only eight weight classes and only one champion in each—when winning a title really meant something. In those days, being a contender meant something too. In the history of boxing there have been some truly great fighters who, for various reasons, never won a world championship. They weren't all Sam Langfords, but—titles or no—they deserve to be remembered. What follows is a look at some of boxing's great contenders. They all were somebody.

Knocked Out by the Color Line

Just as many of baseball's best players in the decades before Jackie Robinson never got a chance to play in the major leagues, so,

through racism, was a generation of black boxers deprived of the chance to fight for a title.

The first and one of the greatest of these men was Peter Jackson, an Australian born in the West Indies. Jackson, who in 1891 fought Jim Corbett to a no-contest decision over sixty-one rounds—in the first bout ever conducted in the United States under the Marquess of Queensberry rules—stood six feet, one inch (185 cm) and weighed two hundred pounds (91 kg). He was an elegant boxer with a dangerous punch. But he never fought for the title. The champion in Jackson's day, John L. Sullivan, had drawn what came to be known as the color line, proclaiming, "I will never fight a Negro." When Corbett won the title, in 1892, he had no interest in facing so tough an opponent again and he too shunned Jackson. Peter Jackson died in 1901, at the age of forty, the victim of tuberculosis as well as what must have been bitter disillusionment.

Several more great black heavyweights followed Jackson, fighting their way along the same path of frustration. The greatest, of course, was Sam Langford, a fighter who might have won championships in every division from welterweight through heavyweight. Langford had company in another brilliant heavyweight named Joe Jeannette. Jeannette, a strong, fast 185-pounder (84 kg) from New Jersey, fought Langford a total of fourteen times and also faced Jack Johnson on nine different occasions, beating the future champ once in 1905 on a foul. But, like Langford, Jeannette

remained shut out of championship matches, though he continued to box through 1919.

The third great black heavyweight of the era was Sam McVey, born in Oxnard, California, in 1884. A strong 210-pounder (95 kg), McVey fought Johnson three times—losing twice on twenty-round decisions and once on a knockout in the twentieth-round. He faced Jeannette five times, winning once, drawing twice, and losing twice (once via a TKO in the fiftieth round in Paris). And he took on Langford fifteen times between 1911 and 1920, winning three times. McVey died in 1921 in New York City.

Johnson himself, once he took the title, helped reinforce the old color line, even as a large part of America was screaming for a white hope to recapture the championship.

After Johnson lost the title to Willard in 1915, the clamor for a white hope died, but not the color line. Though there had long been black champions and mixed bouts in the lighter weights, the heavyweight ranks, because of their prominence, remained effectively segregated. During the reign of Demp-

For every kid who ever wrapped his fists and tied on a pair of gloves, the dream is to become a champion. Only a few make it. Yet greatness is measured in more than title belts; in the great contenders it is measured in the heart.

sey, a fighter named Harry Wills punched his way into the position of top contender. Wills, known as the Brown Panther and eventually as the Black Menace, fought and beat all the top heavyweights of the era. He became, as Nat Fleischer termed it, "Dempsey's perennial shadow." Twice Wills was matched with Dempsey (tickets were even printed for a September 6, 1924, bout in Jersey City), but both times the fight fell through. Promoter Tex Rickard, who had put on the Jack Johnson–Jim Jeffries fight in 1910, which resulted in race riots across the country after Johnson's victory, said he would never again promote a mixed bout for the heavyweight championship. And despite the insistence of the New York State boxing board that Dempsey and Rickard honor their commitment to the number-one challenger, Dempsey signed with Gene Tunney for a fight in Yankee Stadium. The board refused to sanction the bout, and it was held in Philadelphia. There Tunney beat Dempsey, and Wills was left in limbo.

In the years that followed, the color line dissolved. Though blacks continued to face greater obstacles than whites in their ring careers, the heavyweight title was no longer out of bounds. The success of Joe Louis ensured that the best fighters would get their shots.

The Best of the Rest

A. J. Liebling once wrote of Billy Graham—the New York welterweight, not the Florida evangelist—that "he was as good as a fighter can be without being a hell of a fighter." Graham, a technically superior boxer and a flashy combination puncher, who fought from 1941 to 1955, came close. He lost on a fifteen-round decision to then-welterweight champion Kid Gavilan in New York in 1951, a fight many at ringside thought Graham had won. He had beaten Gavilan once the previous year, before the Kid won the title, and he would win, lose,

and draw in three fights against future welter- and middleweight champion Carmen Basilio. But Graham never made that final leap. Liebling's description remains an accurate, if poignant, one.

Throughout the history of boxing there have been many fighters like Graham, fighters just a step away from greatness. There have also been plenty of world champions who never fit the "hell of a fighter" category. Most interesting, though, are the fighters who do measure up to that intangible but definite standard and yet never win a world championship.

For many years, such great black fighters as Sam McVey (above) and Sam Langford (right) were barred from fighting for the heavyweight title. Without the "color line" both might have been champion.

Courtesy Boxing Illustrated

© AP/Wide World Photos

Timing, of course, is a big part of it—just ask Langford, McVey, and Jeannette—and the years 1917 to 1925 were rotten ones during which to be a lightweight. Those were the years, of course, that Benny Leonard ruled the division. Three fighters who were particularly oppressed by Leonard's presence were Lew Tendler, Richie Mitchell, and Charley White. In any other era, all three might well have won the title.

Charley White, the fighter whose left hook Ernest Hemingway rated second only to God's, came close to beating Leonard in 1920, when he belted the champion through the ropes in Benton Harbor, Michigan. White had finished forty-one other opponents, but Leonard climbed back into the ring and knocked him out three rounds later. Perhaps White was simply not bright enough to be champion. Nat Fleischer once wrote that Charley's "high, intellectual brow hid a slow-thinking brain." Still, Fleischer saw fit to rank White among the ten greatest lightweights he had ever seen.

Mitchell, too, had Leonard down during their 1921 title bout, but couldn't keep him there. Leonard finished Mitchell, the Milwaukee Marvel, in the sixth round. Tendler, a southpaw from Philadelphia, fought two classic bouts with Leonard in 1922 and 1923, the first a twelve-round no-decision, the second a fifteen-round loss. Tendler, who never again fought for the title, must have wished he'd been born just a few years later.

William Lawrence Stribling, known always as Young Stribling, was born in Georgia in 1905 and started boxing professionally as a bantamweight in 1921. By the time he died in a motorcycle accident in 1933, Young Stribling was a leading contender for the heavyweight title. He fought 286 bouts, winning 222, still an all-time record for career wins; 126 of those wins were by knockout, the most by any fighter in history until Archie Moore.

During his career Stribling came achingly close, but he never won a title. He fought a ten-

round draw against light heavyweight champion Mike McTigue in 1923 and the following year battled McTigue to a twelve-round no-decision. The newspapers gave Stribling that one, but McTigue kept the belt. In 1926, he lost to Paul Berlenbach, the man who'd beaten McTigue. Stribling would never again fight for the light heavyweight title, though he went on to beat three different light heavyweight champions, all before they won their titles. Though he beat several top heavyweights, Stribling lost in his only bid for the heavyweight crown when he was stopped in the fifteenth round by Max Schmeling in 1931. Still, Young Stribling was a hell of a fighter.

Jerry Quarry was a strong, fast, and gifted heavyweight who just happened to come along at the same time as Joe Frazier and Muhammad Ali. Which is to say, he never had a chance. Quarry was born in Bellflower, California, into a large and combative family (his

The wrong place at the wrong time. Jerry Quarry (above, on the right) was unfortunate to come along in the era of Ali and Frazier. Smokin' Joe stopped the California Irishman twice.

© AP/Wide World Photos

brother Mike became a light heavyweight contender in the early seventies, one unlucky enough to earn a match with champion Bob Foster—and Foster's deadly left hook). The 1965 National Golden Gloves heavyweight champion, Quarry, as a pro, developed into one of the most skillful and dangerous counterpunchers among recent heavyweights. He beat, among others, Floyd Patterson, Brian London, Thad Spencer, Buster Mathis, Ron Lyle, and Earnie Shavers. But he never won the big one. In 1968 he lost a fifteen-round split decision to Jimmy Ellis in the final of the WBA heavyweight title elimination tournament. And then, of course, there were Ali and Frazier. Quarry fought them both twice, and never made it past the seventh round. That sort of frustration might explain why, in 1990, at the age of forty-five, Jerry Quarry was talking about a comeback.

The Amateurs

Amateur boxing is a world unto its own, covering everything from seven- and eight-year-olds flailing away at each other for three rounds under a tent at the state fair, to the finals of the Olympic Games. While almost every professional fighter out there started in the amateur ranks, the two disciplines can almost be considered different sports—especially today, as the bootleg cards and unsanctioned smokers give way to highly organized amateur programs operating under the umbrella of the U.S.A. Amateur Boxing Federation.

Amateur boxing today is set up to reward busyness over effectiveness. The aim is to land more punches than your opponent—not necessarily harder punches. The rules state that a knockdown blow should score no more than a cleanly landed jab. Bouts last only three rounds, so there is little time for anything but all-out flurrying. Even the knockout has been eliminated. Fights that end prematurely now

receive the designation "RSC," for "referee stops contest." Once again, while virtually all fighters spend at least some time competing as amateurs, clearly many are less suited to the style than others. Mike Tyson, for instance, failed to make the U.S. Olympic team in 1984. His rough, puncher's style cost him points with the judges. One imagines that for Tyson it was a relief—indeed a release—to turn pro.

Taking the first step. In amateur clubs across the country, kids learn the fundamentals of the sport. Some will go on—through Golden Gloves and national competition—to the pros. Others may never compete. All will learn the ways of the ring.

There are many levels of amateur boxing. Most young fighters start out in their local Golden Gloves tournament. The first such tournament was sponsored by the New York *Daily News* in 1927 (the year of the Dempsey-Tunney long count). The following year, the Chicago *Tribune* joined the *Daily News,* sponsoring a tournament in Chicago. The New York and Chicago winners met to determine an Inter-City champion. Until 1962, regional champions, determined through competitions sponsored by the *Daily News* and the *Tribune,* met in Eastern and Western regionals, the winners going on to the Inter-City tournament. In 1962, the Golden Gloves of America was formed and since then a national tourament has been held every year. New York and Chicago continue to have their own annual tournaments.

Beyond the Golden Gloves, boxers compete in USAABF (the United States of America Amateur Boxing Federation)–sponsored competitions leading up to annual national championships. The nationals, which used to be held under the auspices of the old AAU (Amateur Athletic Union), determine membership of various national teams for international competition and, every four years, serve as a qualifier for the Olympic trials. The Olympic team is chosen through, first, an Olympic trials tournament, which yields a champion in each weight class, and finally an Olympic Box-Off, pitting the trials champion against an opponent deemed most worthy. The winner of the Box-Off makes the Olympic team.

Golden Gloves

A glance down the rolls of the national Golden Gloves champions since 1962 reads like a Who's Who of boxing. Here are just some of the Gloves champs who went on to glory:

Emanuel Steward. 1962 bantamweight champion. Head of the Kronk Gym and long-time manager of Tommy Hearns.

Billy Douglas. 1963 middleweight champion. Father of James (Buster) Douglas.

Sugar Ray Leonard. 1973 lightweight; 1974 light welterweight. Five-time world champion, 1979–89.

Michael Spinks. 1974 light middleweight; 1976 middleweight. Light heavyweight and heavyweight champion of the world, 1981–87.

Aaron Pryor. 1975, 1976 lightweight. Junior welterweight world champion, 1980–84.

Thomas Hearns. 1977 welterweight. Five-time world champion, 1980–89.

Donald Curry. 1980 welterweight. WBA welterweight champion, 1983–86.

Mike Tyson. 1984 heavyweight. Heavyweight champion of the world, 1986–90.

Evander Holyfield. 1984 light heavyweight. Cruiserweight champion of the world, 1986–88. Heavyweight champion of the world, 1990–.

In other countries, amateur boxing is generally conducted within a club system, with age-group competition leading to regional and eventually to national competition—all under the auspices of a national governing body. For many years the Eastern Bloc nations, with their state-supported "amateur" programs, dominated international competition. Until recently, Soviet and East German boxers, for instance, faced no difficult choices about turning professional: They didn't have to. The best boxers were taken onto national teams where they received financial support and the attentions of the country's best coaches and trainers.

With the recent changes in Eastern Europe, many of the national "sports machines" have been dismantled. Several Soviet boxers have turned professional, with more to come. Cuba remains the lone hold-out. Traditionally one of the strongest countries in the world in amateur boxing—since the days of heavyweight legend Teofilio Stevenson—Cuba continues to support its sports programs at the national level, and Cuban boxers continue to dominate at the international level.

© JD/LPI/FPG International

The Olympic Games

Boxing has been a part of the modern Olympics since 1904 (with the exception of the 1912 Games in Stockholm, that is; boxing was outlawed in Sweden). It remains one of the most popular sports of the Games.

Certainly the Olympic tournament is the most prestigious event in international amateur boxing. For boxers from the Soviet-bloc countries the Olympics have long been their only showcase, the pinnacle of a career. For boxers from the West, an Olympic medal can lead directly to a lucrative professional career. With so much at stake and so much attention focused on it, the competition is often marked by fierce nationalism and politicized judging. In the 1988 Games in Seoul, referee Harry Walker of New Zealand was assaulted by an outraged Korean security guard who felt that Walker had treated a Korean boxer unfairly. The Korean boxer himself staged a sitdown protest in the center of the ring. Such theatrics are nothing new in the Olympic arena. Still, despite such distractions, Olympic boxing has produced some memorable moments and memorable figures, over the course of twenty-one Olympiads.

Looking at a golden future. For many boxers, the Olympic Games are the culmination of a career. For others they are merely the beginning. In 1984, Pernell Whitaker (*left*) of the United States stood on the victory platform in Los Angeles. Since then, "Swee'Pea" has gone on to greater glory—and greater riches—as a professional, becoming the undisputed lightweight champion of the world.

Only seven athletes have won more than one Olympic boxing title.

The three-time champions are:

Laszlo Papp (Hungary), middleweight gold medalist in 1948; light middleweight champion in 1952 and 1956.

Teofilio Stevenson (Cuba), heavyweight gold medalist 1972, 1976, and 1980.

The two-time winners are:

Oliver Kirk (USA), bantamweight and featherweight gold medalist in 1904. The only man ever to win two weight classes in the same Games.

Harry Mallin (Great Britain), middleweight gold medalist in 1920 and 1924.

Boris Lagutin (USSR), light middleweight gold medalist in 1964 and 1968.

Jerzy Kulej (Poland), light welterweight gold medalist in 1964 and 1968.

The Val Barker Trophy has been awarded by the International Amateur Boxing Association at each Olympics since 1936. The trophy honors the outstanding boxer of the Games.

1936 Louis Lauria (USA). Lauria, a flyweight, was only the bronze medalist.

1948 George Hunter (South Africa). Hunter, a light heavyweight, beat out Laszlo Papp and future professional world champ, flyweight Pascual Perez of Argentina.

1952 Norvel Lee (USA). Lee was the light heavyweight champion. What about middleweight gold medalist Floyd Patterson?

1956 Dick McTaggart (Great Britain). Lightweight gold medalist McTaggart got the trophy over American heavyweight champ Pete Rademacher, who in his professional debut in 1957 met Floyd Patterson for the heavyweight championship. In the same Games, Laszlo Papp won his third gold medal, beating the U.S.'s Jose Torres (a future professional light heavyweight champion) in the final.

1960 Giovanni Benvenuti (Italy). Benvenuti, the welterweight gold medalist and hometown hero, took the award over Cassius Clay.

1964 Valeriy Popentschenko (USSR). Popentschenko won the middleweight gold medal and the Barker Trophy in a Games that also included Joe Frazier.

1968 Philip Waruingi (Kenya). The featherweight bronze medalist, Waruingi topped George Foreman, as well as Boris Lagutin and Jerzy Kulej and their second titles.

1972 Teofilio Stevenson (Cuba). Heavyweight champ Stevenson, the knockout sensation of the Games, earned the trophy over Sugar Ray Seales and others, including Waruingi, who this time won the featherweight silver medal.

1976 Howard Davis (USA). Davis, the lightweight champion, was the only one of the five U.S. gold medalists in Montreal not to go on to a professional title.

1980 Patrizio Oliva (Italy). Oliva won the lightweight gold medal. Other top names included Teofilio Stevenson, with his third title, and light heavyweight gold medalist Slobodan Kacar of Yugoslavia, a future professional champ.

1984 Paul Gonzales (USA). Gonzales, the light flyweight gold medalist, was the lightest of the U.S.'s record nine gold medalists. Other stars at the Los Angeles Games included U.S. super heavyweight champ Tyrell Biggs; middleweight silver medalist Virgil Hill of the U.S., a future world light heavyweight champ as a pro; and welterweight gold medalist Mark Breland, everybody's choice of outstanding boxer going into the Games.

1988 Roy Jones (USA). Jones, robbed of the gold medal in the middleweight final, earned the trophy over light flyweight silver medalist Michael Carbajal, the first of the 1988 Olympians to win a professional world championship.

Going Pro

George Foreman, the man who destroyed Joe Frazier in two rounds to win the heavyweight championship of the world, the man who gave new life to the over-forty set with his remarkable comeback, the man with the highest knockout percentage of any heavyweight ever, still says the greatest moment of his boxing career was winning a gold medal in the 1968 Olympic Games in Mexico City.

Foreman, of course, is far from thé only professional champ to have won an Olympic title. In recent years, the Games have become a springboard to big-time pro contracts. Whether other Olympians-turned-pro feel or felt the same way as old George is unknown.

The following is a list of Olympic champions who have gone on to win professional titles.

Frankie Genaro (USA). 1920 Olympic flyweight champion. Held world flyweight title (NBA version) from February 6, 1928 to March 2, 1929.

Fidel La Barba (USA). 1924 Olympic flyweight champion. Held world flyweight title from January 21 to August 23, 1927.

Jackie Fields (USA). 1924 Olympic featherweight champion. Held world welterweight title from July 25, 1929 to May 9, 1930 and from January 28, 1932 to February 22, 1933.

Willie Smith (South Africa). 1924 Olympic bantamweight champion. Held world bantamweight title (British version only) from 1927–1928.

Pascual Perez (Argentina). 1948 Olympic flyweight champion. Held world flyweight title from November 26, 1954 to April 16, 1960.

Floyd Patterson (USA). 1952 Olympic middleweight champion. Held world heavyweight title from November 30, 1956 to June 26, 1959 and from June 20, 1960 to September 25, 1962.

Nino Benvenuti (Italy). 1960 Olympic welterweight champion. Held world junior middleweight title from June 18, 1965 to June 25, 1966. Held world middleweight title from April 17 to September 28, 1967 and from March 4, 1968 to November 7, 1970.

Muhammad Ali (USA). 1960 Olympic light heavyweight champion. Held world heavyweight title from February 25, 1964 to 1967; from October 30, 1974 to February 15, 1978; from September 15, 1978 to 1979.

Joe Frazier (USA). 1964 Olympic Heavyweight champion. Held world heavyweight title from February 16, 1970 to January 22, 1973.

George Foreman (USA). 1968 Olympic heavyweight champion. Held world heavyweight title from January 22, 1973 to October 30, 1974.

Mate Parlov (Yugoslavia). 1972 Olympic light heavyweight champion. Held WBC world light heavyweight title from January 7 to December 2, 1978.

Sugar Ray Leonard (USA). 1976 Olympic light welterweight champion. Held world welterweight title from November 30, 1979 to June 20, 1980 and from November 25, 1980 to November 9, 1982. Won WBA world junior middleweight title June 25, 1981. Won WBC world middleweight title April 6, 1987. Won WBC world light heavyweight title November 7, 1988. Won WBC super middleweight title December 7, 1989.

Leo Randolph (USA). 1976 Olympic flyweight champion. Held WBA world junior featherweight title from May 4 to August 9, 1980.

Leon Spinks (USA). 1976 Olympic light heavyweight champion. Held world heavyweight title from February 15 to September 15, 1978.

Michael Spinks (USA). 1976 Olympic middleweight champion. Held world light heavyweight title from July 18, 1981 to 1985. Held IBF world heavyweight title from September 22, 1985 to 1987.

Slobodan Kacar (Yugoslavia). 1980 Olympic light heavyweight champion. Held IBF world middleweight title from December 31, 1985 to 1986.

Patrizio Oliva (Italy). 1980 Olympic light welterweight champion. Held WBA world junior welterweight title from March 15, 1986 to July 7, 1987.

Frank Tate (USA). 1984 Olympic light middleweight championship. Held IBF middleweight title from October 10, 1987 to July 28, 1988.

Mark Breland (USA). 1984 Olympic welterweight champion. Held WBA world welterweight title from February 6 to August 22, 1987 and February 4, 1989 to July 8, 1990.

Pernell Whitaker (USA). 1984 Olympic lightweight champion. Won world lightweight title February 18, 1989.

And Don't Forget...

Ingemar Johansson (Sweden). Disqualified in 1952 Olympic heavyweight finals for not fighting. Held world heavyweight title from June 26, 1959 to June 29, 1960.

Evander Holyfield (USA). Disqualified in 1984 Olympic light heavyweight quarterfinals. Held world cruiserweight title from July 20, 1986 to 1988. Won world heavyweight championship October 25, 1990.

Gold is not always a guarantee. Whitaker's teammate, Tyrell Biggs, the 1984 Olympic super heavyweight gold medalist, has had less success as a pro, running into Mike Tyson in 1987. Tyson kayoed Biggs in seven.

The Business of Boxing

Who Controls Boxing Or, How Did We Get in this Alphabet Soup?

*I*t wasn't always like this. Once upon a time, a boxing fan knew where he stood. There were eight weight classes and one champion in each class. Not any more. By the end of 1990, there were sixteen weight divisions, with as many as three different champions in each. That's a possible total of forty-eight "world" champions—and a situation of utter confusion for even the diehard boxing buff.

This could only happen in boxing, where—unlike any other major professional sport—no central governing body has ever existed. To appreciate the history and structure of boxing, to begin to understand how the sport got to its present, muddled state, don't look for a rule book. Instead, like Woodward and Bernstein, follow the money. Money controls boxing. And, despite the huge drawing power of the great champions, the fighters do not control the money in the sport. The promoters do.

Tex, Uncle Mike, the Octopus, and a King Named Don

The first of the great boxing promoters was George Lewis Rickard, known to any and all as Tex. Tex Rickard, born in Clay County,

Missouri, in 1871, within shooting distance of the James brothers' ranch, started his career as a cowboy. At twenty-four, he was the marshall of Henrietta, Texas. A year later he was in Alaska. There, during the great Gold Rush, Rickard ran gambling houses in the Yukon. He made and lost a couple of fortunes before selling out and heading to South Africa to look for diamonds.

Rickard's first boxing promotion was the 1906 Joe Gans–Battling Nelson fight. Rickard was never really a fight fan. It was said that even when he was the promoter at Madison Square Garden, Tex could name only two or three of the reigning world champions. But Tex Rickard understood a successful promotion, and when the Gans–Nelson bout left him $13,215 richer, he was hooked on boxing. He would go on to promote some of the most famous fights of his—or any—era, including the Jack Johnson–James J. Jeffries heavyweight title match in 1910.

Rickard's biggest break came when he hooked up with Jack Dempsey. Dempsey, perhaps the greatest attraction in the history of the sport, understood Rickard's power.

"In every fight Rickard ever put on, he himself brought in at least 50 percent of the

gate," said Jack. "No matter who the fighters were, they never accounted for more than the other 50 percent."

Together, Dempsey and Rickard produced five million-dollar gates during the twenties. It was a golden era for the sport and Rickard was largely responsible. In 1925, Tex built the "new" Madison Square Garden, the arena that would remain the center of the boxing world for more than three decades. When he died in 1929, Tex Rickard was laid out in the great hall of the Garden. That the general public would mourn the death of a boxing promoter seems difficult to imagine these days, but thousands of New Yorkers stood in line for hours just to view the body. One wag commented that they must have tied Rickard down in the casket, "or else old Tex would be spinning to see so many people getting in free!"

Boxing is about money, a fact of fistic life that Don King and Mike Tyson *(opposite page)* clearly appreciate. King, the dominant promoter of his era, presented then-heavyweight-champ Tyson with this tidy bonus after Iron Mike's one-round kayo of Carl "The Truth" Williams in 1989.

Rickard himself probably would have said —as he did about so many of the extraordinary events of his life—"I never seen anything like it."

With the passing of Rickard, boxing entered the dark ages. Dempsey and Tunney had both retired, and the heavyweight title was in an ugly muddle. The Depression was cutting into attendance and gate receipts everywhere. But there were two new faces on the horizon— one in the ring, and one out. The fighter was Joe Louis. The man behind the scenes was Michael Strauss Jacobs. Jacobs, better known as Uncle Mike, was a Broadway ticket broker and onetime consultant to Rickard. Jacobs broke into promoting in 1934, with the annual Milk Fund boxing show at the Garden. By 1935, his new Twentieth Century Sporting Club was beginning to bring interest back to the sport. Jacobs heard about the young Louis, still fighting out of New York at the time, and he eagerly sought him out. Like Rickard with Dempsey, Jacobs and Louis together controlled boxing for more than ten years. The stretch of midtown block where Uncle Mike kept his offices became known as Jacobs's Beach, commanding as it did, all of the New York fight scene.

It was Jacobs who opened the door to the most significant development in boxing history: television. He contracted with the Gilette company to sponsor weekly televised fight cards. The move changed the sport forever. It also nearly killed it.

The first king of promoters was George Lewis Rickard known as Tex Rickard (shown here posing with his premier attraction, heavyweight champ Jack Dempsey). Together, these two men were responsible for the sport's first million-dollar gates—as well as some of its greatest fights.

What more could a television producer or sponsor want from a sport than what boxing offers? Just two main characters; basic, often brutal, action; a contained, easily-photographed setting; and all broken up into neat three-minute segments with a minute in between for commercials. It was too good to be true. Ironically, as television embraced boxing, it began to destroy it. With free boxing on the tube twice a week, even the die-hard fan had little incentive to go out to a local club for a live bout. The small clubs began to fold. In turn, there began to be fewer places for young boxers to develop. A. J. Liebling called it technological unemployment. Television, eating up fighters every week, began to find fewer and fewer to replace them with. It was a painful process to watch, but one that took a while —like seeing an old champion slowly cut up and battered into defeat.

Jacobs, his health failing, didn't stick around to see the results of his initiative. In 1949, he signed over his syndicate—and with it the "rights" to the about-to-retire Louis's heavyweight championship—to a man named James D. Norris. Norris, heir to a great farming fortune and part owner of the Detroit Red Wings hockey team, was also the head of something called the International Boxing Club. Over the next ten years, the IBC would become better known as Octopus, Inc. for its total—and less-than-savory, control of boxing. Norris, bound by his TV contracts and increasingly in need of fighters, hitched up with mobster Frankie Carbo. Carbo supplied the fighters and managers, but for a price. Fights were fixed, clubs were closed, the mob controlled the sport. Jimmy Cannon, the syndicated columnist, once called boxing, "the red-light district of sports." Never was that description more accurate. The Octopus was strangling boxing. Finally, in 1960, the Kefauver Antitrust Committee of the U.S. Senate conducted a full-scale investigation into the situation. Norris was forced out of boxing, but the sport was left battered and barely alive.

The savior, of course, was Ali. The new heavyweight champion's consummate skills and showmanship brought interest and fun back to the prize ring—brought young people and women and others who had never watched boxing flocking to their TV sets and to the closed-circuit theatres. Boxing was entertaining again.

At the same time that Ali was sweeping across the nation's consciousness, boxing was opening up internationally as never before. And that's really the beginning of how boxing got in the shape its in now. In 1962, the National Boxing Association, a loose-knit collection of United States boxing commissioners, voted to change its name to the World Boxing Association. Nobody paid too much attention. The fight crowd viewed the WBA as the "only game in town," but it carried very little real weight.

Soon enough, the WBA was joined by another organization, the World Boxing Council (WBC). A more international group, the WBC changed the face of the sport again. Where once any self-respecting fight fan could easily rattle off the names of single champions in each of the eight weight divisions, today that fan is confronted with a possible total of forty-eight world champions, in sixteen weight divisions and a constantly growing roster of sanctioning bodies. While it seems no one who cares for the sport would put up with such a situation, it will remain as long as the promoters and television big-wigs continue to prosper.

The king of today's promoters, of course, is King—Don King. The shock-haired former numbers runner from Cleveland has stepped into the shoes of Rickard and Jacobs and more than filled them. It was King who barnstormed Ali around the globe in the '70's, pulling in big money from foreign governments and international closed-circuit TV. And it is King, today, who—though challenged by rivals such as Bob Arum and the Duva clan—continues to play the sport for all it's worth,

most recently through pay-per-view telecasts and his control of boxing's biggest draw, Mike Tyson. Only, as King would say, in America. Only in boxing.

The Manager

In a touching scene in the original *Rocky* movie (the only one of the series that had anything to do with boxing), Mickey, the crusty old fight trainer played by Burgess Meredith, arrives at Rocky's apartment. "I wanna be your manager," says Mickey. Rocky is skeptical. Mickey tells the Rock about a fight he had when he was young, back in 1923—"the same night Dempsey fought Firpo." Mickey knocked his man out, he tells Rocky. The old man pauses. "But guess who got all the publicity?" he growls. "Dempsey! And you know why?"

" 'Cause he was the champ," says Rocky.

"Because he had a manager!" rasps Mickey. "He had a manager."

Mickey's logic underscores the view of most boxing managers—that what goes on in the ring bears but a fleeting relationship to the ultimate success of a fighter. It's the management that counts, Mickey and his colleagues would insist.

Of course, Dempsey did have a manager, perhaps the ultimate boxing manager, in John Leo McKernan—better known as Doc Kearns. In a career that started in the Klondike and spanned five decades, Kearns handled such champions as Mickey Walker, Joe Maxim, and Archie Moore in addition to Dempsey. A hard drinker and a hard gambler, the little, jug-eared Kearns carried the traditional manager's self-inclusion a step further. Where other managers said "we" when they meant the fighter —as in, "We just signed to fight Robinson and we're going to take him in six"—Kearns saw no reason to share the billing. He dispensed with the fighter altogether. "I won the title off Willard in 1919," Kearns would pipe. "I knocked Firpo down seven times."

Under Kearns's freewheeling guidance, Dempsey fought his way out of the mining towns of the west to the heavyweight championship of the world. Kearns was a master showman. Together with Tex Rickard he created the first million-dollar gates in the sport, when Dempsey faced Carpentier and later Firpo. Though Dempsey and Kearns would later split over money matters (Kearns, it seems, had the same trouble distinguishing between his money and Dempsey's that he had distinguishing between himself and the fighter), the two remained close friends until Kearns's death in 1963.

After the break with Dempsey, Kearns hooked up with Mickey Walker. The Walker–Kearns match was one made in heaven—or at least at the bar of a Broadway speakeasy. Walker was as great a drinker as Kearns, and both men were ready to take on the world in any fight. With the Doctor in his corner, the five foot, seven inch (170 cm) Walker not only won the middleweight championship of the world, but fought his way awfully close to the heavyweight crown as well.

Of Maxim, the first of his two light heavyweight champions of the fifties, Kearns used to offer the dubious endorsement, "He's as great as Dempsey was, only he don't hit so hard." That's like saying you have a performer who's as entertaining as Fred Astaire, only he don't dance so well. Kearns's second light heavyweight champ was Moore. In fact, Moore won the title from Maxim in 1952. Kearns had arranged before the bout to claim a piece of Moore's contract should he beat Maxim. "Looking out for me and mine," was how Doc put it. Despite all his wheeling and dealing, Kearns remained a respected figure in the boxing world. When the Kefauver Committee conducted its investigation into corruption in boxing in 1960, Kearns testified at length. After the investigation was concluded, Senator Kefauver was asked if there were any honest managers in boxing.

John Leo McKernan, better known as Jack (Doc) Kearns, came out of the Klondike to guide the careers of some of boxing's greatest champions, including Jack Dempsey and Archie Moore.

"Some, of course," said Kefauver. "Jack Kearns impressed me. He was the best we talked to, the highest class."

The Doctor could not have said it better himself.

Kearns, of course, is not the only colorful or important manager in boxing history. From the days of Bill Brady, who handled both Corbett and Jeffries, to Lou Duva and Emanuel Steward today, managers have frequently brought as much or more interest to the sport as their fighters.

A good manager can do much to further his boxer's career. A bad manager can ruin a fighter. Matchmaking is a very important part of the equation, especially for a young, still-developing boxer. Rush the kid along too fast and you risk getting him beaten, hurt, and discouraged. Shelter him too much and he never learns anything—even if he gets a title shot, he won't be ready. Compare the developments of two relatively recent heavyweight prospects. Gerry Cooney, the hard-punching white hope of the early eighties was fed a diet of barely ambulatory stiffs by his managers at the time, Mike Jones and Dennis Rappaport. He won twenty-five fights in a row, but never went more than eight rounds and he was never extended. When he met Larry Holmes for the title in 1982, he was woefully unprepared. Holmes stopped him in the thirteenth round.

Evander Holyfield, on the other hand, was prepared meticulously for his shot at the heavyweight title. Under the guidance of Dan and Lou Duva each one of his fights taught him something and moved him along in his career. They weren't there just to fatten his record. Holyfield won the cruiserweight title in just his twelfth pro fight, a bruising fifteen-rounder against Dwight Muhammad Qawi. And when Holyfield moved up to the heavyweight ranks, the Duvas made certain his opponents would test him and teach him. When Holyfield faced Buster Douglas for the heavyweight title on October 25, 1990, he was as prepared as a fighter has ever been.

Of course, a manager can only do so much. Despite what Mickey would say, it's the guy in the ring who ultimately has to win the fight. Benny Leonard, who was managed by a man named Billy Gibson, came home from his second bout against Freddie Welsh—a bout he'd lost—and complained to his father about how elusive Welsh had been. "I chased him all over the ring," said Benny. "and where was Mr. Gibson?" said his father.

There's an old joke about fight managers.

"Why," it is asked, "don't sharks eat managers?" The answer of course is: "Professional courtesy."

But for all the sharks swimming in the fistic waters, there have been some great and even honorable managers as well. To the list of Kearns and Brady and Steward (the head of the Kronk gym and the architect of Thomas Hearns's brilliant career) add these names:

Jack Hurley. Hurley, who lived from 1897 to 1972, managed dozens of fighters, the best being Billy Petrolle. Damon Runyon once wrote, "There are two honest managers in boxing. The one is Jack Hurley and I can't remember the name of the other."

John Roxborough and **Julian Black.** It can't be hard to manage well if your fighter is Joe Louis. Still, Roxborough and Black, despite the overshadowing presence of promoter Mike Jacobs, deserve much of the credit for the development of Louis into both one of the greatest fighters and perhaps the greatest attraction in boxing history.

Al Weill. Weill, officially the matchmaker for the IBC, was Rocky Marciano's de facto manager. Described by A. J. Liebling as "one of the most realistic fellows in a milieu where illusions are few," Weill controlled a whole string of fighters before the war. But his masterpiece was Marciano.

Charlie Johnston. Johnston managed both featherweight champ Sandy Saddler and, before Kearns horned in, light heavyweight Archie Moore.

Cus D'Amato. The eccentric trainer, D'Amato was an equally eccentric manager. He was an extremely cautious matchmaker with his fighters, yet still guided Floyd Patterson and Jose Torres to world championships —and set the course for Mike Tyson's career.

Yank Durham. Durham was the man behind the scenes of Joe Frazier's career, taking Frazier from a Philadelphia slaughterhouse to the heavyweight championship.

The Great Venues

In its earliest years, boxing had no permanent home. The sport was illegal, its practitioners and fans outlaws. A prize fight was liable to be stopped at any moment by the police—if the police could find it, that is. Spectators were often required to tramp for miles over muddy fields to take their places beside rings pitched in secluded spots. Later, in the United States, fights were held on barges anchored midstream and in the back rooms of saloons.

On Christmas Eve 1880 an up-and-coming John L. Sullivan challenged "Professor" John Donaldson, the 160-pound (73 kg) "Champion of the West," in one such match—held in a back room of the Atlantic Garden in Cincinnati. Donaldson, a clever boxer, wanted nothing to do with Sullivan's power and spent the bout in full retreat, sprinting about the ring. Sullivan finally caught him—and knocked him out—in the tenth round. The next day, Christmas, the Cincinnati police arrested Sullivan for engaging in a prize fight. He was brought to court where the judge, who had himself attended the match, asked a witness, "Did you see a prize fight?" "No, your honor," replied the witness. "I saw a foot race. Mr. Sullivan was trying to catch up to Mr. Donaldson, but he couldn't." The judge dismissed the charges.

Once legalized, boxing came in from the cold—at least figuratively—into the arenas and stadiums. Some of these, like the outlaw rings of old, were specially built for a given bout. Only now, construction was carried out in the glare of publicity.

In 1919, when Jess Willard signed to defend his heavyweight title against Jack Dempsey, promoter Tex Rickard paid $100,000 to builder James McLaughlin to construct an eighty-thousand seat wood arena on the shores of Maumee Bay near Toledo, Ohio. McLaughlin used 1,750,000 feet (533,400 m)

of fresh-cut pine for the stadium, which the New York *Sun* called, "the most remarkable structure of wood ever erected for a sporting event." Rickard's arena even had a special section set up for female spectators—separated from the rest of the stands by barbed wire. In the end, a nationwide train strike, misleading newspaper reports about the unavailability of tickets and hotel rooms, and the blazing July heat held attendance down to fewer than twenty thousand paid. Rickard wound up selling his stadium to a local contractor for $25,000 cash after the fight.

In 1921, Rickard built another stadium far greater even than the one in Toledo for the Dempsey-Carpentier match. The site was Boyle's Thirty Acres, a tract of land in Jersey City just across the Hudson River from Manhattan. Again the newspapers devoted pages to describing the arena's construction. A vast wooden saucer, Rickard's stadium was built to hold ninety-one thousand fans. On July 2, 1921, it was full and boxing had its first million-dollar gate. During the excitement of the bout, in which Dempsey knocked Carpentier out in four rounds, the huge saucer swayed, and fans in the cheapest seats fled in panic down the aisles. But the stadium remained standing and indeed was used for title fights for many years.

Of course, despite the success of such specially built arenas, the greatest of all boxing venues was thriving. The original Madison Square Garden, situated naturally enough at Madison Square in New York City, opened in 1871, though it wasn't given its name until 1879. The original Garden played host to horse shows and revival meetings, concerts and theatrical extravaganzas. P. T. Barnum was a part owner for a while. In 1889, the first Garden was torn down and replaced, a year later, by a beautiful $4.5-million pale yellow building of brick and terra cotta designed by the famous architect Stanford White. White's building featured a 341-foot (104 m) tower

© Paul Thompson/FPG International

capped with a gilded statue of the goddess Diana. White himself was murdered there, in his rooftop garden, on June 25, 1906. In one of the age's great scandals, Harry Thaw, a Pitts-burgh playboy, shot White in a quarrel over his wife, Evelyn Nesbit.

The Old Garden, as White's structure will forever be remembered, housed a vast arena, capable of seating nearly fourteen thousand for boxing matches. They also held the six-day bicycle races there and marathon footraces. Of course, they also held boxing matches. Sullivan fought there, as did Young Griffo, Jess Willard, and George Dixon. The Walker Bill of 1920 legalized boxing in New York State and brought a steady stream of championship bouts to the Garden's ring. Dempsey, Leonard, Harry Greb—the greatest champions of the era defended their titles in the Old Garden.

In 1925, the Old Garden was torn down and replaced with a new, much less elegant struc-ture on Eighth Avenue—no longer anywhere near Madison Square, though the name

remained. While not the architectural land-mark that the Old Garden was, the "New Gar-den"—also called "the House that Rickard Built," in honor of Tex Rickard, then the Garden's resident promoter—continued the tradition of landmark fights.

In the first fight at the third Garden, on December 11, 1925, Paul Berlenbach beat Jack Deleney over fifteen rounds to successfully defend his light heavyweight title. From then through 1967, some of the most famous bouts in boxing history took place in the big arena between 49th and 50th Streets. Joe Louis defended his title there eight times. He was also knocked out in the Garden's ring, in 1951 by the young Rocky Marciano. It was the last time Joe fought.

Henry Armstrong won his first world title in the Garden, beating Petey Sarron in 1937, and lost his last one there as well, when Fritzie Zivic beat him in 1940. Ray Robinson became a champion for the first time there six years later, when he decisioned Tommy Bell for the vacant welterweight crown. Sandy Saddler

and Willie Pep fought the first two of their four classic wars in the Garden, and it was in a corner of the Garden's ring that Benny (Kid) Paret took his fatal beating at the hands of Emile Griffith in 1962. Muhammad Ali stopped Zora Folley in the 50th Street Garden in 1967, his last fight as champion before going into three and a half years of exile. The next time Ali fought for the heavyweight championship, he was once again in Madison Square Garden—but he was sixteen blocks farther down Eighth Avenue.

The fourth Madison Square Garden opened in 1968, an eighteen-thousand seat modern arena atop the Pennsylvania Railroad Station. A new building, a new set of heroes. Roberto Duran mugged Ken Buchanan there in 1972 to win the lightweight championship and estab-lish himself as the greatest fighter of his era. But the new-new Garden's most famous fight was the one that marked the return of Ali to championship competition, his 1971 show-down with Joe Frazier. On that March night, as so often before, a twenty-foot (6-m) square

APWide World Photos

patch of canvas in a New York building known as Madison Square Garden, was the focus of the sporting world.

That the Ali–Frazier fight could be held in Madison Square Garden in 1971 points out one very significant change in the way fights have come to be presented. For, as great as the Garden—in all its manifestations—had been, it had never been big enough to house the real blockbuster bouts. Dempsey–Tunney, Louis–Schmeling, Louis–Conn, all were fought in the big ballparks where there were enough seats to handle the crowds of fifty thousand or more that would produce million-dollar gates. Television changed all that, especially closed-circuit television. The live gate became incidental compared to the revenue generated in theatres around the country, indeed around

the world. The first Ali–Frazier fight drew 20,455 fans to the Garden. The live gate was $1,352,951—the first million-dollar gate since the second Louis–Conn fight in 1946—but that was just a drop in the bucket compared to the TV money. Indeed, it fell far short of even covering the fighters' guarantees of $2.5 million each.

The decade that followed saw the biggest fights going on around the globe: in Venezuela, Zaire, and Manila. Third-World governments themselves put up the funds, and promoters cashed in on the vast closed-circuit audience.

The past fifteen years could be called the era of the casinos. Las Vegas and Atlantic City have been the only spots able to afford the huge fees demanded for major bouts. And so, up go

the temporary stadiums—on the tennis courts at Caesars Palace, in the parking lot at the Mirage—just like Rickard's old wooden bowls in Toledo and Jersey City.

Throughout its four incarnations, New York's Madison Square Garden has remained the most famous boxing arena in the world. The photo above shows the third Garden—the "House that Rickard Built"—site of scores of championship bouts from 1925 through 1967. Boyle's Thirty Acres *(opposite page),* the greatest of the outdoor arenas. Built by Rickard in 1921 for the Dempsey–Carpentier fight, the huge wooden bowl held ninety-one thousand fans.

Ringside

Writing the Fights

With the exception of baseball, no other sport has so captured the imagination of the writer as boxing. There is no body of classic football literature, no canon of track-and-field writing. But since the earliest days of the sport the finest writers of the era have found themselves drawn to the ring. Maybe it's the elemental nature of the conflict, one man against another in an empty square. Maybe it's the violence. Or the rich backdrop of character and atmosphere. Whatever the reasons, readers have been treated over the years to an astonishing range of great writing, both reportage and fiction, on the subject of boxing.

The first of the great fight writers was Pierce Egan, whose 1812 volume, *Boxiana; Or Sketches of Ancient and Modern Pugilism,* provides a sparkling and comprehensive history of the English Prize Ring from the early 1700s to Egan's own time. Egan's enthusiasm for the sport is unmatched and his accounts of the major battles of the day are vigorous and vivid. It was Egan who first referred to boxing as "The Sweet Science of Bruising!" Equally satisfying in *Boxiana* is the portrait that comes through of an age; of a time and place and class of people.

No one has yet matched Egan in scope, but there have been great boxing writers in every generation—and great writers who wrote about boxing. A. Conan Doyle, creator of Sherlock Holmes, was an ardent fan and wrote several boxing stories. George Bernard Shaw wrote a boxing novel called *Cashel Byron's Profession.* Jack London was a passionate boxing fan who wrote a number of boxing stories and novels, including *The Game, The Mexican,* and "A Piece of Steak." London was also the man who sounded the call for a Great White Hope when Jack Johnson was heavyweight champion. Nelson Algren, Budd Schulberg, John O'Hara, and Irwin Shaw all wrote boxing stories. Ernest Hemingway, a lifelong boxing fan and boxer, wrote with grace about fights and fighters.

More recently, Edward Hoagland's *The Circle Home* and Leonard Gardner's *Fat City* are both fine novels on their own terms that also happen to be about boxing. The best boxing novel, however, remains W. C. Heinz's *The Professional,* which Hemingway himself called "the only good novel about a fighter I've ever read." First published in 1958 and reissued in 1984, the book is the story of middleweight contender Eddie Brown and his preparation for a fight. It captures the world of the training camp and the characters of the sport with unsentimental realism.

In most cases, however, the best boxing writing is not to be found in fiction, but in reporting. From the days of Damon Runyon and Ring Lardner to the present, some of the finest sportswriting—that most demanding of disciplines—has concerned boxing and boxers. Much more than from the films—or even from what we might have been lucky enough to see with our own eyes—our images of the great fights and fighters come from the writers.

While not among the great stylists, Nat Fleischer must rank as one of the most prolific and influential of the old-time boxing writers. A reporter for the *New York Press* and later for the *New York Telegram,* Fleischer founded *Ring Magazine*—the self-proclaimed Bible of the sport—in 1922. He was also a tireless historian of the ring, producing dozens of books, everything from his autobiography, *Fifty Years at Ringside,* to a multivolume history of the early black prize fighters.

George Plimpton, in one of his participatory journalism episodes, got in the ring for three rounds with Archie Moore when Moore was still light heavyweight champion. Plimpton came away with a bloody nose and a quick story for *Sports Illustrated.* He continued to write about boxing off and on for the maga-

Since the earliest days of the sport, many of the best writers of the day have been fascinated by the ring and by the great champions—such as Jack Dempsey *(opposite page, on the left)* in his 1920 match against Bill Brennan.

George Bernard Shaw, pacifist, vegetarian, and socialist, wrote a fine boxing novel called *Cashel Byron's Profession,* and also befriended heavyweight champ Gene Tunney.

zine over the next twenty years. In 1977 he produced a lovely book called *Shadow Box,* as much about writers as about fighters, though full of wonderful images of Ali from the time of the first Liston fight through the Foreman match in 1974.

The best boxing writers provide more than just a round-by-round account—no matter how vivid—of a fight. The best provide a sense of why the fight went the way it did, and always they provide a sense of who the fighters really

are. Boxing is a strange and at times troubling activity. It is too easy to sit back and see it only from the outside. Red Smith, Jimmy Cannon, Barney Nagler—all bring a sense of connectedness to their fight pieces.

To the reader, by the final bell, the bylines become as much a part of the fight as the boxers—Mike Katz, Mark Kram, Pat Putnam, Ed Schuyler, Britain's Hugh McIlvanney—their moves are woven in there with the punches and the footwork.

A. J. Liebling

For many readers, A. J. Liebling's *The Sweet Science*—a collection of the boxing essays he wrote for *The New Yorker* in the early fifties—remains, pound-for-pound and page-for-page, the best of all boxing books, the standard against which all other fight writing is measured. From its elegant opening paragraph, in which Liebling traces his "rapport with the historic past" through "a series of punches on the nose," to its final essay, a rich and illuminating report on the 1955 Rocky Marciano–Archie Moore fight, entitled "Ahab and Nemesis," *The Sweet Science* brings the ring alive in unmatched prose.

Liebling, best remembered beyond the boxing world for his witty and acerbic "Wayward Press" columns in *The New Yorker* and for his 1961 biography of Earl Long, *The Earl of Louisiana,* was a journalist of great scope. Born in New York City in 1904, educated at Dartmouth (for a while at least; he was thrown out for cutting chapel) and the Columbia Journalism School, he worked as a newspaper reporter for several years before settling in at *The New Yorker* in 1935. There, at that most genteel of periodicals, Liebling covered what editor Harold Ross termed "low-life." The beat included the minor Broadway entertainers, gamblers, sharpsters, con men, and characters of New York City—and, of course, boxers.

From 1939 to 1945 Liebling served as *The New Yorker*'s war correspondent, reporting

Jack London, author of *White Fang* and *Call of the Wild,* was also a great boxing fan who wrote several novels and stories set in the ring.

from Europe and North Africa. After the war he turned his attention to press criticism. In 1951, he returned to covering boxing, "the way," as he put it, "you take a notion that you would like to see an old sweetheart." For the next twelve years, until his death in 1963, he would prove an affectionate and attentive consort.

That Liebling wrote for *The New Yorker* is lucky. It is hard to imagine any other publication welcoming a mention of Ibn Khaldun, "the immortal Tunisian contemporary of Chaucer,"

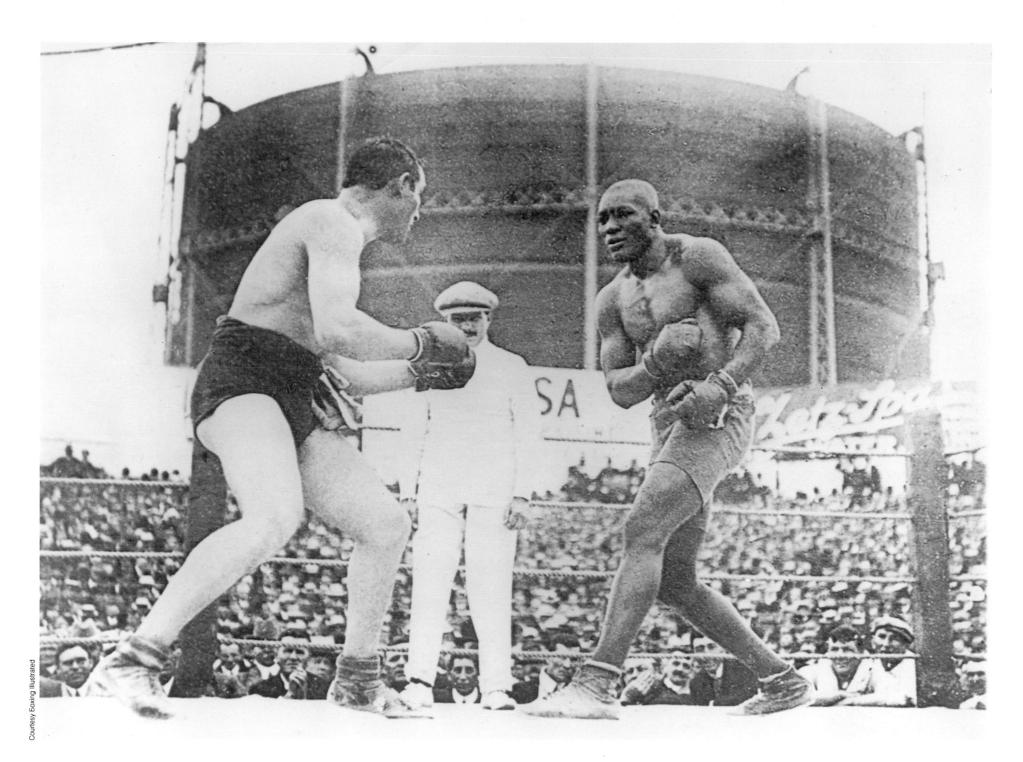

in the middle of a report on a heavyweight championship fight, but it is just that sort of juxtaposition that makes Liebling so delightful.

He describes Moore getting knocked down by minor challenger Harold Johnson: "It was as if Vladimir de Pachmann had been assaulted by a piano stool."

The Liebling style—leisurely, digressive, and scrupulously observed—banishes all sentimentality, all sensationalism, allowing the reader simply to see what was going on in and around the ring and to understand. There was none of what he once termed the "blinded-by-blood-he-swung-again-school

When Jack Johnson battered Tommy Burns to take the heavyweight championship, in Sydney, Australia, in 1908, London issued his infamous call for a "Great White Hope" to wrest the title back.

of fight writing," in Liebling. His great hero was Pierce Egan, the "Thucydides" of the prize ring, and he quotes him often and with great relish in *The Sweet Science.* In the end, though, Liebling's voice is unmistakenly his own:

"I reflected with satisfaction that old Ahab Moore could have whipped all four principals on that card within fifteen rounds," he wrote at the end of *The Sweet Science,* "and that while Dempsey was a great champion, he had less to beat than Marciano. I felt the satisfaction because it proved that the world isn't going backward, if you can just stay young enough to remember what it was really like when you were really young."

Papa in the Ring

Ernest Hemingway never really covered boxing, never filed a ringside report. But of all the major writers who called themselves enthusiasts, none was as close to the sport.

Throughout his life, Hemingway thought of himself as a boxer. As a young man, he earned money working as a sparring partner in the tough gyms of Kansas City (he claimed to have boxed both Jack Blackburn and Sam Langford). When he and his wife Hadley first sailed to Europe, Hemingway broke up the monotony of the voyage by shadow boxing on deck and by organizing a sparring exhibition between himself and another passenger, a professional middleweight named Henry Cuddy. According to Hemingway, he had Cuddy on the verge of a knockout in the third and final round of the match. There were, however, no reporters present at ringside to verify that account.

Hemingway continued to spar wherever he lived, often with professionals in local gyms, such as the one on the Boulevarde Raspail in Paris, but more often with his friends— anyone he could get to lace on the gloves. The list of Hemingway's sparring partners

includes some unlikely pugilists. In the early twenties in Paris he taught Ezra Pound to box (Pound, reported Hemingway, had the "general grace of a crawfish" and led with his chin), and worked regularly with the painter Henry Strater. In a famous incident, Hemingway and the Canadian novelist Morley Callaghan were sparring at the American Club in Paris, with

F. Scott Fitzgerald as the timekeeper. Fitzgerald, enthralled with the action, let the round run on for an extra three minutes while Callaghan battered Hemingway. This led to a brief strain on the Hemingway–Fitzgerald friendship.

As a boxer, Hemingway—a full-fledged heavyweight at six feet (183 cm) and over two hundred pounds (91 kg)—was no Gentleman

Jim. By all reports, even his own, he was skill-ful, if not overly fast, possessed of a good short left hook and not above some dirty stuff now and then. Once, in Cuba, Hemingway and Tunney were sparring when Hemingway, taking advantage of the former champion's easygoing style, threw a low blow that hurt Tunney. Tunney immediately fired back a deadly combination, stopping the blows just millimeters from Hemingway's exposed face. "Don't ever do that again," said Tunney. Hemingway never referred to the incident.

Hemingway's letters were full of critiques of the top fighters of his day and assessments of upcoming matches. He even spoke of his writing in terms of boxing, referring to his first novel as "going fifteen rounds."

And of course Hemingway incorporated boxing and boxers into his fiction, in such stories as "Fifty Grand," "The Battler," and "Light of the World." The character Robert Cohn in *The Sun Also Rises* was "once middle-weight boxing champion of Princeton." In his fiction, however, Hemingway was much less interested in what went on in the ring than he was in how the boxer—most often the beaten or fading boxer—faced his world. For Hemingway, the boxer was the ultimate individualist.

Throughout his life, Ernest Hemingway (*opposite page,* with his second wife, Pauline Pfeiffer) considered himself a boxer. By all reports, the Nobel prize winner possessed a good short left hook. *Right:* Hemingway was clearly fond of other kinds of fighting as well. Here, he and his fourth wife, Mary, take in the action at Madrid's *Plaza de Toros.*

Lights, Camera, Punch!   Boxing goes to the Movies

The motion picture camera got its first look at a boxing match on September 8, 1894. On that Saturday morning in Orange, New Jersey, heavyweight champion Jim Corbett took on a Trenton fighter named Peter Courtney inside Thomas Edison's Kinetoscope theatre —basically a fifteen-foot (4.5 m) wide wooden box. The fight was a full-fledged championship match, though each round lasted only until the film ran out—after about a minute and a half—and the rest periods went on for more than two minutes each, as that's how long it took to change the film. Corbett knocked Courtney out in the sixth round.

Since that day, filmmakers have returned again and again to the ring, adding plot, dialogue, music, sophisticated camera work, and special effects. They have made some classic movies, but they have yet to improve on Edison's simple and eloquent vision.

The trouble with Hollywood boxing films is that they never can leave well enough alone. You'll find scant evidence of the Sweet Science when the movies are in the ring. Every punch becomes a haymaker, every round seems to feature multiple knockdowns and buckets of blood. Even the best boxing movies, such as *Raging Bull* or *Fat City,* can't help stylizing the action.

What's worse, moviemakers discovered early on that boxing—which the late Jimmy Cannon once termed "the red-light district of sports"—is a perfect vehicle for melodrama. In boxing movies, gangsters lurk behind every ring post, manipulating both the sport and the fighters' lives. Remember Marlon Brando as Terry Malloy, spitting the words back at his brother, Charley, in *On the Waterfront?* "Kid, this ain't your night. We're going for the price on Wilson." Or Kirk Douglas as Midge Kelly in *Champion,* being told by his manager, Tommy Haley (played by Paul Stewart), to throw a fight. "This one

Hollywood heavyweights, Sylvester Stallone *(left)* as *Rocky,* and Robert DeNiro *(right)* as Jake LaMotta in *Raging Bull.*

you lose." In the movies, fighters take more dives than Olympic gold medalist Greg Louganis. In the end, what's missing is a sense of the everyday professionalism of the sport. There's too much Life and Death; too much Good and Evil, and not enough plain boxing.

Still, it is impossible to deny the appeal of some of the classic boxing movies, hard for even the toughest ring purist not to cheer when Rocky belts Apollo Creed or thrill when Jake LaMotta, played by an extremely fit Robert DeNiro, spits out, "You never put me down, Ray. You never put me down." And we all believe, inside, that Brando coulda been a contender.

Ring Champions by Years

Heavyweights

1882–1892	John L. Sullivan (a)
1892–1897	James J. Corbett (b)
1897–1899	Robert Fitzsimmons
1899–1905	James J. Jeffries
1905–1906	Marvin Hart
1906–1908	Tommy Burns
1908–1915	Jack Johnson
1915–1919	Jess Willard
1919–1926	Jack Dempsey
1926–1928	Gene Tunney*
1928–1930	vacant
1930–1932	Max Schmeling
1932–1933	Jack Sharkey
1933–1934	Primo Carnera
1934–1935	Max Baer
1935–1937	James J. Braddock
1937–1949	Joe Louis*
1949–1951	Ezzard Charles
1951–1952	Joe Walcott
1952–1956	Rocky Marciano*
1956–1959	Floyd Patterson
1959–1960	Ingemar Johansson
1960–1962	Floyd Patterson
1962–1964	Sonny Liston
1964–1968	Cassius Clay* (Muhammad Ali) (c)
1970–1973	Joe Frazier
1973–1974	George Foreman
1974–1978	Muhammad Ali
1978–1979	Leon Spinks (d); Muhammad Ali*
1978	Ken Norton (WBC); Larry Holmes (WBC) (e)
1979	John Tate (WBA)
1980	Mike Weaver (WBA)
1983	Michael Dokes (WBA)
1984	Tim Witherspoon (WBC); Pinklon Thomas (WBC); Greg Page (WBA)
1985	Tony Tubbs (WBA); Michael Spinks (IBF)
1986	Trevor Berbick (WBC); Tim Witherspoon (WBA); James "Bonecrusher" Smith (WBA); Mike Tyson (WBC)
1987	Michael Spinks; Mike Tyson
1988–1990	Mike Tyson
1990	James "Buster" Douglas
1990	Evander Holyfield

(a) London Prize Ring (bare knuckle champion).
(b) First Marquess of Queensberry champion.
(c) Title declared vacant by the World Boxing Association and other groups in 1967 after Clay's refusal to fulfill his military obligation. Joe Frazier was recognized as champion by New York, five other states, Mexico, and South America. Frazier ko'd Jimmy Ellis on February 16, 1970.
(d) After Spinks defeated Ali, the WBC recognized Ken Norton as champion. Norton subsequently lost his title to Larry Holmes.
(e) Holmes was stripped of his WBC title in 1984. He was the International Boxing Federation champion when he lost to Michael Spinks.

Light Heavyweights

1903	Jack Root, George Gardner
1903–1905	Bob Fitzsimmons
1905–1912	Philadelphia Jack O'Brien*
1912–1916	Jack Dillon
1916–1920	Battling Levinsky
1920–1922	George Carpentier
1922–1923	Battling Siki
1923–1925	Mick McTigue
1925–1926	Paul Berlenbach
1926–1927	Jack Delaney*
1927–1929	Tommy Loughran*
1930–1934	Maxey Rosenbloom
1934–1935	Bob Olin
1935–1939	John Henry Lewis*
1939	Melio Bettina
1939–1941	Billy Conn*
1941	Anton Christoforidis (won NBA title)
1941–1948	Gus Lesnevich; Freddie Mills
1948–1950	Freddie Mills
1950–1952	Joey Maxim
1952–1960	Archie Moore
1961–1962	vacant
1962–1963	Harold Johnson
1963–1965	Willie Pastrano
1965–1966	Jose Torres
1966–1968	Dick Tiger
1968–1974	Bob Foster,* John Conteh (WBA)
1975–1977	John Conteh (WBC); Miguel Cuello (WBC); Victor Galindez (WBA)
1978	Mike Rossman (WBA); Mate Parlov (WBC); Marvin Johnson (WBC)
1979	Victor Galindez (WBA); Matthew Saad Muhammad (WBC)
1980	Eddie Mustava Muhammad (WBA)
1981	Michael Spinks (WBA); Dwight Braxton (WBC)
1983	Michael Spinks
1986–1987	Bobby Czyz (IBF); Dennis Andries (WBC); Marvin Johnson (WBA)
1987	Charles Williams (IBF); Thomas Hearns (WBC); Leslie Stewart (WBA); Virgil Hill (WBA)
1987–1988	Don LaLonde (WBC)
1988	Sugar Ray Leonard (WBC)
1989–1990	Jeff Harding (WBC)
1990	Dennis Andries (WBC)

Middleweights

1884–1891	Jack "Nonpareil" Dempsey
1891–1897	Bob Fitzsimmons*
1897–1907	Tommy Ryan*
1907–1908	Stanley Ketchel, Billy Papke
1908–1910	Stanley Ketchel
1911–1913	vacant
1913	Frank Klaus, George Chip
1914–1917	Al McCoy
1917–1920	Mike O'Dowd
1920–1923	Johnny Wilson
1923–1926	Harry Greb
1926–1931	Tiger Flowers, Mickey Walker
1931–1932	Gorilla Jones (NBA)
1932–1937	Marcel Thil
1938	Al Hostak (NBA); Solly Krieger (NBA)
1939–1940	Al Hostak (NBA)
1941–1947	Tony Zale
1947–1948	Rocky Graziano
1948	Tony Zale; Marcel Cerdan
1949–1951	Jake LaMotta
1951	Ray Robinson; Randy Turpin; Ray Robinson*
1953–1955	Carl "Bobo" Olson
1955–1957	Ray Robinson
1957	Gene Fullmer; Ray Robinson; Carmen Basilio
1958	Ray Robinson
1959	Gene Fullmer (NBA); Ray Robinson
1960	Gene Fullmer (NBA); Paul Pender
1961	Gene Fullmer (NBA); Terry Downes
1962	Gene Fullmer; Dick Tiger (NBA); Paul Pender*
1963	Dick Tiger
1963–1965	Joey Giardello
1965–1966	Dick Tiger
1966–1967	Emile Griffith
1967	Nino Benvenuti
1967–1968	Emile Griffith
1968–1970	Nino Benvenuti
1970–1977	Carlos Monzon*
1977–1978	Rodrigo Valdez
1978–1979	Hugo Corro
1979–1980	Vito Antuofermo
1980	Alan Minter; Marvin Hagler
1980–1987	Marvin Hagler
1987	Sugar Ray Leonard (WBC)
1987–1988	Thomas Hearns (WBC); Frank Tate (IBF); Sumbu Kalamby (WBA)
1988	Michael Nunn (IBF)
1988–1989	Iran Barkley (WBC)
1989	Mike McCallum (WBA)
1989–1990	Roberto Duran (WBC)
1990	Julian Jackson (WBC)

Welterweights

1892–1894	Mysterious Billy Smith
1894–1896	Tommy Ryan
1896	Kid McCoy*
1900	Rube Ferns; Matty Matthews
1901	Rube Ferns
1901–1904	Joe Walcott
1904–1906	Dixie Kid; Joe Walcott; Honey Mellody
1907–1911	Mike Sullivan
1911–1915	vacant
1915–1919	Ted Lewis
1919–1922	Jack Britton
1922–1926	Mickey Walker
1926	Pete Latzo
1927–1929	Joe Dundee
1929	Jackie Fields
1930	Jack Thompson; Tommy Freeman
1931	Tommy Freeman; Jack Thompson; Lou Brouillard
	Jackie Fields
1933	Young Corbett; Jimmy McLarnin
1934	Barney Ross; Jimmy McLarnin
1935–1938	Barney Ross
1938–1940	Henry Armstrong
1940–1941	Fritzie Zivic
1941–1946	Fred Cochrane
1946	Marty Servo*; Ray Robinson
1946–1950	Ray Robinson
1951	Johnny Bratton (NBA)
1951–1954	Kid Gavilan
1954–1955	Johnny Saxton
1955	Tony De Marco; Carmen Basilio
1956	Carmen Basilio; Johnny Saxton; Basilio
1957	Carmen Basilio*
1958–1960	Virgil Akins; Don Jordan
1960	Benny Paret
1961	Emile Griffith; Benny Paret
1962	Emile Griffith
1963	Luis Rodriguez; Emile Giffith
1964–1966	Emile Giffith*
1966–1969	Curtis Cokes
1969–1970	Jose Napoles; Billy Backus
1971–1975	Jose Napoles
1975–1976	John Stracey (WBC); Angel Espada (WBA)
1976–1979	Carlos Palomino (WBC); Pipino Cuevas (WBA)
1979	Wilfredo Benitez (WBC); Sugar Ray Leonard (WBC)
1980	Roberto Duran (WBC); Thomas Hearns (WBA); Sugar Ray Leonard (WBC)
1981–1982	Sugar Ray Leonard*
1983	Donald Curry (WBA); Milton McCrory (WBC)
1985	Donald Curry
1986–1990	Lloyd Honeyghan
1987	Mark Breland (WBA)
1987–1990	Marion Sterling (WBA/WBC)
1987–1988	Jorge Vaca (WBC)
1988	Simon Brown (IBF)
1989–1990	Mark Breland (WBA)
1990	Aaron Davis (WBA); Meldrick Taylor (WBA); Maurice Blocker (WBC)

Lightweights

1896–1899	Kid Lavigne
1899–1902	Frank Erne
1902–1908	Joe Gans
1908–1910	Battling Nelson
1910–1912	Ad Wolgast
1912–1914	Willie Ritchie
1914–1917	Freddie Welsh
1917–1925	Benny Leonard
1925	Jimmy Goodrich; Rocky Kansas
1926–1930	Sammy Mandell
1930	Al Singer; Tony Canzoneri
1930–1933	Tony Canzoneri
1933–1935	Barney Ross*
1935–1936	Tony Canzoneri
1936–1938	Lou Ambers
1938	Henry Armstrong
1939	Lou Ambers
1940	Lew Jenkins
1941–1943	Sammy Angott
1944	Sammy Angott (NBA); J. Zurita (NBA)
1945–1951	Ike Williams (NBA later universal)
1951–1952	James Carter
1952	Lauro Salas; James Carter
1953–1954	James Carter
1955	James Carter; Bud Smith
1956	Bud Smith; Joe Brown
1956–1962	Joe Brown
1962–1965	Carlos Ortiz
1965	Ismael Laguna
1965–1968	Carlos Ortiz
1968–1969	Teo Cruz
1969–1970	Mando Ramos
1970	Ismael Laguna; Ken Buchanan (WBA)
1971	Mando Ramos (WBC); Pedro Carrasco (WBC)
1972–1979	Roberto Duran* (WBA)
1972	Pedro Carrasco; Mando Ramos; Chango Carmona; Rodolfo Gonzalez (all WBC)
1974–1976	Guts Ishimatsu (WBC)
1976–1977	Esteban De Jesus (WBC)
1979	Jim Watt (WBC); Ernesto Espana (WBA)
1980	Hilmer Kenty (WBA)
1981	Alexis Arguello (WBC); Sean O'Grady (WBA); Arturo Frias (WBA)
1982–1984	Ray Mancini (WBA)
1983	Edwin Rosario (WBC)
1984	Livingstone Bramble (WBA); Jose Luis Ramirez (WBC)
1985–1987	Hector (Macho) Camacho (WBC)
1985–1986	Jimmy Paul (IBF)
1986–1987	Greg Haugen (IBF)
1987	Jose Luis Ramirez (WBC); Julio Cesar Chavez (WBA/WBC)
1987–1988	Vinnie Pazienza (IBF)
1989	Pernell Whitaker

Featherweights

1892–1900	George Dixon (disputed)
1900–1901	Terry McGovern; Young Corbett*
1901–1912	Abe Attell
1912–1923	Johnny Kilbane
1923	Eugene Criqui; Johnny Dundee
1923–1925	Johnny Dundee*
1925–1927	Kid Kaplan*
1927–1928	Benny Bass; Tony Canzoneri
1928–1929	Andre Routis
1929–1932	Battling Battalino*
1932–1934	Tommy Paul (NBA)
1933–1936	Freddie Miller
1936–1937	Petey Sarron
1937–1938	Henry Armstrong*
1938–1940	Joey Archibald
1942–1948	Willie Pep
1948–1949	Sandy Saddler
1949–1950	Willie Pep
1950–1957	Sandy Saddler*
1957–1959	Hogan (Kid) Bassey
1959–1963	Davey Moore
1963–1964	Sugar Ramos
1964–1967	Vicente Saldivar*
1968–1971	Paul Rojas (WBA); Sho Saijo (WBA)
1971	Antonio Gomez (WBA); Kuniaki Shibada (WBC)
1972	Ernesto Marcel* (WBA); Clemente Sanchez* (WBC); Jose Legra (WBC)
1973	Eder Jofre (WBC)
1974	Ruben Olivares (WBC); Alexis Arguello (WBA); Bobby Chacon (WBC)
1975	Ruben Olivares (WBC); David Kotey (WBC)
1976	Danny Lopez (WBC)
1977	Rafael Ortega (WBA)
1978	Cecilio Lastra (WBA); Eusebio Pedrosa (WBA); Salvador Sanchez (WBC)
1980	Salvador Sanchez (WBC)
1982	Juan LaPorte (WBC)
1984	Wilfredo Gomez (WBC); Azumah Nelson (WBC)
1985	Barry McGuigan (WBA)
1986	Steve Cruz (WBA)
1986–1988	Antonio Rivera (IBF)
1987	Antonio Esparragoza (WBA)
1988	Jorge Paez (IBF)
1988–1990	Jeff French (WBC)
1990	Marcos Villasana (WBC)

THIS DATE IN BOXING

JANUARY

1, 1907 Joe Gans kayos Kid Herman in 8 rounds to retain lightweight title.

2, 1957 Gene Fullmer beats Ray Robinson for middleweight title championship.

3, 1914 Benny Leonard outpoints Charlie Barry over 10 rounds.

5, 1955 Sugar Ray Robinson kayos Joe Rindone in 6 rounds.

7, 1925 Mike McTigue retains light heavyweight title on 12-round no-decision against Mickey Walker.

8, 1903 Philadelphia Jack O'Brien and Joe Grimm fight to 6-round no-decision.

9, 1788 Richard Humphreys defeats Daniel Mendoza.

10, 1949 Archie Moore kayos the Alabama Kid in 4 rounds.

11, 1935 Joe Louis kayos Hans Birkie in 10 rounds.

13, 1922 Gene Tunney outpoints Battling Levinsky over 12 rounds to win American light heavyweight title.

14, 1984 Ray Mancini kayos Bobby Chacon in 3rd to win WBA lightweight title.

15, 1972 Joe Frazier stops Terry Daniels in 4 rounds to retain heavyweight title.

16, 1950 Willie Pep kayos Charley Riley in 5 rounds to retain featherweight title.

17, 1791 Big Ben Brain defeats Tom Johnson for English heavyweight crown.

18, 1956 Sand Saddler kayos Flash Elorde in 13 rounds to retain featherweight title.

19, 1906 Joe Gans kayos Mike "Twin" Sullivan in 15 rounds to win vacant welterweight title.

20, 1973 Roberto Duran kayos Jimmy Robertonson in 5 rounds to retain lightweight title.

21, 1938 James J. Braddock outpoints Tommy Farr over 10 rounds.

22, 1973 George Forcman kayos Joe Frazier in second round to win heavyweight title.

23, 1982 Milt McCrory kayos Randy Shields in 8 rounds.

24, 1976 George Foreman kayos Ron Lyle in 4 rounds.

25, 1894 James J. Corbett knocks out Charley Mitchell in three rounds to defend heavyweight title.

26, 1948 Ike Williams outpoints Freddie Dawson over 10 rounds

27, 1954 Archie Moore outpoints Joey Maxim over 15 rounds to retain light heavyweight title.

28, 1974 Muhammad Ali outpoints Joe Frazier over 12 rounds.

29, 1952 Archie Moore outpoints Harold Johnson over 10 rounds.

30, 1962 Joey Giardello beats Henry Hank in 10 rounds.

31, 1941 Joe Louis kayos Red Burman in 5 rounds to retain heavyweight title.

FEBRUARY

1, 1965 Floyd Patterson outpoints George Chuvalo in 12 rounds.

2, 1980 Salvador Sanchez kayos Danny Lopez in 13 rounds to win WBC featherweight title.

3, 1980 Larry Holmes stops Lorenzo Zanon in 6 rounds to retain WBC heavyweight title.

4, 1979 Alexis Arguello kayos Alfredo Escalera in 13 rounds to retain WBC junior lightweight title.

5, 1943 Beau Jack outpoints Fritzie Zivic over 10 rounds.

6, 1967 Muhammad Ali outpoints Ernie Terrell over 15 rounds to retain heavyweight title.

7, 1882 John L. Sullivan kayos Paddy Ryan in 9 rounds to win bare-knuckle heavyweight title.

8, 1924 Pancho Villa outpoints Georgie Marks to retain flyweight title.

9, 1974 Carlos Monzon kayos Jose Napoles in the 7th round to retain middleweight title.

10, 1908 Tommy Burns kayos Jack Palmer in 4 rounds to retain heavyweight title.

11, 1990 "Buster" Douglas kayos Mike Tyson in 10 rounds to win heavyweight title.

12, 1977 Esteban DeJesus kayos Buzzsaw Yamabe in 6 rounds to retain WBC lightweight title.

13, 1952 Rocky Marciano kayos Lee Savold in 6 rounds.

14, 1951 Sugar Ray Robinson kayos Jake LaMotta in the 13th round to win first of five middleweight championships.

15, 1978 Leon Spinks beats Muhammad Ali over 15 rounds to win heavyweight title.

16, 1968 Joe Frazier kayos Jimmy Ellis in four rounds to win heavyweight title.

17, 1941 Joe Louis kayos Gus Dorazio in 2 rounds to retain heavyweight title.

18, 1989 Pernell Whitaker outpoints Greg Haugen over 12 rounds to win IBF lightweight title.

19, 1945 Willie Pep outpoints Phil Terranova over 15 rounds to retain featherweight title.

20, 1976 Muhammad Ali kayos Jean Pierre Coopman in 5 rounds to retain heavyweight championship.

21, 1941 Sugar Ray Robinson outpoints Bobby McIntire over 6 rounds

22, 1928 and **1929** Mickey Walker outpoints Cowboy Jack Willis, both over 10 rounds.

23, 1906 Tommy Burns decisions Marvin Hart over 20 rounds to win heavyweight title.

24, 1989 Roberto Duran outpoints Iran Barkley over 12 rounds to win WBC middleweight title.

25, 1964 Cassius Clay stops Sonny Liston in seven rounds to win heavyweight championship.

26, 1926 Tiger Flowers outpoints Harry Greb over 15 rounds to win middleweight title.

27, 1975 Ishimatsu Suzuki outpoints Ken Buchanan over 15 rounds to retain WBC lightweight title.

28, 1949 Ezzard Charles outpoints Joey Maxim over 15 rounds.

29, 1890 Joe Walcott kayos Tom Powers in 2 rounds.

MARCH

1, 1934 Primo Carnera decisions Tommy Loughran over 15 rounds to retain heavyweight title.

2, 1971 Bob Foster kayos Hal Carroll in 4 rounds to retain light heavyweight title.

3, 1927 Jack Sharkey kayos Mike McTigue in 12 rounds.

4, 1968 Joe Frazier stops Buster Mathis in 11 rounds to win N.Y. State heavyweight title.

5, 1913 Frank Klaus outpoints Billy Papke over 20 rounds to win middleweight title.

6, 1976 Wilfred Benitez outpoints Antonio Cervantes over 15 rounds to win junior welterweight title.

7, 1951 Ezzard Charles outpoints Jersey Joe Walcott over 15 rounds to retain heavyweight title.

8, 1971 Joe Frazier defeats Muhammad Ali over 15 rounds.

9, 1984 Tim Witherspoon outpoints Greg Page over 12 rounds to win WBC heavyweight title.

10, 1909 Jack Johnson fights Victor McLaglen to a 6-round no decision.

11, 1989 Evander Holyfield stops Michael Dokes in 10 rounds.

12, 1987 Jose Luis Ramirez outpoints Pernell Whitaker to retain WBC lightweight title.

13, 1963 Muhammad Ali beats Doug Jones in 10 rounds.

14, 1906 Jack Johnson outpoints Joe Jeannette over 15 rounds.

15, 1975 Alexis Arguello kayos Leonel Hernandez in 8 rounds to retain WBA featherweight title.

16, 1966 In his last fight, Willie Pep loses 6-rounder to Calvin Woodland.

17, 1897 Bob Fitzsimmons kayos James J. Corbett in 14 rounds to win the heavyweight championship.

18, 1959 Davey Moore kayos Hogan "Kid" Bassey in 13 rounds to win featherweight title.

19, 1972 Rafael Herrera kayos Ruben Olivares in 8 rounds to win bantamweight title.

20, 1945 In his pro debut Paddy DeMarco outpoints Sal Giglio over 4 rounds.

21, 1941 Joe Louis stops Abe Simon in 13 rounds to retain heavyweight title.

22, 1967 Muhammad Ali kayos Zora Folley in 7 rounds to retain heavyweight title.

23, 1979 Larry Holmes stops Osvaldo Ocasio in 7 rounds to retain WBC heavyweight title.

24, 1975 Muhammad Ali stops Chuck Wepner in 15 rounds to retain heavyweight title.

25, 1958 Ray Robinson decisions Carmen Basilio to win middleweight championship.

26, 1909 Stanley Ketchel and Philadelphia Jack O'Brien fight 10-round no-decision bout.

27, 1942 Joe Louis kayos Abe Simon in 6 rounds to retain heavyweight title.

28, 1917 Willie Meehan outpoints Jack Dempsey over 4 rounds.

29, 1940 Joe Louis kayos Johnny Paychek in 2 rounds to retain heavyweight title.

30, 1984 Marvin Hagler kayos Juan Roldan in 10 rounds to retain middleweight title.

APRIL

1, 1938 Joe Louis kayos Harry Thomas in 5 rounds to retain heavyweight title.

3, 1971 Ruben Olivares beats Chucho Castillo in 15 rounds to regain bantamweight title.

4, 1928 Max Schmeling outpoints Franz Diener over 15 rounds to win German heavyweight title.

5, 1915 Jess Willard kayos Jack Johnson in the 26th round to win heavyweight title.

6, 1987 Sugar Ray Leonard outpoints Marvin Hagler over 12 rounds.

8, 1941 Joe Louis stops Tony Musta in 9 rounds to retain heavyweight title.

9, 1988 Evander Holyfield kayos Carlos DeLeon in 8 rounds to win WBC cruiserweight title.

10, 1950 Sandy Saddler kayos Reuben Davis in 8 rounds.

11, 1981 Larry Holmes outpoints Trevor Berbick over 15 rounds to retain heavyweight title.

12, 1948 Archie Moore kayos Dusty Wilkerson in 7 rounds.

13, 1985 Marvin Hagler kayos Thomas Hearns in 3 rounds to retain middleweight title.

14, 1926 In his pro debut James J. Braddock fights 4-round no-decision with Al Settle.

15, 1795 John Jackson beats Richard Humphries for English championship.

16, 1983 "Buster" Douglas kayos Jesse Clark in 2 rounds.

17, 1860 In first ever world title fight Tom Sayers of England and John Heenan of the U.S. fight to a draw in 36 rounds at Farnborough, England.

18, 1908 Tommy Burns kayos Jewey Smith in 5 rounds to retain heavyweight title.

19, 1986 Michael Spinks outpoints Larry Holmes over 15 rounds to retain heavyweight title.

20, 1882 John L. Sullivan kayos John McDermott in 3 rounds.

21, 1984 Donald Curry kayos Elio Diaz in 7 rounds to retain WBA welterweight title.

22, 1969 Joe Frazier kayos Dave Zyglewicz in 1 round to retain N.Y. State heavyweight title.

23, 1937 Archie Moore kayos Karl Martin in 1 round.

24, 1931 Tony Canzoneri kayos Jack Kid Berg in 3 rounds.

25, 1981 Matthew Saad Muhammad kayos Murray Sutherland in 9 rounds to retain WBC light heavyweight title.

26, 1975 George Foreman fights five opponents in one night in exhibition.

27, 1968 Jimmy Ellis outpoints Jerry Quarry over 15 rounds to win vacant heavyweight title.

28, 1966 Joe Frazier kayos Don "Toro" Smith in 3 rounds.

29, 1932 Mickey Walker outpoints King Levinsky over 10 rounds.

30, 1976 Muhammad Ali outpoints Jimmy Young over 5 rounds to retain heavyweight title.

MAY

1, 1957 Ray Robinson kayos Gene Fullmer to regain middleweight title.

2, 1955 Archie Moore outpoints Nino Valdes over 15 rounds.

4, 1984 Julio Cesar Chavez kayos Ramon Avitia in 6 rounds.

5, 1973 Eder Jofre beats Jose Legra in 15 rounds to win featherweight title.

6, 1898 James J. Jeffries outpoints Tom Sharkey over 20 rounds.

7, 1937 Lou Ambers outpoints Tony Canzoneri over 15 rounds to retain lightweight title.

9, 1908 Stanley Ketchel kayos Twin Sullivan in 20 rounds to win middleweight title.

10, 1935 Tony Canzoneri outpoints Lou Ambers over 15 rounds to win vacant lightweight title.

11, 1900 James J. Jeffries kayos James J. Corbett in 23 rounds.

12, 1902 Joe Gans kayos Frank Erne in 1 round to win lightweight title.

14, 1883 John L. Sullivan kayos Charley Mitchell in 3 rounds.

15, 1983 Bobby Chacon beats Cornelius Boza-Edwards in 12 rounds to retain WBC junior lightweight title.

16, 1955 Rocky Marciano stops Don Cockell in 9 rounds to retain heavyweight title.

18, 1973 In his pro debut, Marvin Hagler kayos Terry Ryan in 2 rounds.

19, 1909 Jack Johnson fights Philadelphia Jack O'Brien to 6-round no-decision.

20, 1983 Larry Holmes outpoints Tim Witherspoon over 12 rounds to retain WBC heavyweight title.

21, 1966 Muhammad Ali stops Henry Cooper in 6 rounds to retain heavyweight title.

22, 1976 Roberto Duran kayos Lou Bizzarro in 14 rounds to retain lightweight title.

23, 1941 Joe Louis beats Buddy Baer on a disqualification in 7 rounds to retain heavyweight title.

24, 1968 Bob Foster kayos Dick Tiger in 4 rounds to win light heavyweight title.

25, 1965 Muhammad Ali retains heavyweight title with one-round knockout of Sonny Liston.

26, 1972 Joe Frazier stops Ron Stander in 5 rounds to retain heavyweight title.

27, 1983 Marvin Hagler kayos Wilford Scypion in 4 rounds to retain middleweight title.

28, 1986 Evander Holyfield kayos Terry Mims in 5 rounds.

29, 1982 Rafael Limon kayos Rolando Navarrete in 12 rounds to win WBC junior lightweight title.

30, 1951 Ezzard Charles outpoints Joey Maxim over 15 rounds to retain heavyweight title.

31, 1976 Wilfred Benitez outpoints Emiliano Villa over 15 rounds.

JUNE

1, 1984 Livingstone Bramble stops Ray Mancini in 14 rounds to win WBA lightweight title.

2, 1973 Carlos Monzon beats Emile Griffith in 15 rounds to retain middleweight title.

3, 1935 Marcel Thil outpoints Ignacio Ara over 15 rounds to retain middleweight title.

4, 1908 Stanley Ketchel outpoints Billy Papke in 10 rounds to retain middleweight title.

5, 1952 Jersey Joe Walcott outpoints Ezzard Charles over 15 rounds to retain heavyweight title.

6, 1921 Benny Leonard and Rocky Kansas fight 20-round no-decision.

7, 1970 Ismael Laguna stops Ishimatsu Suzuki in 13 rounds to retain lightweight title.

8, 1963 Emile Griffith outpoints Luis Rodriguez over 15 rounds to regain welterweight title.

9, 1899 James J. Jeffries kayos Bob Fitzsimmons in 11 rounds to win heavyweight title.

11, 1982 Larry Holmes stops Gerry Cooney in 13 rounds to retain heavyweight title.

12, 1930 Max Schmeling defeats Jack Sharkey on a foul in four rounds to win vacant heavyweight championship.

13, 1935 James J. Braddock outpoints Max Baer in 15 rounds to win heavyweight championship.

14, 1934 Max Baer knocks out Primo Carnera in 11 rounds to win heavyweight title.

15, 1858 Tom Sayers defeats Tom Paddock in 21 rounds to win English heavyweight championship.

16, 1949 Jake LaMotta stops Marcel Cerdan in 10 rounds to win middleweight title.

17, 1979 Danny Lopez kayos Mike Ayala in 15th round to retain featherweight title.

18, 1941 Joe Louis knocks out Billy Conn in 13 rounds to retain heavyweight title.

19, 1957 Joe Brown stops Orland Zulueta in 15 rounds to retain lightweight title.

20, 1980 Roberto Duran beats Sugar Ray Leonard over 15 rounds to win welterweight title.

21, 1932 Jack Sharkey outpoints Max Schmeling in 15 rounds to win heavyweight title.

22, 1937 Joe Louis knocks out James J. Braddock in eight rounds to become heavyweight champion.

23, 1969 Joe Frazier stops Jerry Quarry in 7 rounds to retain N.Y. State heavyweight title.

25, 1948 Joe Louis knocks out Jersey Joe Walcott in 11 rounds to retain heavyweight title.

26, 1972 Roberto Duran stops Ken Buchanan to win lightweight title.

27, 1972 Bob Foster kayos Mike Quarry in 4 rounds to retain light heavyweight title.

28, 1939 Joe Louis kayos Tony Galento in 4 rounds to retain heavyweight title.

29, 1933 Primo Carnera stops Jack Sharkey in six rounds to win heavyweight title.

30, 1909 Jack Johnson beats Tony Ross in 6 rounds.

JULY

1, 1975 Muhammad Ali outpoints Joe Bugner over 15 rounds to retain heavyweight title.

2, 1921 In boxing's first million-dollar gate Jack Dempsey stops George Carpentier in four rounds.

3, 1905 Marvin Hart kayos Jack Root in 12 rounds to claim vacant heavyweight title.

4, 1919 Jack Dempsey kayos Jess Willard in 3 rounds to win heavyweight championship.

5, 1909 Stanley Ketchel outpoints Billy Papke in 20 rounds to retain middleweight title.

8, 1990 Aaron Davis kayos Mark Breland in 9 rounds to win WBA welterweight championship.

9, 1926 Pete Latzo retains welterweight title on a 4th-round foul from George Levine.

10, 1951 Randy Turpin decisions Ray Robinson to win middleweight championship.

13, 1980 Matthew Saad Muhammad kayos Yaqui Lopez in 14 rounds to retain WBC light heavyweight title.

14, 1990 Terry Norris outpoints Rene Jacquot over 12 rounds to retain WBC super welterweight title.

15, 1989 Evander Holyfield kayos Aldison Rodrigues in 2 rounds.

16, 1947 Rocky Graziano wins middleweight title with 6-round kayo of Tony Zale.

17, 1976 Pipino Cuevas kayos Angel Espada in 2 rounds to win WBA welterweight title.

18, 1951 Jersey Joe Walcott kayos Ezzard Charles in 7th round to win heavyweight title.

19, 1967 Joe Frazier stops George Chuvalo in 4 rounds.

20, 1986 Evander Holyfield outpoints Dwight Muhammad Qawi over 15 rounds to win WBA and IBF cruiserweight titles.

21, 1989 Mike Tyson kayos Carl Williams in 1 round to retain heavyweight title.

22, 1963 Sonny Liston kayos Floyd Patterson in 1 round to retain heavyweight title.

23, 1981 In his second pro fight James "Buster" Douglas outpoints Michael Lear over 4 rounds.

24, 1968 Jose Legra kayos Howard Winstone in 5 rounds to win vacant WBC featherweight title.

25, 1902 James J. Jeffries kayos Bob Fitzsimmons in 8 rounds to retain heavyweight title.

26, 1928 Gene Tunney stops Tom Heeney in 11 rounds to retain heavyweight title.

27, 1918 Jack Dempsey kayos Fred Fulton in 18 seconds of the first round.

28, 1990 Dennis Andries kayos Jeff Harding in 8 rounds to regain WBC light heavyweight title.

29, 1957 Floyd Patterson stops Tommy Jackson in 10 rounds to retain heavyweight title.

30, 1884 Jack Dempsey kayos George Fulljames in 22 rounds to win middleweight title.

31, 1971 Hedgemon Lewis kayos Ariel Green in 6 rounds.

AUGUST

1, 1917 Jack Dempsey kayos Al Norton in 1 round.

3, 1974 Jose Napoles stops Hedgemon Lewis in 9 rounds to retain welterweight title.

4, 1970 George Foreman stops George Chuvalo in 3 rounds.

5, 1990 Vinnie Pazienza outpoints Greg Haugen over 10 rounds.

6, 1966 Muhammad Ali kayos Brian London in 3 rounds to retain heavyweight title.

7, 1982 Dwight Qawi kayos Matthew Saad Muhammad in 6 rounds to retain WBC light heavyweight title.

8, 1952 Rex Layne outpoints Ezzard Charles over 10 rounds.

10, 1949 Ezzard Charles stops Gus Lesnevich in 8 rounds to retain heavyweight title.

11, 1944 Archie Moore kayos Louie Mays in 3 rounds.

12, 1925 Harry Greb kayos Pat Walsh in 2 rounds.

13, 1974 Marvin Hagler kayos Peachy Davis in 1 round.

14, 1903 James J. Jeffries kayos James J. Corbett in 10 rounds to retain heavyweight title.

15, 1966 Jose Torres beats Eddie Cotton in 15 rounds to retain light heavyweight title.

16, 1967 Carlos Ortiz outpoints Ismael Laguna to retain lightweight title.

17, 1914 In his first recorded bout Jack Dempsey fights to a 6-round draw with Young Herman.

18, 1979 Matthew Saad Muhammad beats John Conteh in 15 rounds to win light heavyweight title.

19, 1966 Sonny Liston kayos Amos Johnson in 3 rounds.

20, 1904 Tommy Burns kayos Cyclone Kelly in 4 rounds.

21, 1973 Bob Foster beats Pierre Fourie in 15 rounds to retain light heavyweight title.

22, 1969 Ruben Olivares kayos Lionel Rose in 5 rounds to win bantamweight title.

23, 1977 Michael Spinks kayos Jasper Brisbane in 2 rounds.

24, 1908 Tommy Burns kayos Bill Squires in 13 rounds to retain heavyweight title.

25, 1904 James J. Jeffries stops Jack Munroe in 2 rounds to retain heavyweight title.

26, 1934 Max Schmeling kayos Walter Neusel in 9 rounds.

27, 1928 Micky Walker kayos Armand Emanuel in 7 rounds.

28, 1959 Gene Fullmer kayos Carmen Basilio in 14 rounds to win middleweight title.

29, 1985 Evander Holyfield kayos Rick Myers in 1 round.

30, 1937 Joe Louis decisions Tommy Farr over 15 rounds to retain heavyweight title.

31, 1984 Pinklon Thomas outpoints Tim Witherspoon over 12 rounds to win WBC heavyweight title.

SEPTEMBER

1, 1973 George Foreman kayos Jose Roman in 1 round to retain heavyweight title.

2, 1908 Tommy Burns kayos Bill Lang in 6 rounds to retain heavyweight title.

3, 1906 Joe Gans beats Battling Nelson on a foul in the 42nd round, to retain lightweight title.

4, 1916 Freddie Welsh outpoints Charlie White over 20 rounds to retain lightweight title.

5, 1898 Mysterious Billy Smith retains welterweight title on a 25-round draw with Andy Walsh.

6, 1920 Jack Dempsey kayos Billy Miske in three rounds to retain heavyweight title.

7, 1892 James J. Corbett knocks out John L. Sullivan in New Orleans in the first heavyweight championship fight fought with gloves under the Marquess of Queensberry rules.

8, 1973 Roberto Duran stops Ishimatsu Suzuki in 10 rounds to retain lightweight title.

9, 1909 Jack Johnson fights Al Kaufman to 10 round no decision.

10, 1966 Muhammad Ali stops Karl Mildenberger in 12 rounds to retain heavyweight title.

11, 1941 Chalky Wright kayos Jocy Archibald in 11 rounds to win featherweight title.

12, 1951 Ray Robinson kayos Randy Turpin in 10th round to regain middleweight title.

13, 1950 Jake LaMotta kayos Laurent Dauthuille in 15th round to retain middleweight title.

14, 1886 Stanley Ketchel born in Grand Rapids, Michigan; 1923, Jack Dempsey kayos Luis Angel Firpo in second round.

15, 1978 Muhammad Ali wins heavyweight title for third time with 15-round decision over Leon Spinks, in New Orleans.

16, 1981 Ray Leonard stops Tommy Hearns in 14 rounds to unify welterweight title.

17, 1954 Rocky Marciano kayos Ezzard Charles in 8 rounds to retain heavyweight title.

18, 1946 Joe Louis kayos Tami Mauriello in 1 round to retain heavyweight title.

19, 1917 Jack Dempsey kayos Charley Miller in 1 round.

20, 1939 Joe Louis kayos Bob Pastor in 11 rounds to retain heavyweight title.

21, 1955 Rocky Marciano kayos Archie Moore in 9 rounds to retain heavyweight title.

22, 1927 In the Battle of the Long Count, Gene Tunney beats Jack Dempsey over 10 rounds to defend his heavyweight title.

23, 1926 Gene Tunney defeats Jack Dempsey on 10-round decision to win heavyweight title.

24, 1953 Rocky Marciano stops Roland LaStarza in 11 rounds to retain heavyweight title.

25, 1962 Sonny Liston wins heavyweight championship with one-round kayo of Floyd Patterson.

26, 1972 Bob Foster kayos Chris Finnegan in 14 rounds to retain light heavyweight title.

27, 1946 Tony Zale kayos Rocky Graziano in six rounds.

28, 1976 Muhammad Ali outpoints Ken Norton over 15 rounds to retain heavyweight title.

29, 1941 Joe Louis stops Lou Nova in 6 rounds to retain heavyweight title.

30, 1961 Benny Kid Paret outpoints Emile Griffith over 15 rounds to regain welterweight title.

OCTOBER

1, 1975 Muhammad Ali stops Joe Frazier in 14 rounds to retain heavyweight title.

2, 1906 Tommy Burns kayos Fireman Jim Flynn in 15 rounds to retain heavyweight title.

3, 1981 Mike Weaver outpoints James Tillis over 15 rounds to retain WBA heavyweight title.

4, 1940 Sugar Ray Robinson makes pro debut, knocking out Joe Escheverria in 2 rounds.

5, 1974 Carlos Monzon kayos Tony Mundine in 7 rounds to retain middleweight title.

6, 1979 Jorge Lujan kayos Roberto Rubaldino in 15 rounds to retain bantamweight title.

7, 1898 Mysterious Billy Smith outpoints Charley McKeever over 25 rounds to retain welterweight title.

8, 1975 Rodolfo Martinez outpoints Hisami Numata over 15 rounds to retain WBC bantamweight title.

9, 1989 Terry Norris outpoints Jorge Vaca over 10 rounds.

10, 1972 In his last fight before winning heavyweight title, George Foreman kayos Terry Sorrels in 2 rounds.

11, 1913 George Chip kayos Frank Klaus in 6 rounds to win middleweight title.

12, 1975 Alexis Arguello kayos Royal Kobayashi in 5 rounds to retain WBA featherweight title.

13, 1904 Tommy Sullivan kayos Abe Attell in 5 rounds to win vacant featherweight title.

14, 1949 Ezzard Charles kayos Pat Valentino in 8 rounds to retain heavyweight title.

16, 1909 Jack Johnson knocks out Stanley Ketchel in 12 rounds to retain heavyweight title.

17, 1969 Jose Napoles outpoints Emile Griffith over 15 rounds to retain welterweight title.

20, 1979 John Tate outpoints Gerrie Coetzee over 15 rounds to win WBA heavyweight title.

21, 1953 Bobo Olson outpoints Randy Turpin over 15 rounds to win vacant middleweight title.

22, 1789 Tom Johnson defeats Isaac Perrins to retain English heavyweight championship.

23, 1982 Donald Curry outpoints Marlon Starling over 12 rounds.

24, 1939 Henry Armstrong outpoints Jimmy Garrison over 10 rounds to retain welterweight title.

25, 1990 Evander Holyfield kayos Buster Douglas in 3 rounds to win heavyweight title.

26, 1970 Muhammad Ali returns to ring after three-year exile with three-round TKO of Jerry Quarry.

27, 1976 Pipino Cuevas kayos Shoji Tsujimoto in 6 rounds to retain welterweight title.

28, 1960 Joe Brown outpoints Cisco Andrade over 15 rounds to retain lightweight title.

29, 1960 Muhammad Ali, then Cassius Clay, makes professional debut with six-round decision over Tunney Hunsaker.

30, 1974 Muhammad Ali kayos George Foreman in eight rounds to regain heavyweight championship.

31, 1974 Roberto Duran kayos Jose Vasquez in 2 rounds.

NOVEMBER

1, 1980 Jim Watt stops Sean O'Grady in 12 rounds to retain WBC lightweight title.

2, 1907 Jack Johnson kayos Fireman Jim Flynn in 11 rounds.

4, 1932 Tony Canzoneri outpoints Billy Petrolle over 15 rounds to retain lightweight title.

5, 1917 Pete Herman outpoints Frankie Burns over 20 rounds to retain bantamweight title.

6, 1981 Larry Holmes stops Renaldo Snipes in 11 rounds to retain heavyweight title.

7, 1970 Carlos Monzon kayos Nino Benvenuti in 12 rounds to win middleweight title.

8, 1899 Mysterious Billy Smith outpoints Charley McKeever over 20 rounds to retain welterweight title.

9, 1984 Larry Holmes stops Bonecrusher Smith in 12 rounds to retain heavyweight title.

10, 1978 Larry Holmes kayos Alfredo Evangelista in 7 rounds to retain WBC heavyweight title.

11, 1972 Carlos Monzon beats Bennie Briscoe in 15 rounds to retain middleweight title.

12, 1982 Aaron Pryor kayos Alexis Arguello in 14 rounds to retain WBA junior welterweight title.

13, 1886 John L. Sullivan kayos Paddy Ryan in 3 rounds.

14, 1966 Muhammad Ali stops Cleveland Williams in 3 rounds to retain heavyweight title.

15, 1901 James J. Jeffries stops Gus Ruhlin in 6 rounds to retain heavyweight title.

16, 1934 Bob Olin outpoints Slapsie Maxie Rosenbloom over 15 rounds to win light heavyweight title.

17, 1939 Billy Conn outpoints Gus Lesnevich over 15 rounds to retain light heavyweight title.

18, 1970 Joe Frazier kayos Bob Foster in 2 rounds to retain heavyweight title.

19, 1987 "Buster" Douglas kayos Donny Long in 2 rounds.

20, 1942 Willie Pep outpoints Chalky Wright over 15 rounds to win featherweight title.

21, 1916 Jack Britton outpoints Charley White over 12 rounds to retain welterweight title.

22, 1965 Muhammad Ali stops Floyd Patterson in 12 rounds to retain heavyweight title.

23, 1943 Manuel Ortiz outpoints Benny Goldberg over 15 rounds to retain bantamweight title.

24, 1976 Dong-Kyun Yum outpoints Royal Kobayashi over 15 rounds to win WBC junior featherweight title.

25, 1980 Ray Leonard stops Roberto Duran in 8 round, "No Mas" bout.

26, 1982 Larry Holmes outpoints Tex Cobb over 15 rounds to retain heavyweight title.

29, 1906 Honey Mellody stops Joe Walcott in 12 rounds to retain welterweight title.

30, 1979 Ray Leonard kayos Wilfred Benitez in 15th round to win welterweight title.

DECEMBER

1, 1973 Bob Foster beats Pierre Fourie in 15 rounds to retain light heavyweight title.

2, 1978 Marvin Johnson kayos Mate Parlov in 10 rounds to win WBC light heavyweight title.

3, 1981 In his last bout, Joe Frazier fights to a 10-round draw with Jumbo Cummings.

4, 1961 Floyd Patterson kayos Tom McNeeley in 4 rounds to retain heavyweight title.

5, 1947 Joe Louis outpoints Jersey Joe Walcott over 15 rounds to retain heavyweight title.

6, 1805 Hen Pearce beats Jem Belcher to win English heavyweight championship.

7, 1989 Sugar Ray Leonard outpoints Roberto Duran over 12 rounds.

8, 1924 Gene Tunney outpoints Jeff Smith over 15 rounds.

9, 1955 Ray Robinson knocks out Bobo Olsen in 2nd round to win middleweight title.

10, 1968 Joe Frazier outpoints Oscar Bonavena over 15 rounds to retain N.Y. State heavyweight title.

11, 1982 Bobby Chacon beats Rafael Limon in 15 rounds to win WBC junior lightweight title.

12, 1969 Ruben Olivares kayos Alan Rudkin in 2 rounds to retain bantamweight title.

13, 1886 Jack Dempsey kayos Jack Fogarty in 27 rounds to retain middleweight title.

14, 1920 Jack Dempsey knocks out Bill Brennan in 12 rounds.

15, 1971 Vincente Rondon stops Doyle Baird in 8 rounds to retain WBA light heavyweight title.

16, 1940 Joe Louis stops Al McCoy in 6 rounds to retain heavyweight title.

17, 1952 Archie Moore outpoints Joey Maxim over 15 rounds to win light heavyweight title.

18, 1950 Rocky Marciano kayos Bill Wilson in 1 round.

19, 1913 Jack Johnson fights to a 10-round draw with Battling Jim Johnson to retain heavyweight title.

20, 1946 Sugar Ray Robinson beats Tommy Bell to win welterweight title.

21, 1985 Evander Holyfield kayos Anthony Davis in 5 rounds.

22, 1955 Ezzard Charles outpoints Bob Albright over 10 rounds.

23, 1961 Emile Griffith outpoints Isaac Logart over 10 rounds.

24, 1898 Matty Matthews outpoints George Kerwin over 20 rounds.

25, 1903 Honey Mellody outpoints Patsy Sweeney over 12 rounds.

26, 1908 Jack Johnson kayos Tommy Burns in 14 rounds to win heavyweight title.

27, 1901 Jack Johnson and Hank Griffin fight to a 15-round draw.

28, 1956 Ingemar Johansson kayos Peter Bates in 2 rounds.

30, 1918 Jack Dempsey kayos Gunboat Smith in 2 rounds.

31, 1903 Twin Sullivan and Jack Blackburn battle to a 15-round draw.

Page numbers in italics refer to captions, illustrations, and sidebars.

Abrams, Georgie, 82
Algren, Nelson, 115
Ali, Muhammad, 17, *18,* 19, 20, 21, 24, 25, 29, 31, 32, 34, *35, 37, 38–39,* 38–40, *40,* 70–71, *71,* 85, 86–87, *87, 95,* 97, 99, 100, 103, 104, 109, 112–13
Aliano, Eddie, *25*
Amateur boxing, 100–101
Ambers, Lou, 54, 55
Antyllus (Greek writer), *9, 35*
Apparel, 27
Arcel, Ray, *25,* 32, 92, 93
Archer, Joey, 43
Arguello, Alexis, 32, *66,* 66–67
Arizmendi, Baby, 54
Armstrong, Henry, 54–55, *55,* 66, 112
Arum, Bob, 89, 109

Baer, Buddy, 25
Baer, Max, 18, *24*
Barkley, Iran, 45
Barnum, P.T., 111
Barrow, Joe, 41
Barry, Dave, 23, 58, *58–59*
Basilio, Carmen, *41,* 43, *43*
Behr, Johnny, 83
Belcher, Jem, 12
Bell, Tommy, 43, 112
Bellows, George, 65
Benitez, Wilfred, 44
Benvenuti, Giovanni, 103
Benvenuti, Nino, 104
Berbick, Trevor, 40
Berlenbach, Paul, 51, 99, 112
Biggs, Tyrell, 103, *104–5*
Bimstein, Whitey, *25,* 31, 32
Black, Julian, 111
Blackburn, Jack, 25, *33–34,* 49, 72, 78, 89, 118
Body punching, 19–20
Bonavena, Oscar, 38
Boxing history, 9–14
Boxing literature, 115–19
Braddock, Jim, 78, 88
Brady, Bill, 110
Bradyl (boxing patron), 12
Breland, Mark, 103, 104
Brennan, Bill, 64, *114–15*
Brian, Benjamin, *12*
British boxing, 11–15
Britt, Jimmy, 53, 76
Britton, Jack, 46, 51
Broughton, Jack, 11, *13,* 26
Brown, Bundini, 70, 86, 87
Brown, Freddie, *25,* 32
Buchanan, Ken, 44, 45, 112
Bulger, Jack, 51
Burke, James, 13
Burke, Sailor, *23*
Burns, Tommy, 37, 86, *117*
Bush, Red, 51

Business of boxing, 107–13
Byrne, Simon, 13

Callaghan, Morley, 118
Camacho, Hector, 27
Cannon, Jimmy, 82, 83, 109, 116
Capone, Al, 57
Carbajal, Michael, 37, 103
Carbo, Frankie, 109
Carnera, Primo, 37
Carpentier, Georges, 57, 64, 76, 110, 111
Chambers, Arthur, 15
Charles, Ezzard, *61,* 72, *94–95*
Chavez, Julio Cesar, 22–23
Christodoulou, Stanley, 67
Chuvalos, George, 97
Cicero (orator), *11*
Citro, Ralph, *25*
Clancy, Gil, 32, *34*
Clay, Cassius. *See* Ali, Muhammad
"Color line", 97–98
Combination punches, 20–21
Conn, Billy, 78, *79,* 113
Cooney, Gerry, 37, 110
Cooper, Henry, 25
Corbett, James J., 17, 19, 21, 23, 27, 37, 97, 110
Corcoran, Peter, 12
Corner, 24–25
Crawley, Peter, *12*
Cribb, Tom, 12–13
Crusinberry, James, 64
Cuba, 101
Cuddy, Henry, 118
Curry, Donald, 101
Czyz, Bobby, 25

Daggert, Charlie, 73, *73*
D'Amato, Cus, 19, 20, 21, 32, 111
Darts, Bill, 12
Davis, Howard, 103
Defense, 21
DeJesus, Esteban, 44–45
Dekuh, Arthur, *50–51*
Deleney, Jack, 112
Dempsey, Jack, 20, 21, 23, *24,* 24, 31, *35,* 46, 51, 56–59, *57, 58–59, 64,* 64–65, 76, 82, *84,* 88–89, *88–89,* 98, 101, 107, 108, *108,* 109, 110, 111, 112, 113, *114–15,* 118
de Pachmann, Vladimir, 117
Dickens, Charles, 14
Dipley, Walter, 61
Dixon, George, 112
Donaldson, Arthur, *22,* 54, 89
Dorgan, Tad, 52
Douglas, Billy, 101
Douglas, Buster, 17, 20, 24, 37, 101, 110
Douglas, John Sholto, 15
Dowling, Francis, *34, 35*
Downes, Terry, *43,*
Doyle, Arthur Conan, 115
Dundee, Angelo, *25,* 32, 34, 38, 87, 90, 91

Duran, Roberto, 21, *24, 28–29,* 32, *44,* 44–45, *45,* 52, 69, 92–93, *92–93,* 112
Durham, Yank, 111
Duva, Dan, 89, 109, 110
Duva, Lou, 109, 110

Earp, Wyatt, 23
East Europe, 101
Edgerton, Walter, 52
Egan, Pierce, 12, *12,* 24, 115, 118
Ellis, Jimmy, 100
Equipment, 26–27
Erne, Frank, 52, 52–53, 76
Ernst, Billy, 52
Ertle, Harry, 80, 81
Escheverria, Joe, 43

Fields, Jackie, 103
Fifth Street Gym (Miami), 34
Figg, James, 11, 32
Finnegan, Mickey, 47
Firpo, Luis Angel, 23, 57, *64,* 64–65, 82, 109
Fitzgerald, F. Scott, 118
Fitzsimmons, Bob, 19, 27
Fleischer, Nat, *23,* 24, 31, 47, 48, 86, 98, 99, 115
Flowers, Tiger, *16–17,* 51
Flynn, Jim, 49
Folley, Zora, 112
Foreman, George, 17, 29, 38–40, 70, 86, 87, 103, *103,* 104
Foster, Bob, *61,* 100
Frazier, Joe, 19, 20, 24, 27, 32, 38, 40, *40,* 70–71, *71,* 86, 94–95, *95,* 99, 100, 103, 104, 111, 112 13
Fullmer, Gene, 19, 43
Fulton, Fred, 57
Futch, Eddie, 24, 32, 71

Gainford, George, 41
Galento, Tony, *35*
Gallagher, Jack, 65
Gallagher, Johnny, 57
Gallico, Paul, 51, 57
Game, The (London), 115
Gans, Joe, 49, 52–53, *52–53,* 76–77, *77,* 107
Garcia, Ceferino, 54
Gardner, Leonard, 115
Gavilan, Kid, 98
Genaro, Frankie, 103
Gibbons, Tom, 57, 64
Gibson, Billy, 47, 110
Giosa, Eddie, 47
Gladiators, 11
Gloves, 26–27
Godoy, Arturo, 23
Golden Gloves tournament, 101
Goldman, Charlie, *25,* 30, 32, 95
Goldstein, Ruby, 23, 41, 82
Gonzales, Paul, 103
Graham, Billy, 98

Graves, Jackie, 21
Graziano, Rocky, *31,* 32, 82–83, *83*
Greb, Harry, *16–17,* 50, *61,* 112
Greece (ancient), 9
Greenspan, Bud, 46
Griffith, Emile, 23, 32, 112
Griffo, Young, 112
Gyms, 33–34

Hagler, Marvin, *19,* 34, 45, 68–69, *69*
Hague, Iron, 49
Hallmark, Tim, 34
Harris, Willie, *23*
Haukaup, Johnny, 46
Hawkins, Dal, 52
Head protectors, 27
Hearns, Thomas, 29, 30, 32, 34, 44, 68–69, *69,* 101
Heenan, John C., *14,* 14
Heinz, W. C., 115
Heller, Peter, 54
Hemingway, Ernest, 19, 60, 99, 115, 118–19
Herford, Al, 52
Herman, Young, 59
Hill, Virgil, 103
Hoagland, Edward, 115
Hogarth, William, 11
Holmes, Larry, 20, 32, 34, 40, *61,* 110
Holyfield, Evander, *31,* 34, *35,* 101, 104, 110
Humphries, Richard, 12, 24
Hunsaker, Tunney, 40
Hunter, George, 103
Hurley, Jack, 111
Hyfield, Hannah, *12*

Igoe, Hype, 65
Iovino, Al, 54, 55

Jab, *17*
Jackson, John *12,* 12
Jackson, Peter, 97
Jacobs, Mike, 89, 108, 111
Jeannette, Joe, 97, 99
Jeffries, James J., 23, 60, 98, 107, 110
Jiminez, Julio, 47
Joh, Billy, *23*
Johansson, Ingemar, 18, 31, 104
Johnson, Alexander, 61
Johnson, Harold, 117
Johnson, Jack, 48, 49, *60,* 61, 86–87, *86–87,* 97–98, 107, 115, *117*
Johnson, Tom, 12, 24
Johnston, Charlie, 111
Jolson, Al, 54
Jones, Doug, 97
Jones, Mike, 110
Jones, Roy, 103
Juchan, Tom, 12

Kacar, Slobodan, 103, 104
Kansas, Rocky, 46
Katz, Mike, 116

Kearns, Doc, 50, 51, 57, 65, 89, 109–10, *110,* 111
Kefauver, Estes, 109, 110
Kessler, Harry, *23*
Ketchel, Stanley, 17, 31, 49, *60,* 60–61
Khaldun, Ibn, 116
Kilrain, Jake, *13, 26*
King, Don, 89, *106–7,* 109
Kirk, Oliver, 103
Kram, Mark, 116
Kronk gym (Detroit), 34
Kulej, Jerzy, 103

La Barba, Fidel, 103
La Guardia, Fiorello, 49
Lagutin, Boris, 103
Laing, Kirkland, 44
LaMotta, Jake, 41, 43
Lane, Mills, 23
Langford, Sam, 20, *48,* 48–49, 97, *98,* 99, 118
Lardner, John, 61
Lardner, Ring, 115
Latzo, Pete, 51
Lauria, Louis, 103
Lee, Norval, 103
Left hook, 19
Leonard, Benny, 17, 23, 46–47, *47,* 80–81, *81, 92,* 92–93, 99, 110, 112
Leonard, Eddie, 46
Leonard, Sugar Ray, *18, 19, 21, 44,* 44, 45, *61,* 69, 90–91, 101, 104
Lewis, Ted, 27
Liebling, A. J., 19, 20, 29, 31, *33,* 33, 49, 72, 98, 109, 111, 116–18
Liston, Sonny, 17, 25, 29, *37,* 38, 40, 86, 87
LoBianco, John, 44
London, Brian, 100
London, Jack, 115, *116, 117*
Louis, Joe, 17, 18, *20,* 20, *24,* 25, 27, 31, 32, *33–34, 35,* 41, 54, *61,* 72, 78, *79, 84,* 88–89, *88–89,* 98, 108, 111, 112, 113
Lyle, Ron, 100
Lyons, Waterman, 12

McCoy, Al, 78
McCrory, Milton, 34
Mace, Jem, *12,* 14
McFadden, George, 52
McGovern, Terry, 52, 76
McIlvanney, Hugh, 116
McLaglen, Victor, 24–25
McLarnin, Jimmy, 47
McLaughlin, James, 111
McPartland, Kid, 52
McTaggart, Dick, 103
McTigue, Mike, 23, 51, 99
McVey, Sam, 97, *98,* 99
McVicker, Jack, 49
Madison Square Garden, 33, 107, 111–13
Mallin, Harry, 103
Managers, 109–11

Marciano, Rocky, 19, *23, 25,* 30, 31, 32, 72–73, *73, 85,* 94–95, *94–95,* 111, 112, 116, 118
Marcos, Ferdinand, 70
Marcos, Imelda, 70
Marles, Jack, 27
Marquess of Queensberry rules, 15
Masterson, Bat, 23
Mathis, Buster, 100
Maxim, Joe, 41, 109, 110
Meade, Eddie, 54
Meggs, George, 12
Mendoza, Carlos, 45
Mendoza, Daniel, *12,* 12, 24
Mercante, Arthur, Jr., 87
Meredith, Burgess, 109
Milsom, Baker, 12
Minter, Alan, 69
Mitchell, Richie, 46–47, 80, 99 .
Miteff, Alex, *38–39*
Molineaux, Tom, 12
Montanez, Pedro, *55*
Monzon, Carlos, 61
Moore, Archie, 20, 21, *23, 61,* 94, 99, 109, 110, 111, 115, 116, 117, 118
Moore, Davey, 45
Moorer, Michael, 34
Morris, Jim, 57
Morrison, Ian, 27
Morrissey, John, 14
Mouthpieces, 27
Mugabi, John, 69

Nagler, Barney, 116
Nelson, Battling, 53, 76–77, *77,* 107
Nesbit, Evelyn, 112
Norfolk, Battling, 49
Norris, James, D., 109
Norton, Ken, 32, 70

O'Brien, Jack, 17, 24, 29, 49, 61
O'Hara, John, 115
Oliva, Patrizio, 103, 104
Oliver, Stephen, *12*
Olsen, Bobo, 43
Olympic Games, 102–3
Orsini, Joe, 51

Paddock, Tom, 14
Padilla, Carlos, 93
Papke, Billy, 60–61
Papp, Laszlo, 103
Paret, Benny, 23, 112
Parlov, Mate, 104
Pastor, Bob, 78
Patterson, Floyd, 18, 21, 31, 32, *40,* 100, 103, 111
Pearce, Hen, 12
Pender, Paul, 43
Pep, Willie, 17, 21, *61,* 112
Perez, Pascual, 103
Patrolle, Billy, 111
Plimpton, George, 115–16
Police Athletic League, 34

Popentschenko, Valeriy, 103
Pound, Ezra, 118
Protective cups, 27
Pryor, Aaron, *66,* 66–67, 101
Punches, 17–21
Putnam, Pat, 66, 116

Qawi, Dwight Muhammad, 110
Quarry, Jerry, 32, *34,* 38, 86, *99,* 99–100

Racism, 97–98
Rademacher, Pate, 103
Raft, George, 54
Randolph, Leo, 104
Rappaport, Dennis, 110
Referee, 22–23
Richmond, Bill, 12
Rickard, Tex, 57, 64, 76, 89, 98, 107, *108,* 110, 111, 112
Right cross, 18–19
Rings, 27
Ringside Gym (Las Vegas), 34
Risko, Johnny, 51
Robinson, Jackie, 97
Robinson, Sugar Ray, 17, 19, 23, 29, *41,* 41–43, *43,* 55, *84,* 90–91, 112
Rome (ancient), 9–11
Ross, Barney, 54, 55
Rothstein, Arnold, 47
Roxborough, John, 111
Runyon, Damon, 51, 111, 115
Ruth, Babe, 57

Saddler, Sandy, 37, 111, 112
Sarron, Petey, 54, 55, 112
Savold, Lee, 78
Sayers, Tom, *14,* 14
Schlossberg, Phil, 25
Schmeling, Max, 18, *20,* 51, 78, 88, 99, 113
Schulberg, Bud, 115
Schuyler, Ed, 116
Seales, Sugar Ray, 103
Segregation, 97–98
Sellers, Harry, 12
Severinsen, Doc, 69
Sharkey, Jack, 51
Shavers, Earnie, 100
Shaw, George Bernard, 115, *116*
Shaw, Irwin, 115
Shilstone, Mackie, 34
Shuler, James, 69
Siddons, George, 52
Siler, George, 77
Simmons, Brad, 49
Slack, Jack, *12,* 12, *13*
Slider, Chester, 55
Smith, Jim, 61
Smith, Red, 116
Smith, Tiger, 49
Smith, Willie, 103
Soviet Union, 101
Spencer, Thad, 100
Spinks, Leon, 40, 104

Spinks, Michael, 20, 32, 34, 101, 104
Spoldi, Aldo, 54
Steele, Richard, 22–23, 69, 90
Stevens, Bill, *12,* 12
Stevenson, Teofilio, 101, 103
Steward, Emanuel, 32, 69, 101, 110
Stillman, Lou, 33
Stillman's Gym, *33,* 33
Strater, Henry, 118
Stribling, Young, 99
Sullivan, Jack, 60, 61
Sullivan, John L., *13.* 17, 21, 26, 27, 97, 111, 112
Sullivan, Mike, 53

Tate, Frank, 104
Taylor, Estelle, 57
Taylor, George, 11
Taylor, Meldrick, 22–23
Television, 109
Tendler, Lew, 46, 47, *47,* 80–81, *81,* 99
Thackeray, William, 14
Thaw, Harry, 112
Thompson, Maurice, 60
Tocco, Johnny, 34
Torres, Jose, 20, 21, 32, 103, 111
Tracy, Kid, 61
Trainers, 24, 32
Training, 29–35
Tunney, Gene, 23, 57–58, *58–59,* 59, *61,* 65, 98, 101, 108, 113, *116*
Turpin, Randy, 23, 43
Tyson, Mike, 17, 20, 21, 24, 27, *27,* 32, 52, 77, 100, 101, *104–5, 106–7,* 109, 111

Velez, Lupe, *50–51*
Venues, 111–13

Walcott, Jersey Joe, 19, 23, 72–73, *73,* 94
Walker, Harry, 102
Walker, Liz, 51
Walker, Mickey, 23, 31, 50–51, *50–51,* 60, 109, 110
Waruingi, Philip, 103
Weill, Al, 111
Welsh, Freddie, 46, 47, 110
Whitaker, Pernell, *102,* 104
White, Charley, 19, 46, 80, 99
White, Jabez, 53
White, Johnny, 53
White, Stanford, 111
Wilde, Jimmy, 37
Wilkinson, Elizabeth, *12*
Willard, Jess, 20, 37, 56–57, 59, 64, 86, 88, 97, 109, 111, 112
Williams, Carl, *107*
Williams, Charles, 25
Williams, Cleveland, 21, 40
Williams, Mike, 17
Wills, Harry, 85, 98
Woodman, Joe, 48
Writers, 115–19

Zale, Tony, 82–83, *83*
Zivic, Fritzie, 55, 112